Lecture Notes of the Institute for Computer Sciences, Social Informatics and Telecommunications Engineering   296

More information about this series at http://www.springer.com/series/8197

Ghada Bassioni · Cheikh M. F. Kebe ·
Assane Gueye · Ababacar Ndiaye (Eds.)

Innovations and Interdisciplinary Solutions for Underserved Areas

Third EAI International Conference, InterSol 2019
Cairo, Egypt, February 14–15, 2019
Proceedings

Editors
Ghada Bassioni
Ain Shams University
Cairo, Egypt

Cheikh M. F. Kebe
Ecole Superieure Polytechnique
Dakar, Senegal

Assane Gueye
Université Alioune Diop de Bambey
Bambey, Senegal

Ababacar Ndiaye
Université Assane Seck de Ziguinchor
Ziguinchor, Senegal

ISSN 1867-8211   ISSN 1867-822X (electronic)
Lecture Notes of the Institute for Computer Sciences, Social Informatics
and Telecommunications Engineering
ISBN 978-3-030-34862-5   ISBN 978-3-030-34863-2 (eBook)
https://doi.org/10.1007/978-3-030-34863-2

This Springer imprint is published by the registered company Springer Nature Switzerland AG
The registered company address is: Gewerbestrasse 11, 6330 Cham, Switzerland

Preface

The third edition of InterSol was held during February 14–15, 2019, in Cairo, Egypt. Cairo's Ain Shams University hosted this annual international meeting under the leadership of Prof. Ghada Bassioni. Just like the previous edition, InterSol 2019 was a forum for scientific exchange and experience shared by people from all over the world. Faithful to its main objectives, the conference served as a framework for the participants to present their work addressing issues and problems in underserved and unserved areas. In fact, populations living in underserved areas face problems in almost all sectors: energy, water, communication, climate, food, health, education, transportation, social development, economic growth, etc.

Through InterSol, researchers contribute to the remediation of these problems by proposing innovative solutions. However, given the nature of the problems, it is obvious that the proposed solutions can be sustainable, relevant, and effective only if they integrate the interdisciplinary dimension. In other words, they must combine different disciplines while taking into account geographical, social, economic, and environmental specificities, among others. These are characteristics that make InterSol unique in the African and even international scientific landscape. Its major strength resides in the number, diversity, and quality of participants.

InterSol 2019 gathered researchers, scientists, educators, students, NGOs and industry from Africa, Europe, Asia, and the Americas.

This volume includes, on the one hand, results of research efforts that were submitted and selected to be presented at the InterSol 2019 conference. On the other hand, the volume also includes selected articles that were presented at the Conference on Research in Computer Science and its Applications (CNRIA 2019). The CNRIA conference was held during April 25–28, 2019, on the campus of the Université Gaston Berger (UGB) of Saint-Louis, Senegal. In this volume, there is a total of 18 papers (9 from InterSol and 9 from CNRIA) that treat different themes including: energy, agriculture, electronics, networks and telecoms, health, social sciences, just to name a few.

We believe that this volume will serve as a good distributor to widely spread the great work presented at InterSol 2019 and CNRIA 2019. It shall also serve as a medium to share the solutions presented by the scientists, who have participated in this international gathering and are dedicated to tackling issues in underserved areas. Indeed, the primary goal of InterSol is to contribute to alleviate living standards for people in these areas, and InterSol 2019 has been another giant step towards this goal.

August 2019

Ghada Bassioni
Cheikh M. F. Kebe
Assane Gueye
Ababacar Ndiaye

Organization

Steering Committee

Imrich Chlamtac   Create-Net and University of Trento, Italy
Cheikh M. F. Kebe   Université Cheikh Anta Diop, École Supérieure
                               Polytechnique, Senegal
Assane Gueye   Univerity of Maryland, College Park, USA,
                               and Universite Alioune Diop, Senegal

Organizing Committee

General Chair

Ghada Bassioni   Ain Shams University, Egypt

General Co-chair

Cheikh Mouhamed   Université Cheikh Anta Diop, Senegal
  Fadel Kebe

TPC Chair and Co-chairs

Assane Gueye   Université Alioune Diop de Bambey, Senegal,
                               University of Maryland, College Park, USA
Melissa Densmore   UCT, South Africa
Tembine Hamidou   New York University, USA
Moustapha Diop   University of Maryland, Baltimore College, USA

Sponsorship and Exhibit Chair

Abdulhameed Mambo   Nile University of Nigeria, Nigeria

Workshops Chair

Wilfred Ndiffon   African Institute of Mathematical Sciences, Kigali,
                               Rwanda

Publicity and Social Media Chair

Jessica Thorn   University of York, UK, African Climate and
                               Development Initiative, South Africa, and African
                               Institute for Mathematical Sciences, Rwanda

Publications Chair

Ababacar Ndiaye   Université Assane Seck de Ziguinchor, Senegal

Web Chair

Babacar Mbaye   Université Alioune Diop de Bambey, Senegal

Posters and PhD Track Chair

Maimouna Diouf   Aix-Marseille University, France

Tutorials Chair

Narcisse Talla Tankam   University of Ngaoundere, Cameroon

Local Arrangement Committee

Tamer Zaki   Egyptian Petroleum Research Institute, Egypt
Ayman Fareed   Ain Shams University, Egypt
Gehan Adel   Ain Shams University, Egypt
Heba Soliman   Ain Shams University, Egypt
Karima Ali   Ain Shams University, Egypt
Ali Korin   Ain Shams University, Egypt
Alaa Mohsen   Ain Shams University, Egypt
Ahmed Abdelhameed   Ain Shams University, Egypt
Walid Hisham   Ain Shams University, Egypt
Mohamed Abdelaal   Ain Shams University, Egypt
Ayman Mohammed   Ain Shams University, Egypt

Technical Program Committee

Mbaye, Mamadou Lamine   UASZ, Senegal
Garba, Aminata   CMU, Rwanda
Travaly, Youssef   NEF, Rwanda
Nelson, Kara   UCB, USA
Coulibaly, Pane Jeanne   INERA, Burkina Fasso
  d'Arc
Sadouanouan, Malo   UPB, Burkina Fasso
Kane, El Hadji Malick   HEFR, Switzerland
Gueye, Bamba   UCAD, Senegal
Thorn, Jessica P. R.   University York, UK, ACDI, South Africa, and AIMS,
                           Rwanda
Talla Tankam, Narcisse   University of Ngaoundere, Cameroon
Gueye, Assane   UADB, Senegal, and UMCP, USA
Ba, Mouhamadou Lamine   UADB, Senegal
Camara, Gaoussou   UADB, Senegal
Kabore, Francois   Jesuit University Institute, Ivory Coast, and GU, USA
  Pazisnewende
Kebe, Cheikh M. Fadel   UCAD, Senegal
Densmore, Melissa   UCT, South Africa
Diop, Alassane   UVS, Senegal

Bassioni, Ghada	Ain Shams University, Egypt
Diop, Moustapha	UMBC, USA
Mbodji, Senghane	UADB, Senegal
El Sherif, Rabab	Cairo University, Egypt
Hamidou, Tembine	NYU, USA
Ndiaye, Ababacar	UASZ, Senegal
Mambo, Abdulhameed	Nile University, Nigeria
Mahmoudi, Charif	NIST, USA
Pal, Joyojee	University of Michigan, USA
Van Stam, Gertjan	SIRDC, Zimbabwe

Contents

A Survey of Game Theoretic Solutions for Cloud Computing Security Issues

Bernard Ousmane Sane[1]([envelope]), Cheikh Saliou Mbacke Babou[1], Doudou Fall[2], and Ibrahima Niang[1]

[1] University Cheikh Anta Diop of Dakar, Fann Bp 5005, Dakar, Senegal
{bernardousmane.sane,cheikhsalioumbacke.babou,
ibrahima1.niang}@ucad.edu.sn
[2] Nara Institute of Science and Technology, Ikoma, Nara 630-0192, Japan
doudou-f@is.naist.jp

Abstract. Cloud computing has become quintessential to information technology as it represents the foundation of all the emerging paradigms. Cloud computing uses virtualization to maximize resources utilization. Despite its benefits, organizations are still reluctant to adopt cloud computing due to its numerous security issues. Among the solutions that have been provided to solve cloud security issues, game theoretic proposals showed great potentials. In this paper, we survey the most representative game theoretic approaches to solve cloud computing security issues. We classify these approaches or methods based on their security scenarios and their respective solutions. We overview different solutions to control cloud vulnerabilities and threats using game theory. We also investigate and identify the limitations of these solutions and provide insights of the future of cloud security particularly on virtual machines, hypervisors and data security.

Keywords: Cloud computing · Game theory · Security · Countermeasures · Virtualization

1 Introduction

Cloud computing has become quintessential to information technology (IT) as it represents the foundation of all the emerging technologies: big data, Internet of Things (IoT), artificial intelligence (AI), etc. The security issues of cloud computing are numerous and complex, and greatly participate on preventing its widespread adoption [13,23]. The existing security solutions are not suitable for the dynamic aspect of cloud computing because they depend on traditional security models (BellLaPadula (BLP) model, Biba model, etc.), that are more adequate for static attack scenarios [33]. Additionally, the traditional cybersecurity solutions are lagging behind in terms of quantitative analysis and decision-making frameworks. Several solutions have been proposed to tackle the security

© ICST Institute for Computer Sciences, Social Informatics and Telecommunications Engineering 2019
Published by Springer Nature Switzerland AG 2019. All Rights Reserved
G. Bassioni et al. (Eds.): InterSol 2019, LNICST 296, pp. 1–12, 2019.
https://doi.org/10.1007/978-3-030-34863-2_1

Table 1. A summary of useful survey papers in cloud computing and (or) the domain of game theory.

Cloud computing					
Reference	Year	Data	VMs	Hypervisor	Method countermeasure using game theory	Mathematical perspective on game theory
[33]	2016	No	No	No	Yes	Yes
[23]	2016	No	Yes	Yes	Yes	No
[13]	2014	Yes	Yes	Yes	No	No
[14]	2019	Yes	Yes	No	Yes	No
This paper	2019	Yes	Yes	Yes	Yes	Yes

issues of cloud computing. Among them, game theory methods have particularly been effective [21, 28]. As mentioned in paper [33], game theory and cybersecurity have similar features. Indeed, in game theory, a player's payoff depends on his strategy and the strategies of the other players. In cybersecurity, the security of an information system depends both on the administrator's security policy and on the attacker's strategies. This commonality makes game theory an essential mathematical tool for cloud computing security.

This manuscript is a survey of game theoretic methods for cloud computing security issues. We first classify game theoretic methods based on their security scenarios and respective solutions. Furthermore, from the threats and vulnerabilities on cloud computing, we study related security solutions that are based on game theory. We also provide research perspectives on cloud security, particularly on virtual machine, hypervisor and data security. In Table 1, we show how our paper differs from the existing survey papers – [13, 14, 23, 33] – in this field.

This paper is organised as follows: in Sect. 2, we present cloud computing. In Sect. 3, we give some background and the application of game theoretical concepts to cybersecurity. In Sect. 4, we present a variety of threats associated with cloud computing systems and also their countermeasures by using game theory approaches. This paper ends with the main conclusions and discussion for future research in Sect. 5.

2   Cloud Computing Security

2.1   Cloud Computing:

IT resources have become easy to access with cloud computing where almost everything related to IT can be serviced through the Internet [22]. The major characteristics of cloud computing, such as elasticity (the ability to dynamically adapt to the users resource needs), pay-per-use (which means, you just pay the time services that you use), transfer of risk (a specific risk is passed from the developers to the providers), etc., have revolutionized the way that we make use of computing [29].

We acknowledge that there are many definitions of cloud computing [13, 29, 31]. However, the National Institute of Standards and Technology (NIST) definition seems to cover all essential aspects [30]: "Cloud computing is a model for enabling convenient, on-demand network access to a shared pool of configurable computing resources (e.g., networks, servers, storage, applications, and services) that can be rapidly provisioned and released with minimal management effort or service provider interaction". In summary, there are five essential characteristics: *on-demand self service, broad network access, resource pooling, rapid elasticity*, and *measured service*. Cloud computing has three service models:

- *Software as a Service (SaaS)*, in which ready-to-use applications are serviced to the customers,
- *Platform as a Service (PaaS)*, in which the cloud service providers (CSPs) provide design and development environments to the users
- *Infrastructure as a Service (IaaS)*, in which the CSPs provision manageable virtual machines to the users.

The NIST definition contends that there are four main deployment models in cloud computing:

- *Public clouds*, which are open to anyone,
- *Community clouds*, restricted to groups with similar goals,
- *Private clouds*, restricted to a single organization and,
- *Hybrid clouds*, a combination of the aforementioned.

Despite all its benefits, security is the most important factor that is hindering the wide use of cloud computing. In Subsect. 2.2, we present the classification of cloud vulnerabilities.

2.2 Cloud Computing Security Issues

We present a variety of threats associated with cloud computing systems and classify them into four categories according the services:

Infrastructure as a Service (IaaS)

- **Network threats:** in cloud computing, the virtual machines (VMs) are connected through a network. Adversaries can launch various kinds of attacks (XML Signature Wrapping Attack, Flooding Attack (DDoS), Metadata Spoofing Attack, etc.) in a cloud system through its network which may deteriorate the quality of cloud services.
- **Host threats:** are related to virtual machines, hypervisors and data. In fact, on an existing cloud system, the support for security isolation is limited. Since different VMs are sharing the same resources, the VM-based attacks exploit vulnerabilities in the virtual machines or the underlying hypervisor in the LAN (Local Area Network) to violate data protection and affect the cloud services. Host attacks can be split into subcategories:

- VM to VM attacks: in which we have cross-VM side-channel attacks, scheduler-based attacks, VM migration and rollback attacks, etc.
- VM to Hypervisor attacks: in which we have VM Hopping and VM Escape attacks, etc.
- Data attacks: in which we have Data Confidentiality, Data Integrity, Data Availability, Data Isolation, etc.

Platform as a Service (SaaS)

- **Application threats:** Risks associated with the Applications-based attacks include: Malware injection, steganography attacks, Web services- & protocol-based attacks, Security Misconfiguration, SQL Injection Attack.

Software as a Service (PaaS)

- **Information security policy issues:** the provider is the manager and he defines the security policy and the security mechanisms of the deployed services. Improper Data Sensitization, Information leakage, Vendor Lock-in are the problems that can arise from poor management.

3   Overview of Game Theory

In this section, we elaborate fundamental notions of game theory.

Definition 1. Game [28].
A description of the strategic interaction between cooperative and non-cooperative players where the payoff of a player's choice of action depends on the action of other players.
In game theory, we use the following terms to describe a game:

- **Player:** a participant of the game who is called to make a decision for actions.
- **Action:** an action by a player refers a move in the given game.
- **Payoff:** the recompense or penalty inflicted to a player as a result of his action in the game.
- **Strategy:** the Oxford Dictionary defines strategy as "*a plan of action or policy designed to achieve a major or overall aim*" in a game.

Definition 2. Game theory is a branch of mathematics used to model all situations where we need to make decisions.

Definition 3. Nash equilibrium: or strategic equilibrium, is a stable state of the game in which no player can unilaterally change his strategy and get a better payoff. It is represented by a list of strategies, one for each player.

Definition 4. Non-cooperative game [33]: is a game in which each player is interested by his own gain. The players are said to be selfish.

Table 2. Game models and security issues

Game model			Suitable scenario	Solution	Reference
Non-cooperative games	Static games	Incomplete imperfect	DDoS attacks vs admin network	Bayesian nash equilibrium	*Liu et al.* [18]
			Intrusion detection	Bayesian nash equilibrium	*Liu et al.* [19]
		Complete imperfect	Information warfare	Bayesian Nash equilibrium	*Carin et al.* [6], *Jormakka et al.* [11]
	Dynamic games	Complete imperfect	Intrusion detection	Optimal solution	*Alpcan et al.* [2]
			Network security	Nash equilibrium	*Nguyen et al.* [24]
		Incomplete imperfect	Network security	Nash equilibrium	*Alpcan et al.* [1]
			Network security	Nash and Bayesian	*You et al.* [4]
		Complete perfect	Computer network	Nash equilibrium	*Lye et al.* [20]
			Risk assessment	optimal solution	*Xiaolin et al.* [34]
			Security and intrusion detection	Nash equilibrium	*Nguyen et al.* [25]
		Incomplete perfect	Intrusion detection in mobile ad-hoc network	Nash and Bayesian	*Patcha et al.* [26]
			Information network	Nash equilibrium	*Alpcan et al.* [3]
			Intrusion response	Optimal solution	*Bloem et al.* [5]

Definition 5. Cooperative game [33]: is a competition between groups of players, rather than between individual players. Players who are in the same group cooperate.

Remark 1. In reality, many cybersecurity issues are non-cooperative games [33]. Hence, in the remaining of the paper, we will focus on Non-cooperative games.

3.1   Classification

Based on a number of stages (one or multiple), we have *Static* and *Dynamic games* [33].

- In a *static game* (or strategic game), each player makes a single decision at the beginning of the game at the same time and each of them has no information about the actions of the other players before making their own action.
- A *dynamic game* (or extensive game) is a game that is comprised of multiples steps, and players may have some information about the outcomes of the previous games.

We have the following sub-classes in Static and Dynamic Games:

- perfect information or not;
- complete information or not.

Table 3. Analysis of game theoretic methods for VM to VM attacks and VM to hypervisor attacks in cloud environments.

Cloud Resource Allocation Games, (*Jalaparti et al.* [10], 2010)		
Characteristics	Parameters and assumptions	
a. Define a CRAG (cloud resource allocation game)	Game	CRAG: Static SCRAG: Dynamic
b. Prove that with a function named linear cost functions, the cost to the system at Nash equilibrium is at most a constant factor over the optimal	Game players	Cloud users
c. Define an SCRAG (Stackelberg CRAG) and two types of strategies: Aloof Strategy [10] and Least cost first strategy [10]		Provider
d. Using strategy named Least cost first at the SCRAG, they show the cost to the system at Nash equilibrium is at most $1/\alpha$ times worse compared to the optimal assignment for the CRAG where α is the fraction of jobs to the optimal assignment for the CRAG	Assumptions	- As resource, only CPU is considered for all clients - Selfish clients - The provider's goal is to optimize the total utility of the clients - The cloud has sufficient amount of resources

Game Theoretic Modeling Of Security And Interdependency In A Public Cloud, (*Kamhoua et al.* [12], 2014)		
Characteristics	Parameters and assumptions	
a. Study the interdependence problem in a public cloud	Game	Static
b. Game theory is used to model the scenario in which an indirect attack is considered for independent users	Game players	Cloud users
c. The model is defined so that the hypervisor is not directly compromised	Assumptions	- Players are rational - Each player has two strategies: Invest in security or not

Security Aware Virtual Machine Allocation In Cloud: A Game Theoretic Approach, (*Kwiat et al.* [17], 2015)		
Characteristics	Parameters and assumptions	
	Game	Static
a. Propose a solution that minimize interdependence in [12]	Game players	Cloud users
b. Nash Equilibrium doesn't dependent of the hypervisor's behavior with independent users (malicious or not)		
c. Resolve issues of Interdependency among several users	Assumptions	- Players are rational - Each user runs only one virtual machine

Establishing evolutionary game models for CYBer security information EXchange (Cybex), (*Deepak et al.* [32], 2016)		
Characteristics	Parameters and Assumptions	
	Game	Non-cooperative dynamic game
a. Cybex (CYBer security information EXchange) game formulation and analysis	Game players	Firm
b. To find the optimal Equilibrium solution for the stability of a chosen strategy	Assumptions	- The players are rational - Firms are dynamically evolving and interacting in a non-cooperative manner

Remark 2. All static games are of the sub-class imperfect information because they only have one stage.

Table 2 shows the connection between cybersecurity and game theory. Flagship papers contributed to this relationship [15,16].

4   Discussions on Different Game Theory Methods Applied to Host Threats

We present the state-of-the-art practices to control virtual machines, hypervisors and data vulnerabilities using game theory.

4.1   Game Theoretic Methods Against VM to VM Attacks and VM to Hypervisor Attacks

Based on the independent nature of cloud users, the literature review suggests that using game theory can help solve many issues such as virtual machine allocation [27,35]. Hence, some papers like [10,12,17] focus on game theoretic approaches and their applications to efficient and secure virtual machine resource allocations.

In Table 3, we compare different papers that use game theoretic methods for virtual machine and hypervisor security on cloud computing system [10,12,17, 32].

4.2   Game Theoretic Methods Against Data Attacks

On cloud computing, many users share the same storage platform. This allows malicious (but legitimate) cloud users to get access and alter other users' data. In table 4, we analyse papers [7–9] that talk about data security on cloud computing.

4.3   Discussions and Challenges

In cloud computing, multiple clients share the same resources like CPU that could cause interference between users' tasks. For instance, if we consider the rates per CPU/hours, a client will be paid more when the server is loaded than when it is not. This means that the interaction between customer tasks has an impact on prices. However existing pricing and scheduling schemes do not focus on these interconnectedness between the clients who are hosted in the cloud. As solution, in 2010 *Jalaparti et al.* proposed a game theory method for modeling the complex client-client (CRAG) and client-provider (SCRAG) interactions in a cloud [10]. Unlike traditional solutions, they ensured that the pricing will be optimal and proportional to the resources used by the clients. On the provider side the resources will be used optimally.

On the other hand, a the major factor that makes difficult the adoption of the cloud comes from the danger of sharing the hypervisor. In fact, an attacker can launch an indirect attack on user x by first compromising the VM of user y and then passes on the hypervisor. If the latter is compromised, all the machines which are connected to it will be compromised including that of user x. This is an interdependency problem, where the security of one user may impact the security of another user. It is another interaction between cloud users that

Table 4. Analysis of game theoretic methods for data security in the cloud.

Smart Cloud Storage Service Selection Based on Fuzzy Logic,
Theory of Evidence and Game Theory, (*Esposito et al.* [8],
2015)

Characteristics	Parameters and Assumptions	
	Game	Non-cooperative game with complete information
a. They used fuzzy inference for choosing the best service against the problem of storage service selection		
b. Diverse formulations of the strategies to efficiently find the best solution	Game players	Customers
	Assumptions	-Egoistical players -Each player is interested by how to optimise its own cost without any consideration of the situation of the other players

Data Integrity and Availability Verification Game in
Untrusted Cloud Storage, (*Djebaili et al.* [7], 2014)

Characteristics	Parameters and Assumptions	
	Game	Non-cooperative game
a. Resolve the cloud data check for that they define cloud storage verification game and find the Nash equilibrium for solving the game	Game players	Third party auditor
		Cloud provider
b. Consider more realistic assumptions in their model	Assumptions	- The provider stores the clients data - The third party auditor checks data by using a deterministic schema - Strategy type: Mixed strategy - Third party auditor actions are 'check' or 'not check' - Cloud provider actions are 'delete' or 'modify'

Auditing a Cloud Providers Compliance with Data Backup
Requirements: A Game Theoretical Analysis, (*Ziad Ismail et
al.* [9], 2016)

Characteristics	Parameters and Assumptions	
a. Focus on verifying data availability when data is outsourced to the cloud provider	Game	Non-cooperative static game
b. Third party auditor's optimal verification	Game players	The provider and the Third party auditor(TPA)
c. With a case study, they experiment the analytical results	Assumptions	- Players are rational - Auditor has as strategy to 'check' or 'not check' and the provider, 'replicate' or 'not'

traditional security methods cannot resolve. We contend that game theory is exactly right for this situation. This is because it is described as a mathematical model between opposing, or cooperating decision-makers. Hence, *Kamhoua et al.* viewed attacks on the hypervisor and how to mitigate them from a game theoretical perspective [12]. *Kwiat et al.* [17] proposed a solution against the negative externality issue that was elicited in [12]. However, in [12] and [17] a game player knows other players estimated loss.

A collaboration of security agencies is necessary to cope with future cyber crimes. However, a framework is needed to facilitate the exchanges between the agencies or firms: Cybex (Cybersecurity Information Exchange). The authors in paper [32] studied Cybex using game theory, because Cybex involves firms, i.e., decision-makers. In addition, the connection between game theory and cybersecurty is already established [12,33]. However, the authors considered just two crucial problems related to cybersecurity.

Integrity and availability are the main issues we encounter while storing data in cloud computing systems. Despite the proposal of several verification schemes in the literature, questions are still asked about the frequency of verification schemes and their optimal/efficient usage. The best approach will be to use game theory to achieve the minimum cost, maintain accuracy and consistency. That is why in [7], the authors tried to find the best approach by treating the data integrity check issue as a non-cooperative game, and by deriving the minimum verification resource requirements and the optimal strategy of the verification. Similarly, *Ismail et al.* analyzed the issue of checking availability of the data when it is outsourced to a cloud service provider [9]. They formulated the issue between the cloud provider and the third party auditor as a non-cooperative game for finding an optimal data verification strategy.

As future works, [10] opens exciting challenges such as: the proposition of other game models that take into account different types of resources, including many cloud service providers, and various privacy and security constraints that a user might require, e.g., Client X may not want to be collocated with Client Y. It will be also interesting to redesign the proposal of *Kwiat et al.* [17] as a game with incomplete information and to extend the proposal of *Tosh et al.* [32] with different investment scenarios. The authors of [7] focus on data verification and integrity in cloud computing systems where the provider is dishonest. However, their work requires improvements by considering other assumptions such as the externalization of several types of a data to a provider, replication of data, etc. In [9], the authors experimented with the aforementioned situation by replicating each type of the same data numerous times in the cloud. They featured in limited parameters: size and sensitivity.

5   Conclusion

This survey summarizes the advantages and limitations of several cloud proposals on virtual machine security, hypervisor security and data security, that use game theory. In each category of the proposals, we reviewed the parameters, assumptions and characteristics of the proposed solutions. We notice that game theory solves many security issues that traditional methods cannot solve. Among these problems, we have: interactions between users tasks, interdependency problem between users on the same hypervisor, data verification for achieving minimum cost, maintaining accuracy and consistency data, etc. We observed fundamental limitations in some proposed game model solutions that should be taken into account in future research.

References

1. Alpcan, T., Basar, T.: A game theoretic analysis of intrusion detection in access control systems. In: 2004 43rd IEEE Conference on Decision and Control (CDC) (IEEECat. No.04CH37601), vol. 2, pp. 1568–1573 December 2004
2. Alpcan, T., Basar, T.: An intrusion detection game with limited observations (2005)
3. Alpcan, T., Pavel, L.: Nash equilibrium design and optimization. In: 1st International Conference on Game Theory for Networks, GAMENETS 2009, Istanbul, Turkey, 13-15 May 2009, pp. 164–170 (2009)
4. You, X.Z., Shiyong, Z.: A kind of network security behavior model based on game theory. In: Proceedings of the Fourth International Conference on Parallel and Distributed Computing, Applications and Technologies, pp. 950–954, August 2003
5. Bloem, M., Alpcan, T., Basar, T.: Intrusion response as a resource allocation problem. In: Proceedings of the 45th IEEE Conference on Decision and Control, pp. 6283–6288, December 2006
6. Carin, L., Cybenko, G., Hughes, J.: Cybersecurity strategies: the queries methodology. Computer **41**(8), 20–26 (2008)
7. Djebaili, B., Kiennert, C., Leneutre, J., Chen, L.: Data integrity and availability verification game in untrusted cloud storage. In: Proceedings of 5th International Conference on Decision and Game Theory for Security, GameSec 2014, Los Angeles, CA, USA, 6-7 November 2014, pp. 287–306 (2014)
8. Esposito, C., Ficco, M., Palmieri, F., Castiglione, A.: Smart cloud storage service selection based on fuzzy logic, theory ofevidence and game theory. IEEE Trans. Comput. **65**(8), 2348–2362 (2016)
9. Ismail, Z., Kiennert, C., Leneutre, J., Chen, L.: Auditing a cloud providers compliance with data backup requirements: a game theoretical analysis. IEEE Trans. Inform. Forensics Secur. **11**(8), 1685–1699 (2016)
10. Jalaparti, V., Nguyen, G.D.: Cloud resource allocation games, March 2019
11. Jormakka, J., Mols, J.V.E.: Modelling information warfare as a game. J. Inform. Warfare **4**, 12–25 (2005)
12. Kamhoua, C.A., Kwiat, L., Kwiat, K.A., Park, J.S., Zhao, M., Rodriguez, M.: Game theoretic modeling of security and interdependency in a public cloud. In: 2014 IEEE 7th International Conference on Cloud Computing, pp. 514–521, June 2014
13. Khalil, I., Khreishah, A., Azeem, M.: Cloud computing security: a survey. Computers **3**, 1–35 (2014)
14. Koloniari, G., Sifaleras, A.: Game-theoretic approaches in cloud and P2P networks: issues and challenges. In: Sifaleras, A., Petridis, K. (eds.) Operational Research in the Digital Era – ICT Challenges. SPBE, pp. 11–22. Springer, Cham (2019). https://doi.org/10.1007/978-3-319-95666-4_2
15. Kunreuther, H., Heal, G.: Interdependent security: the case of identical agents. Working Paper 8871, National Bureau of Economic Research, April 2002
16. Kunreuther, H., Kunreuther, H.: Interdependent security: the case of identical agents. J. Risk Uncertain. **26**, 2003 (2002)

17. Kwiat, L., Kamhoua, C.A., Kwiat, K.A., Tang, J., Martin, A.P.: Security-aware virtual machine allocation in the cloud: a gametheoretic approach. In: 8th IEEE International Conference on Cloud Computing, CLOUD 2015, New York City, NY, USA, 27 June - 2 July 2015, pp. 556–563 (2015)
18. Liu, P., Zang, W., Yu, M.: Incentive-based modeling and inference of attacker intent, objectives, and strategies. ACM Trans. Inf. Syst. Secur. **8**(1), 78–118 (2005)
19. Liu, Y., Comaniciu, C., Man, H.: A Bayesian game approach for intrusion detection in wireless ad hoc networks. In: Proceeding from the 2006 Workshop on Game Theory for Communications and Networks, GameNets 2006. ACM, New York(2006)
20. Lye, K.-W., Wing, J.M.: Game strategies in network security. Int. J. Inf. Secur. **4**(1–2), 71–86 (2005)
21. Manshaei, M.H., Zhu, Q., Alpcan, T., Bacşar, T., Hubaux, J.-P.: Game theory meets network security and privacy. ACM Comput. Surv. **45**(3), 25:1–25:39 (2013)
22. Marston, S., Li, Z., Bandyopadhyay, S., Zhang, J., Ghalsasi, A.: Cloud computing - the business perspective. Decis. Support Syst. **51**(1), 176–189 (2011)
23. Narwal, P., Kumar, D., Sharma, M.: A review of game-theoretic approaches for secure virtual machine resource allocation in cloud. In: Proceedings of the Second International Conference on Information and Communication Technology for Competitive Strategies (2016)
24. Nguyen, K.C., Alpcan, T., Basar, T.: Security games with incomplete information. In: 2009 IEEE International Conference on Communications, pp. 1–6, June 2009
25. Nguyen, K.C., Alpcan, T., Basar, T.: Stochastic games for security in networks with interdependent nodes. In: 1st International Conference on Game Theory for Networks, GAMENETS 2009, Istanbul, Turkey, May 13-15, 2009, pp. 697–703 (2009)
26. Patcha, A. Park, J.: A game theoretic approach to modeling intrusion detection in mobile ad hoc networks. In: Proceedings from the Fifth Annual IEEE SMC Information Assurance Workshop, pp. 280–284, June 2004
27. Pillai, P.S., Rao, S.: Resource allocation in cloud computing using the uncertain-typrinciple of game theory. IEEE Syst. J. **10**(2), 637–648 (2016)
28. Roy, S., Ellis, C., Shiva, S., Dasgupta, D., Shandilya, V., Wu, Q.: A survey of game theory as applied to network security. In: 2010 43rd Hawaii International Conference on System Sciences, pp. 1–10, January 2010
29. Shahzad, F.: State-of-the-art survey on cloud computing security challenges, approaches and solutions. Proc. Comput. Sci. **37**, 357–362 (2014). The 5th International Conference on Emerging Ubiquitous Systems and Pervasive Networks (EUSPN-2014)/The 4th International Conference on Current and Future Trends of Information and Communication Technologies in Healthcare (ICTH 2014)/Affiliated Workshops
30. Simmon, E., Bohn, R.B.: An overview of the NIST cloud computing program and reference architecture. In: Concurrent Engineering Approaches for Sustainable Product Development in a Multi-Disciplinary Environment - Proceedings of the 19th ISPE International Conference on Concurrent Engineering (ISPE CE 2012), Trier, Germany, 3–7 September 2012, pp. 1119–1129 (2012)
31. Takabi, H., Joshi, J., Ahn, G.-J.: Security and privacy challenges in cloud computing environments. IEEE Secur. Priv. **8**, 24–31 (2011)
32. Tosh, D.K., Sengupta, S., Kamhoua, C.A., Kwiat, K.A.: Establishing evolutionary game models for cyber security information exchange (CYBEX). J. Comput. Syst. Sci. **98**, 27–52 (2018)

33. Wang, Y., Wang, Y., Liu, J., Huang, Z., Xie, P.: A survey of game theoretic methods for cyber security. In: 2016 IEEE First International Conference on Data Science in Cyberspace (DSC), pp 631–636, June 2016
34. Xiaolin, C., Xiaobin, T., Yong, Z., Hongsheng, X.: A Markov game theory-based risk assessment model for network information system. In: 2008 International Conference on Computer Science and Software Engineering, vol. 3, pp. 1057–1061, December 2008
35. Xu, X., Yu, H.: A game theory approach to fair and efficient resource allocation incloud computing. Math. Probl. Eng. 1–14(04), 2014 (2014)

New Approach for the Evaluation of Carbon Sequestration Capacity: Case of Closed Plant Formations and Gallery Forests

Narcisse Talla Tankam[1,2(✉)], Janvier Fotsing[2],
Maurice Ndikwé Dourwé[2], Idriss Landry Kouedjou[2],
and Michel Tchotsoua[2]

[1] Automatic and Applied Computer Engineering Laboratory,
University Institute of Technology Fotso Victor,
University of Dschang, Dschang, Cameroon
narcisse.talla@univ-dschang.org
[2] Geomatic Laboratory FALSH, University of Ngaoundere,
Ngaoundere, Cameroon

Abstract. Many techniques for the assessment of Carbone sequestration are developed for classic forests. But less researchers are interested in the evaluation of the Carbone sequestration capacity of marginal forests. In this paper, we propose an innovative technique of evaluating the capacity of Carbon sequestration of marginal forests, based on a new allometric equation and a new technique of colored and multiband image classification.

Based on a series of 151 plots identified and characterized in 15 training representative sites, we identify the various species present on the site of study and we customize the Brown allometric equation. The obtained equation is successfully used to assess the capacity of Carbone sequestration of marginal forests in Adamawa Cameroon. Finally, we obtain that the gallery forests of Mayo Paro sequestered 194.22 t/ha while closed plant formations of Vina sequestered 108.85 t/ha. These results are validated through a verification mission on the site of study.

Keywords: Colored image classification · Vina closed plant formations · Gallery forest · Allometric equation · Carbone sequestration · Marginal forest

1 Introduction

The increase in greenhouse gases (GHGs) concentration in the atmosphere, mainly carbon dioxide (CO2) and methane (CH4), is recognized as one of the causes of current climate change. This increase in GHGs in the atmosphere is, nowadays, one of the most studied issues. Thus, a great scientific interest has developed around forests with their ability to sequester carbon in their biomass via photosynthesis. This stored carbon is lost and abandoned in the nature when the forest is destroyed and combusted, inducing the increase of the proportion of this chemical element in the atmosphere. According to [1] and [2], CO2 emissions from land-use change is the second leading cause of increased atmospheric CO2 concentration, after emissions from fossil fuel combustion.

© ICST Institute for Computer Sciences, Social Informatics and Telecommunications Engineering 2019
Published by Springer Nature Switzerland AG 2019. All Rights Reserved
G. Bassioni et al. (Eds.): InterSol 2019, LNICST 296, pp. 13–25, 2019.
https://doi.org/10.1007/978-3-030-34863-2_2

In Cameroon, forests cover 41.3% of the national territory and represent 10% of Congo watershed forests [3]. According to [4], greenhouse gas emissions in Cameroon in 1994 were estimated at 43 988 Gg of CO_2, equivalent with 50.44%, 37.83% and 7.36% caused respectively by land use change, agriculture and energy.

In order to limit the increase of CO_2 in the atmosphere, strategies such as the Clean Development Mechanism (CDM) and REDD have been developed to reduce GHG emissions such as methane and CO_2. The REDD mechanism, introduced at the Bali Conference in 2007, is to compensate developing countries that reduce deforestation and forest degradation over a period of time. In order to benefit from the financial or technological revenues linked to these mechanisms, it is essential, if not imperative, to know the amount of carbon stored in forests. However, few data on biomass or carbon stock in sub-Saharan Africa, notably in Cameroon, are available to date and most of the studies that have been conducted there have been conducted in the dense forests of greater South-Cameroon, part of the Congo watershed [5–7]. The state of the literature on the issue in the Sudano-Guinean savannahs of Adamawa reveals a need for knowledge on the quantification of the carbon stock in this ecosystem and mainly on closed plant formations. The studies carried out by [8] and [9] constitute reference frames in the Sudano-Guinean savannahs of Adamawa. To evaluate the carbon stock in the ecosystem, the authors used the classical allometric equation [10] as if the site of study were in the dense forest of Congo watershed.

In this study, based on the spatialization and quantification of Gallery forests and closed plant formations, we propose a new methodology of sequestered hypogeous carbon stock evaluation. The proposed approach, thank to an inventory of various species present in the site of study, customizes the classical allometric equation for sequestered carbon estimation and describes an accurate methodology of carbon stock evaluation, based on a new technique of colored image classification, adapted for marginal forests.

The remaining paper is organized as follows: we first present, in the next section, the site of study, then in the 3rd section, we present the materials, data and methods. In the 4 section before the conclusion, we present and discuss some relevant results obtained.

2   Site of Study

The site of study is located in the Cameroonian Adamawa region (Fig. 1), between 12° and 15° East Longitude and between 6° and 8° North Latitude. The Mayo Paro watershed is located in the district of Tignère, the capital of the Division of Faro-et-Déo, Adamawa Region. It is located between latitudes 6°60' and 7°24' North and longitudes 12°30' and 12°42' East. Limited in the West by the Galim-Tignère sub-division, it shares its northern borders with the Mayo Lolti watershed, in the South with the Mayo Poutghou watershed and in the East with the Mayo Tignère watershed. The catchment area covers an area of approximately 56 118.7134 ha, occupied by 12 villages: Loungtoung, Walkossam, Mayo-Toloré, Laura, Sadeck, Mayo rounkongo 1 and 2, Paro lewel 1 and 2, Gassanguel, Carrefour Galim, and Paro Ndjidda. The climate is equilibrated by a rainy season and a dry season. The temperature varies from 12° to 34°. The main activity in the study site is breeding.

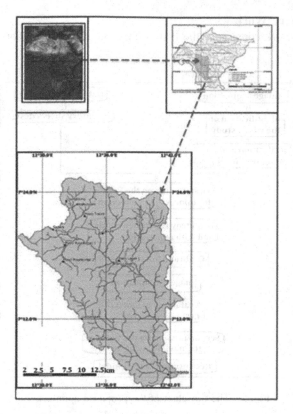

Fig. 1. Localization of the site of study.

3 Materials, Data and Methods

3.1 Materials and Data

To carry out the inventory, we used: a GPS (Global Positioning System) terminal for the acquisition of geographic coordinates of eligible trees in selected plots; a tape measure to measure the circumference of individuals (eligible trees); a digital camera for taking pictures of trees to determine their height; inventory sheets to copy auxiliary data; machetes to facilitate progression in the forest and to bark trees and a meter board to calibrate the height of individuals for the height evaluation process.

As data, we used Landsat images taken on May 2014, with 30 m spatial resolution, for the extraction of information related to the areas of the closed plant formations of the site of study. We also used Google EarthView images to locate the site of study.

3.2 Methods

Following is the flowchart of the proposed approach (Fig. 2).

3.2.1 Preliminary Work

The preliminary work consists of the first five actions of the flowchart.

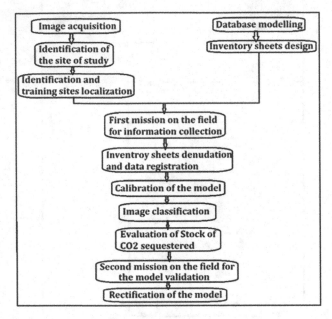

Fig. 2. The flowchart of the proposed approach.

From the laboratory, on the one hand, the conceptual model of data is built and the relational model is derived for the inventory sheets building. On the other hand, from the Landsat image acquired, the site of study is identified and extracted. From the site of study, the various training sites are localized and their geographical coordinates extracted.

3.2.2 Field Missions

Once the preliminary work is done in the laboratory, the first mission is organized on the field. Within this first mission; in the first site of study (closed plant formations), 90 plots of 400 m^2 each are carried out in 09 representative sampling sites. In the second site of study, 61 plots of 400 m^2 each are carried out in 6 sampling sites. The sampling sites were chosen accordingly to the accessibility and representativeness of the plant formation.

The floristic inventory consisted of identifying and characterising, for each plot, all trees of at least 31.5 cm circumference and at least 5 m height within the plot. Individuals that did not meet these criteria were simply identified and registered in the database, without being menstruated. On each of the individuals fulfilling the above conditions, the determination of scientific names was done *in situ*, thanks to the "Ligneux du sahel" [11] book. For unidentified species, specimens were collected for identification at the Cameroon National Herbarium. The circumference was measured in order to deduce the Diameter at Breast Height (DBH). In the forest, some trees had foothills at 1.30 m (DBH). For this category, we measured the circumference beyond the buttress as suggested in [12]. To determine the height of the trees, we used the photograph of the tree calibrated with a meter board, and we determined the height thanks to the software "Mesurim" [13].

3.2.3 Determination of Biomass and Carbon

In order to determine the amount of carbon stored at the individual level and considering the diversity of species, the use of allometric equations for each species would be ideal because of the diversity of forms [14]. But considering this diversity, lack of resources forced many researchers to use the same methodology for all species.

Many authors use regression equations for the most commonly encountered species in sites [15] and [16]. Among the existing equations for estimating biomass, that of Brown et al. [10] was retained because it has been developed under climatic conditions similar to our site of study, with an average annual rainfall varying from 1500 to 4000 mm, including that of Adamawa (1200–2000 mm) and the coefficient of determination between the biomass of the trees and their two parameters (DBH and height) is highly significant ($R^2 = 0.987$). In addition, this formula takes into account the dendrometric factors from our inventory. For a given specie i, this biomass equation is given by:

$$B_i = e^{-\alpha_i + \beta_i * \ln(DBH_i^2 * h_i)} \tag{1}$$

h_i being the total height of the tree of specie i.

For the Berlinia grandiflora specie for example, the coefficients are given by:

$$\alpha_i = -3.1441; \; \beta_i = +0.9719 \tag{2}$$

It is known that the estimation of the carbon contained in a tree is the half of the value of its dry biomass [10]. This relationship has been modeled by the following equation:

$$\text{Stored carbon } (C_i) = \frac{1}{2} B_i \tag{3}$$

The amount of carbon sequestered in a plot j is then obtained by the following equation,

$$SC_j = \frac{1}{2} \sum_i \left(e^{-\alpha_i + \beta_i * \ln(DBH_i^2 * h_i)} \right)_j \tag{4}$$

Since the size of a plot is $P = 20 \text{ m} \times 20\text{m} = 400 \text{ m}^2$, the quantity of sequestered carbon per unit of 1 m^2 in the whole site of study, made of Ns plots, is given by the following equation:

$$SC_u = \frac{1}{2P}\sum_{j=1}^{Ns}\sum_i \left(e^{-\alpha_i + \beta_i * \ln(DBH_i^2 * h_i)}\right)_j \qquad (5)$$

Once the quantity of Carbone sequestered per 1 m^2 is known, we classify the image, using a supervised image classification approach and we calculate the total area of the marginal forest. Then the Total quantity of sequestered Carbone is given by the following equation:

$$SC_t = \frac{A}{2P}\sum_{j=1}^{Ns}\sum_i \left(e^{-\alpha_i + \beta_i * \ln(DBH_i^2 * h_i)}\right)_j \qquad (6)$$

A being the total area of the marginal forest in the area of study, expressed in m^2.

It is then compulsory to estimate the total area of the closed plant formations and gallery forests present in the site of study. For this purpose, we proceed by image classification.

3.2.4 Colored Image Classification

The classification process begins with the development of the predefined classes of land occupation. Eleven (11) thematic classes have been defined: River, Tree savannah, Burns, Grassy savannah, Built, Wooded savannah, Closed plant formations, Clear forest, Cultivated field and Gallery forest.

We opted for the "maximum likelihood" in a supervised classification method because of its fairly widespread use in remote sensing. It is a method based on probabilistic approaches. It consists in calculating the probability of one pixel to belong to one class rather than another. At the end of this operation, each pixel of the image is attached to one of the previously listed land occupation classes.

For this purpose, the first action was the separation of various bands (R, G, B) of the image. Indeed, the remote sensing colored image is a combination of at least three image bands, each being a grey scale image that can be treated separately. On each band, a series of 20 textural parameters is tested and the correlated ones eliminated. At the end of this process, the following textural parameters [Haralick, 1973] were adopted:

(1) The Energy parameter. This textural parameter measures the uniformity of the texture. Its expression, for a given band R, is given by the following equation.

$$ENE_R = \sum_{i=0}^{MaxGS}\sum_{j=0}^{MaxGS}\left(P_{t_R}(i,j)\right)^2. \qquad (7a)$$

Where $MaxGS$ is the maximum grey scale in the R image band, t_R is the translation vector t, linking the pixel of grey scale j to the pixel of grey scale i in band R and $P_{t_R}(i,j)$ is the probability of occurrence of a couple (i, j) linked by this vector t_R in the image. Similarly, the energy parameter for the two other bands is given by respectively by the following equations.

$$ENE_G = \sum_{i=0}^{MaxGS} \sum_{j=0}^{MaxGS} (P_{t_G}(i,j))^2; \quad B_{ENE} = \sum_{i=0}^{MaxGS} \sum_{j=0}^{MaxGS} (P_{t_B}(i,j))^2. \quad (7b)$$

From Eqs. 7a and 7b, Considering that B1 = Red image band; B2 = Green image band and B3 = Blue image band, we define the equation of the energy textural parameter for the coloured image as follows:

$$ENE = \frac{1}{3}(ENE_{B1} + ENE_{B2} + ENE_{B3}) = \frac{1}{3} \sum_{k=1}^{3} \sum_{i=0}^{MaxGS} \sum_{j=0}^{MaxGS} (P_{t_{Bk}}(i,j))^2. \quad (8)$$

(2) The entropy parameter. In contrary to the Energy, this textural parameter measures the untidiness observed in the image. For a given image band Bk (k = 1, 2, 3), its expression is given by the following equation:

$$ENT_{Bk} = \sum_{i=0}^{MaxGS} \sum_{j=0}^{MaxGS} [Log(P_{t_{Bk}}(i,j)) \times P_{t_{Bk}}(i,j)]. \quad (9)$$

According to Eq. 9 and similarly to Eq. 8, the value of the parameter Entropy for the image is given by:

$$ENT = \frac{1}{3} \sum_{k=1}^{3} \sum_{i=0}^{MaxGS} \sum_{j=0}^{MaxGS} [Log(P_{t_{Bk}}(i,j)) \times P_{t_{Bk}}(i,j)]. \quad (10)$$

(3) The correlation parameter. This textural parameter measures the linear dependence (related to the translation vector t) of grey levels in the image. It is neither in correlation with the energy nor the entropy parameters. For a given image band Bk (k = 1, 2, 3), its expression is given by the following equation:

$$COR_{Bk} = \sum_{i=0}^{MaxGS} \sum_{j=0}^{MaxGS} \left[\frac{(i-\mu)(j-\mu)}{\sigma^2} P_{t_{Bk}}(i,j) \right]. \quad (11)$$

According to Eq. 11 and similarly to Eq. 8, the value of the parameter Entropy for the image is given by:

$$COR = \frac{1}{3} \sum_{k=1}^{3} \sum_{i=0}^{MaxGS} \sum_{j=0}^{MaxGS} \left[\frac{(i-\mu)(j-\mu)}{\sigma^2} P_{t_{Bk}}(i,j) \right]. \quad (12)$$

Where μ and σ represent respectively the mean and the standard deviation related to the structural operator.

(4) The contrast parameter. This textural parameter, the last among the selected parameters, deals with the passage of higher to lower grey levels consecutively in the image. Its expression, for a given image band Bk, is given by the following equation:

$$CST_{Bk} = \sum_{i=0}^{MaxGS} \sum_{j=0}^{MaxGS} \left[(i-j)^2 P_{t_{Bk}}(i,j) \right]. \quad (13)$$

According to Eq. 13 and similarly to Eq. 8, the value of the parameter Contrast for the image is given by:

$$COR = \frac{1}{3}\sum_{k=1}^{3}\sum_{i=0}^{MaxGS}\sum_{j=0}^{MaxGS}\left[\frac{(i-\mu)(j-\mu)}{\sigma^2}P_{t_{Bk}}(i,j)\right]. \qquad (14)$$

The value of $P_{t_{Bk}}(i,j)$ is given by the following equation

$$P_{t_{Bk}}(i,j) = \frac{|\{(r,s),(r,s)+t \in Bk/Bk(r,s)=i \text{ and } Bk((r,s)+t)=j\}|}{|(r,s)/(r,s) \in Bk \text{ and } (r,s)+t \in Bk|}. \qquad (15)$$

Where |X| is the cardinal number of the set X.

Centred on each identified plot in the various sites of study, an image window of size 9×9 is extracted. This size was adopted after a series of empirical tests of image window sizes, from 3×3 to 15×15. For each image window W_i, the four adopted textural parameters are calculated to form a textural vector

$$V_{W_i} = (ENE_{W_i}, ENT_{W_i}, COR_{W_i}, CST_{W_i}). \qquad (16)$$

For the Np plots identified on the training site as dominated by a certain information class C, the characteristic textural vector CV_C of the information class C is given by the following equation.

$$CV_C = \frac{1}{N_p}\left(\sum_{i=1}^{N_p} ENE_{W_i}, \sum_{i=1}^{N_p} ENT_{W_i}, \sum_{i=1}^{N_p} COR_{W_i}, \sum_{i=1}^{N_p} CST_{W_i}\right). \qquad (17)$$

Nine information classes have been identified on the training site: Built, Cultivated field, Clear forest, Closed plant formations, Burns, Tree savannah, Wooded savannah, Grassy savannah and Gallery forest.

For each pixel of the image, a 9×9 size image window is extracted and the characteristic vector calculated. The pixel is assigned to the information class that minimises the distance between the characteristic vector of the pixel and its proper characteristic vector. The symmetric border filling method is adopted for the management of border pixels.

4 Results

4.1 Land Cover Analysis

Figure 3 shows the mapping of land cover types in the Vina Division. It shows that natural plant formations are distributed over the entire area. The linear form of construction is located mainly along the roads, which reflects the fact that the roads are development factors. The strong concentration of the Mount in the center of the map, is justified by the fact that, it is the place of junction of the various road axes, materializing the principal city (Ngaoundéré) of the region. Fields and burns are more concentrated around the city. This situation reflects the fact that the populations do not have enough space around their compounds for the practice of agro-pastoral activities.

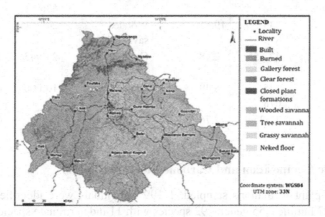

Fig. 3. Land cover types

Figure 3 shows the spatial distribution of closed plant formations in the Vina Division. It appears that these formations are distributed over the whole area but are more concentrated at the northern end of the study area.

The classification quality can be evaluated by the Overall accuracy (OA) statistic parameter, which designates the percentage of correctly classified pixels. In addition to OA, the classification can be evaluated by the use of confusion matrix in term of the designated target C (information class). In this case, the probability detection for a given thematic class C (tree savannah for example) is assimilated to the precision of C signatures detection which corresponds to the pixels correctly classified. Therefore, the probability of false alarms reported in normal site of study becomes equivalent to the commission error to detect the absence of selected thematic class in the studied area [17]. For the present study, the Kappa index was used to evaluate our classification accuracy. It measures accuracy and expresses the proportional reduction of the error obtained by a classification method, compared to the error obtained by a completely random classification technique. The average value of the Kappa Index obtained as part of our classification is 97.25%.

The post-classification treatments made it possible to highlight the areas (in hectares) of the different types of land use (Table 1). Thus, the closed plant formations of the Division of Vina cover an area of 145 678 ha and represent eighth of the total area of this Division.

Table 1. Area of different types of land use

Land cover type	Area (ha)	Percentage (%)	Land cover type	Area (ha)	Percentage (%)
Built	4775	0.28	Tree savannah	848 626	49.45
Culture field	335 815	19.57	Wooded savannah	247 165	14.40
Clear forest	42 555	2.48	Grassy savannah	25 943	1.51
Closed plant formations	145 678	8.49	Gallery forest	10 000	0.6
Burns	47 354	2.76	Unclassified	7 856	0,46

4.2 Floristic Composition and Carbone Stock Per Specie

In the closed plant formations sampled, 1 199 individuals were identified. They are divided into 27 families, 55 genera, 92 species with 11 indeterminate species (Table 2). Syzygium guineense, Vitex doniana, Breonadia salicina, have the highest frequencies respectively 276, 94 and 80 individuals out of the 1 199 individuals identified. The estimated amount of biomass is 783.69 tones for all the plant formations sampled with an average of 217.7 t/ha. The approximate value of the total amount of carbon stored by these sampled formations is 391.845 tones of Carbon with an average of 108.85 t/ha.

Table 2. Distribution of biomass and stored Carbone by family

Species	Quantities	Biomass (Kg)	Stocked Carbone (t)
Myrtaceae	284	156749.39	78.37
Euphorbiaceae	172	73056.79	36.53
Rubiaceae	98	56577.83	28.29
Verbenaceae	187	323918.17	24.06
Ebenaceae	67	35864.33	17.93
Moraceae	57	29903.63	14.95
Mimosaceae	51	27188.97	13.59
Total	916	703259,11	213,72

Species with less than 2 tones of Carbone sequestered are ignored in the table.

4.3 Biomass and Stocked Carbone Quantity Estimation

The estimate of the biomass contained in all the closed plant formations of the site of study was based on the previous data summarized in the following Table 3.

Table 3. Summaries of data used to estimate the global Carbon stock.

Data	Values
Closed plan formations	145 678 ha
Sampled area	3.6 ha
Expansion factor	40 466
Total quantity of stocked Carbone par sample	783 694.16 kg
Total quantity of stocked Carbone par sample	253.95 kg C

The estimate of the biomass contained in all the closed plant formations of the site of study was based on an extrapolation, from an expansion factor (40 466).

Thus, the value of the total biomass contained in the closed plant formations of the zone of study is approximately 20 552 681.4 t. The amount of carbon stored by these closed vegetation formations is estimated at 10 276 340.7 t C.

Knowing that one tone of CO2 reduction is equivalent to one tone of carbon credit [18], one can estimate the amount of total credit of Carbone generated by marginal forests of Adamaoua Cameroon.

4.4 Carbon Credit

There are several carbon estimation programs and methodologies, and carbon credit nomenclature may vary depending on the programs under which the credits in question were recorded:

- Verified Emissions Reduction (VER) are the carbon units generated according to ISO 14 064-2
- The Climate Reserve Tonne (CRT) is the carbon unit recorded by the Climate Action Reserve (CAR), a California registry.

The Verified Carbon Standard (VCS) program names the Verified Carbon Unit (VCU) carbon credits using various methodologies other than the VCS methodology; for example, the Clean Development Mechanism (CDM) methodology and the Climate Action Reserve (CAR) methodology (except for the Forest and Urban Forest methodology). Our approach falls within this program. The vintage of the carbon credit and the methodology used for quantification are some of the factors that influence the price of carbon credit. The vintage is a term for the year of production of the carbon credit, which is the year the GHG reduction occurred [18].

To obtain carbon credits that can be sold on the market, three stages are required:

- The first step is to **quantify its emissions**, that is, the quantification of the reduction according to a protocol or methodology.
- The second step is to validate and/or to verify, by a third party. It is a question of validating the initial hypotheses and the calculation methodology. Verification is always mandatory. An auditor certifies that the protocol and the data used for calculation and mathematical reasoning are accurate.

- Finally, the third step is the registration of carbon credits on a recognized register. This registration creates a unique and traceable serial number. It is this serial number that is sold on the carbon market.

The present project contributes at the first stage.

4.5   Discussion

The plant formations involved in this study are still not continuous in space and hermetically closed. Despite this constraint, a maximum of effort has been made to obtain a representation as close to reality. The good knowledge of the field, coupled with information extracted from Google Earth tool were decisive. The illustration is also given by the statistically acceptable classification rate (Kappa index = 97%).

However, this value of carbon obtained per hectare (108.85 t/ha) in the Division of Vina, combined with the area covered by the closed plant formations of this Division (145 678 ha) show how marginal the forests of the Congo watershed, and particularly that of our site of study, are an integral part of the response to climate change, through its role in reducing the amount of carbon present in the atmosphere.

5   Conclusion

The purpose of this work was to provide an accurate method of estimating the biomass and quantity of Carbon sequestered in the closed plant formations. The Vina Division, located in cameroonian Adamaoua region has been selected as site of study. Taking into account the collection period of the phytogeographic data, these plant formations sequestered about 10 276 340,7 tones of Carbone (tC) in May 2014 (year of image acquisition and month of field mission). The species ensuring the largest carbon stocks are Syzygium guineense (77 tC), Breonadia salicina (27tC), Vitex doniana (20 tC). This study can serve as a reference for future research. This research can be extended by integrating stocks of hypogeous carbon.

Climate change, representing the environmental challenge of the century, including sustainable forest management as a component of REDD+ is an effective way to address this threat. This management requires basic, reliable information on the state of the forest, their evolution and carbon storage potential. This is a major contribution for this issue.

References

1. Ana-Helena, B., Marozzi, F., Maria, S., Fernando Antonio, F., Araujo Crispim, S.M.: Carbon stocks in savannas aboveground biomass of the Nhecolandia Panamal Brazil, 7p. (2012)
2. IPCC: Bilan 2007 des changements climatiques. Contribution des Groupes de travail I, II et III au quatrième Rapport d'évaluation du Groupe d'experts intergouvernemental sur l'évolution du climat, Équipe de rédaction principale Genève, Suisse, 103 p. (2007)
3. EDF (État des Forêts): Les forêts du bassin du Congo, 276 p. (2010)

4. UICN: Comment aborder la REDD+ au Cameroun: Contexte, enjeux et options pour une stratégie nationale. Yaoundé, Cameroun, 103p. (2015)
5. Tayo Gamo, K.Y.: Dynamique de la biodiversité ligneuse et des stocks de carbone dans les systèmes agro forestiers à base de cacaoyer au centre Cameroun: cas de Ngomedzap. Mémoire d'ingénieur, Univ. Dschang 106p. (2014)
6. Dmapo Wambo, J.: Evaluation de la production agricole, variations et relations de quelques indices écologiques et stock de carbone des forets côtières sous un système d'agriculture sur brulis dans le futur parc national de Douala-Edéa. Région du Littoral. Mémoire de master professionnel. Univ. de Yaoundé, 143p. (2012)
7. Vincke, D.: Élaboration d'une méthodologie de la biomasse ligneuse aérienne de populations d'espèces commerciales du Sud-Est du Cameroun. 117p. (2011)
8. Tchobsala: Impacts des coupes de bois sur la végétation naturelle de la zone périurbaine de Ngaoundére (Adamaoua). Thèse de doctorat, univ. De Yaoundé, 207p. (2010)
9. Aoudou Doua, S.: Suivi de l'évolution de la végétation ligneuse de la savane soudanienne dans la haute vallée de la Bénoué au Nord Cameroun. Thèse de doctorat, Univ. De Ngaoundéré, 307p. (2010)
10. Brow et Lugo: Biomass estimation Method for tropical forest with application to forest inventory data. For. sci. **35**, pp. 881–902 (1992)
11. Arbonnier, M., Bonnet, P., Grard, P.: Ligneux du Sahel [électronique Ressource] : outil graphique d'identification, Versailles : Éd. Quae. (2008)
12. Walker, W., Baccini, A., Horning, N., Knight, D., Braun, E., Bausch, A.: Field guide for forest biomass and carbon estimation. Ed. Woods hole research center, 72p. (2011)
13. IFE - Institut français de l'éducation, Mesurim: téléchargement du logiciel - Site des ressources d'ACCES pour enseigner la Science de la Vie et de la Terre (2018). http://acces. ens-lyon.fr/acces/logiciels/applications/mesurim. Accessed 29 oct 2018
14. Ketterings, Q.M., Coe, R., Noordwijk, M., Ambagau, Y., Palm, C.A.: Reducing uncertainty in the use of allometric biomass equations for predicting above-ground tree biomass in mixed secondary forests. For. Ecol. Manage. **120**, 199–209 (2001)
15. IPCC: Good Practice Guidance for Land Use, Land-Use Change and Forestry, 590 p. (2003)
16. Thiams, S., Sambou, B., Mbow, C., Guisse, A.: Elaboration de modèles allométriques d'Acacia Sénégal L Wild pour l'analyse du carbone ligneux en milieu sahélien. Afrique sci. 12p. (2014)
17. Lounis, B., Belhadj-Aissa, A.: Sea SAR images analysis to detect oil slicks in Algerian coasts. J. Math. Model. Algorithms Oper. Res. JMMA **13**(4), 371–386 (2014). https://doi. org/10.1007/s10852-014-9250-3. Print ISSN 2214-2487, Online ISSN2214-2495
18. National Ecocredit: Qu'est-ce qu'un crédit de carbone? (2013). http://www.nationaleco credit.com/le-marche-du-carbone/le-principe-du-marche-du-carbone/quest-ce-quun-credit-de-carbone/

Technical, Economic and Environmental Analysis of Hybrid Energy Solutions for Rural Electrification in the Republic of Chad

Modou Diop[1]([⊠]), Salif Sow[1], Zoutene Pabame[1], Ababacar Ndiaye[1,2], and Cheikh M. F. Kébé[1]

[1] Centre Internationale de Formation et de Recherche en Énergie Solaire (C.I.F.R.E.S), Ecole supérieure polytechnique-UCAD, Fann, BP 5085, Dakar, Sénégal
diopmodou13@yahoo.com, salif.sow01@hotmail.com, zoutenepabame@yahoo.fr, ababacar.ndiay@gmail.com, cmkebe@gmail.com
[2] Université Assane Seck de Ziguinchor, Ziguinchor, Sénégal

Abstract. The use of renewable off grid systems are being more common in the African rural communities. Especially hybrid systems have an important role to play on sustainable energy access for all. Different combinations are possible to ensure intermittent energy production far from the national grids. However, it is important to find the best hybrid combinations for each climate region.

This work focuses on the technical, economic and environmental analysis of a hybrid energy system (SEH), based on **solar-wind-diesel and batteries** applied in the three existing climatic regions of Chad, for the needs of a decentralized rural electrification. The sizing and optimization approach consisted in choosing for each climate region a representative site where the solar and wind potentials data are available. Using HOMER software (Hybrid Optimization Model for Electric Renewable), technical-economic analysis of energy solutions is made for four types of load profiles in each climate region. The system is applied to provide energy separately for domestic use, income generating activities and a telecommunication station all in rural areas. The main performance parameters in which focused the work are the net present cost (NPC), the cost of electricity (COE), the Green House Gases (GHG) emissions and the renewable fraction. The results show that in the Saharan region the best combinations are **PV-wind-diesel-battery** for domestic use, and **PV-diesel-battery** for both water pumping and telecom application. For income generating activities, a **PV-battery** system is the most interesting hybrid system in the Sahelian region. Finally, a sensitivity analysis shows that by increasing the renewable energies fraction in the system, the COE will decrease.

Keywords: Hybrid system · Rural electrification · Homer energy · Optimization · Sensitivity study · Climatic regions · NPC · COE

G. Bassioni et al. (Eds.): InterSol 2019, LNICST 296, pp. 26–37, 2019.
https://doi.org/10.1007/978-3-030-34863-2_3

1 Introduction

The global energy demand ceaseless increasing is one of the major constraint on the preservation of the environment. The satisfaction of this demand is largely based on the use of fossil fuels that have a huge negative impact on the world global warming and the degradation of the ozone layer. In addition, fossil energy resources are in limited quantities, thereby, the need to consider new ways of producing energy for the satisfaction of global demand is necessary [1]. In Africa, The electricity demand in some areas is conventionally supplied by small isolated diesel generators [2]. The operating costs associated with these diesel generators may be unacceptably high due to discounted fossil fuel costs and difficulties in fuel delivery and maintenance of generators [2]. Indeed, the CO_2 emission due to the use of these fossil fuels is one of the principal cause of greenhouse effect on the environment [3].

Renewable energies start playing an important role in the production of electricity in the world. Africa, particularly has a significant renewable energy resources that can help to emphasis energy access without compromising our environment. At the same, most of the African rural population are living far from the countries' national electricity grid.

In this situation, off-grid renewable energy sources, such as solar photovoltaic (PV) and wind turbine generator provide a realistic alternative to supplement diesel generators for electricity supply in rural areas. Indeed, the problem associated to the natural fluctuation of these resources can be partially overcome by combining them to make a hybrid energy system [4]. This is one of the most important systems for developing renewable energies at the moment. That is why we need strategies that are technically, economically and socially viable. Hybrid systems have greater reliability and lower cost than a stand-alone PV or a wind system. In order to have a cost-effective hybrid system, optimal sizing is necessary [5].

Several works have been done to size hybrid systems PV/wind associated with batteries and or diesel generator using different methods [6, 7]. Ramli et al. estimated the energy demand for domestic, industrial, agricultural in a remote village, identified the optimal option for RE based electrification and compared it to conventional grid extension using HOMER software [8]. The results show that a hybrid combination of solar-wind-hydro-battery is cost effective, sustainable, techno-economically and environmentally more viable compared to grid extension.

This paper studies the optimal combination of different energy sources for different load profiles in the three climate region of the republic of Chad. It is conducted for energy supply to the following applications in rural areas: domestic use, income generating actives like shops, telecommunication relay antenna and water pumping. The main elements of the system are solar PV, Wind energy, diesel generator and Batteries. For all the three sites and all the load profiles, the combination of all the components will be the basic system, and homer energy according to the techno-economical parameters gives the best hybrid solution for the different applications in each site. The objective of this paper is to produce a decision support tool for the Government of Chad in the energy sector.

2 Materials and Methods

2.1 Description of the Hybrid System

The photovoltaic array and the wind generator supplies DC phase connected to a bidirectional inverter. The power will be then distributed either directly to the consumers or to the battery bank, depending on the state of charge and state of demand.

The PV modules and the wind turbines work together to satisfy the energy demand. During the day, the renewable energy sources production is first directed to the grid to meet the daily energy needs. If the production from the wind generator and PV array is sufficient, then the other part of the generated power is provided to the battery bank up to its full charge. The batteries can then provide electricity for nocturne energy needs and during cloudy time. In case the batteries have low charge and the PV and wind generators cannot provide enough energy to the system, the diesel generator will be launched automatically to produce the necessary energy to satisfy the demand and charge also the batteries Fig. 1. Depending on the type of load profile and the energy potential in each site, the optimal hybrid system can be with fewer elements. The components not necessary to meet perfectly the demand will be removed from the system.

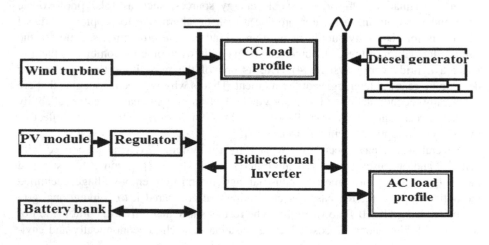

Fig. 1. Block diagram of the hybrid solar-wind-diesel system

2.2 Description of the Sites and Used Data

General Description

The territory of Chad is between 12° and 24° north latitude and 13° and 24° west longitude. Located in north-central Africa, Chad stretches for about 1,800 km from its northernmost point to its southern boundary. It is divided into three (3) major bioclimatic regions, namely the Saharan, Sahelian and Soudanian regions.

The Saharan region covers an area of 600,350 km^2 or 48% of the land area. Dry for nine months of the year, it receives 350 mm (13.8 in) or more of rain, mostly during July and August. The Sahelian region represents about 490,570 km^2. The climate in this transition region between the desert and the southern soudanian region is divided into a rainy season (from June to early September) and a dry period (from October to May). The Soudanian region, is the wettest part of the country. Between April and October, the rainy season brings between 750 and 1,250 mm of precipitation. Temperatures are high throughout the year. For this study we selected one village in each climatic region. The villages are located in the three cities described in Fig. 2.

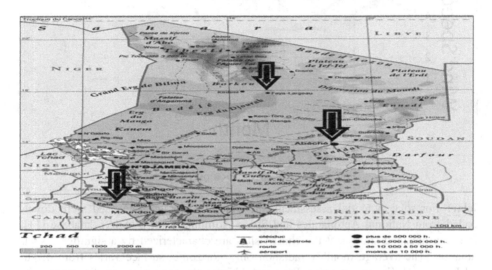

Fig. 2. Sites location

Renewable Energy Potential

Wind: Due to the lack of data from meteorological stations during a long period with a good time resolution, we used the MERRA (Modern-Era Retrospective Analysis for Research and Applications) satellite data from NASA. The wind data are sampled hourly and include wind speed, relative humidity, pressure, temperature and wind directions. It is for a period of ten years between 2005 to 2014 equal to 87648 records for each site. All the data are given for highs from 10 m and more.

Using Matlab for data treatment, the average wind speed variation for the three sites is represented in Fig. 3. It can be seen that for the three climatic regions, Saharan, Sahelian and Soudanian, the mean monthly wind speeds are between 2 and 7.3 m/s at a height of 10 m. Faya located in the north and in the Saharan climate region has more important wind speeds during all the year. The lowest wind speed is about 3.7 m/s, and it can increase up to 7 m/s during a long period of the year. For the two other sites, Abéché and Pala, the wind velocity is not very important. It sometime can attend

4.5 m/s but the yearly average wind speed is just about 3 m/s. Meaning that it is more useful to install wind turbines in Faya compared to the other sites.

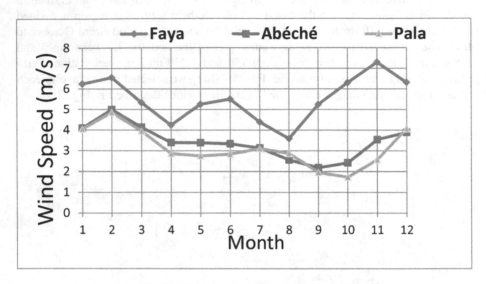

Fig. 3. Wind speed variation over the year

Solar: For solar potential assessment, the monthly average data used were downloaded from National Aeronautics and Space Administration (NASA) database [11]. The data obtained show that the chosen sites are characterized by a significant solar radiation. The average monthly radiation on a horizontal surface varies from 4.7 to 7.4 KWh/m^2/d. For the two sites Faya and Abéché, the lowest solar radiation months are January and December; while for Pala the lowest radiations are registered in June and August Fig. 4.

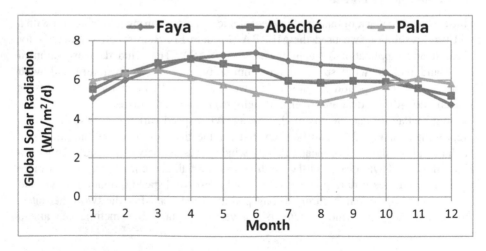

Fig. 4. Global solar radiation

2.3 Method of Analysis

HOMER Simulation Tool

Hybrid optimization Model for electric renewable (Homer) is one of the most used software for sizing and analyzing hybrid systems. HOMER simulation tool is used for the design of micro-power system and comparisons of various powers generating system. HOMER can design grid-connected and off-grid hybrid systems serving electric and thermal loads using different renewable and non-renewable sources along with power conditioning equipment [9]. Optimal system configurations suitable for the different application can be evaluated through this simulation tool. In pre-HOMER phase, physical modeling of hybrid renewable system or the various input parameters to model the system are the load profiles, selected energy components to generate electricity, different energy resources associated with the selected components and optimization constraints. HOMER simulates all possible system configurations that meet the required load demand for a given area under its available energy resources. HOMER simulates thousands of system configurations, optimizes for lifecycle cost, and generates results of sensitivity analyses on most inputs. In the optimization process, HOMER simulates many different system configurations, discards the infeasible ones, ranks the feasible ones according to net present cost and presents and the cost of electricity. Figure 5 shows the block diagram of the operating principle of the Homer software.

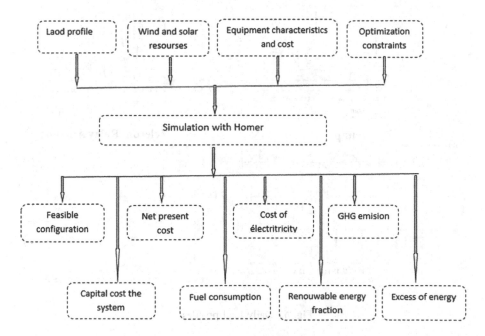

Fig. 5. Principle of operation of the Homer software

2.4   Energy Demand Analysis

For the analysis four of the most used application that needs energy in rural areas are selected. The load profiles represented in Fig. 6 describes the energy demand for domestic use, income generating actives, water pumping and telecommunication relay antenna.

For domestic load estimation, we assumed that all households in a village of 400 inhabitants use electricity. They use appliances like led light bulbs, radios, TVs, sometimes refrigerators and computers. In addition, this load profile takes into account other community infrastructure energy needs. The chosen village type has one health center, a primary school and a church. The total daily energy consumption is then 90 kWh/day for a peak of 7 kW.

The income generating activities consists of three shops, a mill and a sewing workshop. The different types of devices used are: lamps, fan, radio, refrigerator and a sewing machine. All the activities energy needs combined correspond 24.13 kWh/day.

The pump used specially for households' water needs and farming consumes about 5.62 kWh/day with a total power of 5.62 kW. And lastly the total telecom antenna has peak power demand of about 2 kW and the daily energy required is 4.6 kWh. The four energy demand profiles are represented in Fig. 6.

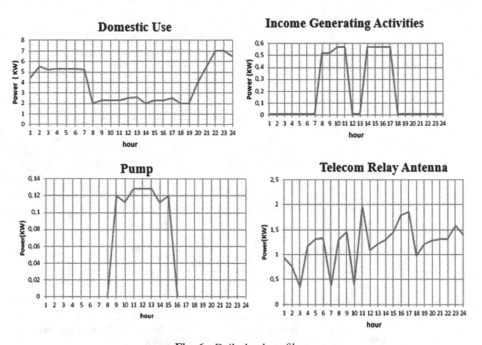

Fig. 6. Daily load profiles

3   Results and Discussions

After computing all the input data needed like load profiles, solar and wind potential, components sizes and costs, HOMER starts running the simulation. All possible systems configurations that can allow to satisfy the energy demand are then given and classified according to the cost of electricity obtained and the net present cost. The feasible solution with the lowest COE is in the top then come the other possible solutions ranked according to their COE. The results obtained for the three sites with the four load profile applications are presented in the following tables. The project life time is assumed to be 25 years.

3.1   Domestics Use

In all the climate regions, the best solution to supply the domestic energy needs is to combine all the basic component of the system. The optimal hybrid system with the lowest price of electricity between 0.264 USD in the Saharan region to 0.362 in the Soudanian region is PV-wind-diesel-batteries. The Sahalian region also has a COE of about 0.304 USD/kWh which is quite high but less compared to the COE in the Soudanian region. The CO_2 emissions in the Saharan, sahalian and soudanian region for the hybrid system are respectively 1078 kg/year, 5946 kg/year and 8437 kg/year. In this case, using PV-wind-diesel-batteries hybrid system is more viable economically than using a standalone solar or wind system in all the three climate region. But it can clearly be noticed that the implementation of this hybrid system is economically more interesting in the Saharan climate region. At the same time, it has less impact on the environment. This is imperatively due to the fact that the solar and wind potential are more available in this region, thus, the diesel generator is not used so much. The results for the domestic application in the three climate region are summarized in Table 1.

Table 1. Optimal solutions for domestic use

Application	Energy Demand	System architecture	Saharian region	Sahalian region	Soudanian region
Domestic use	P = 13,56 kW E = 90 kWh/j	PV generator (KWc)	20	20	20
		Wind generator (kW)	10	10	10
		Diesel generator	4	8	6
		Battery bank (Ah)	25 920	25 920	2880
		CO_2 emissions (Kg/year)	1078	5946	8437
		Renewable energy fraction (%)	98.6	90.2	81.5
		Net present cost (USD)	115,151	132,380	157,574
		Cost of electricity (USD)	0.264	0.304	0.362
		Optimal hybrid system	**PV/Wind/ DG/battery**	**PV/Wind/ DG/battery**	**PV/Wind/ DG/battery**

3.2   Income Generating Activities

The results for the income generating activities energy demand supply differ from a site to another. The optimal solution found for the Saharan region is just the use of a diesel generator. Compared to the other feasible solutions in this site it has the lowest COE, but in practical it does not fit to the objectives of this work. The aim of this study is to find feasible solutions with renewable resources that can replace diesel generator. A PV/battery and a PV/battery/DG are the two optimal systems for the Sahalian and Soudanian. It is normal that a wind generator is not needed in these two sites, the potential is very low. We can clearly notice that the COE obtained 0.830 USD/kWh for the Saharan region, 0.39 USD/kWh for the Sahalian region and 0.451 USD/kWh for the soudanian climate are quite high (Table 2).

Table 2. Optimal solutions for income generating activities

Application	Energy demand	System architecture	Saharian region	Sahalian region	Soudanian region
Income generating activities	P = 4.49 kW E = 24.1 kWh/j	PV generator (KWc)	0	2	1
		Wind generator (kW)	0	0	0
		Diesel generator	2	0	0.57
		Battery bank (Ah)	1440	1440	1440
		CO_2 emissions (kg/year)	2144	0	415
		Renewable energy fraction (%)	0	100	79
		Net present cost (USD)	17,846	8,376	9,701
		Cost of electricity (USD)	0.830	0.390	0.451
		Optimal hybrid system	**Diesel**	**PV/battery**	**PV/DG/ battery**

3.3   Water Pumping

A PV/Diesel/Battery hybrid system is the most viable solution technical-economically in all the three climate regions. Two things can justify this result. In this case, energy is needed only during day time. Secondly the three regions have also an important solar radiation. Therefor the PV array can provide almost all the needed energy. The battery bank and the diesel generator have to supply the system during cloudy time and during a small part of the day. The COE are practically the same and there is also a very small difference in quantity of CO_2 emitted per year. However, it should be noted that the costs and amount of CO_2 emission are lower in the Saharan region. This is clearly because of its solar potential a little more important compared to the other two regions (Table 3).

Table 3. Optimal solutions for water pumping application

Application	Energy demand	System architecture	Saharian region	Sahalian region	Soudanian region
Water pumping	E = 5.62 kWh/j	PV generator (KWc)	1	1	1
		Diesel generator	0.3	0.3	0.3
		Inverter (kW)	0.5	0.5	1
		Battery bank (Ah)	1440	1440	1440
		CO_2 emissions (kg/year)	452	480	525
		Renewable energy fraction (%)	81.6	79.7	76.6
		Net present cost (USD)	8,010	8,153	8,398
		Cost of electricity (USD)	0.372	0.379	0.390
		Optimal hybrid system	**PV/Diesel/ battery**	**PV/Diesel/ battery**	**PV/Diesel/ battery**

3.4 Telecom Relay Antenna

The optimal hybrid system in all the climate regions is a PV-wind-battery combination. For the telecom relay antenna, the needed power is always quite low, so even with quite low wind speeds a small wind turbine can participate to the energy generation to satisfy the demand. During the day, the wind and solar generators produce the energy needed by the antenna and charge also the batteries. When Sun sets, the wind turbine can still continue producing energy depending on the resources, but the most of the needed energy will come from batteries. Despite the fact that the optimal hybrid system is the same, the COE is lower in the Saharan region. As presented in Table 4 the COE are 0.293 USD/kWh, 0.303 USD/kWh and 0.321 USD/kWh respective for the Saharan, sahalian and soudanian region. This is because of the variation of the wind potential which is more important in the North. The impact of the system in the environment is negligible everywhere.

Table 4. Optimal solutions for the Telecom application

Application	Energy demand	System architecture	Saharian region	Sahalian region	Soudanian region
Antenna Telecom	P = 0.57 kW E = 4.6 kWh/j	PV generator (KWc)	10	10	10
		Diesel generator	1	1	2
		Battery bank (Ah)	8640	8640	8640
		CO_2 emissions (kg/year)	241	494	241
		Renewable energy fraction (%)	98.9	97.5	98.9
		Net present cost (USD)	39,462	40,848	43,289
		Cost of electricity (USD)	0.293	0.303	0.321
		Optimal hybrid system	**PV/Wind/ battery**	**PV/Wind/ battery**	**PV/Wind/ battery**

4   Conclusion

The primary objective of this study was to find the optimal hybrid solution adapted to satisfy different energy demand profiles in the rural areas of the three climatic regions in the Republic Chad. The optimal systems also must have trifling impact on the environment. For the country's three climate regions, mainly the same hybrid system is found as optimal to meet perfectly the energy needs of different application. To bring energy for the rural households and some public infrastructure, it is more interesting to install a PV/Wind/Diesel/battery hybrid system in all the three climate regions. However, this hybrid combination is more useful in the Saharan region. The COE is low and the CO_2 emission is negligible.

A PV/Diesel/battery and a PV/Wind/battery hybrid system fits respectively more to a pump and Telecom Relay antenna in all the three selected regions. Unlike the other applications, meeting the energy demand for the identified income-generating activities requires different systems depending on the region. In the Saharan region, it has been found that economically it is more useful to use a Diesel generator for this type of load profile, but this will have important negative consequences in the environment. Using PV associated with batteries is the perfect solution in the two other sites, however a diesel generator need to be added in the Soudanian region.

The results of this study can be used as a decision making tool for deployment of stand-alone hybrid systems to supply cost effective electricity in rural areas in the Republic of Chad while protecting the environment. It might be conducted in other areas to support efficient use of hybrid off systems in remote areas.

References

1. Ould Bilal, B.: Mise en œuvre de nouvelles approches d'optimisation multi-objectif de systèmes hybrides éolien-solaire-batterie-groupe électrogène. Université Cheikh Anta Diop De Dakar Ecole, thèse (2012)
2. Sawle, Y., Gupta, S.C., Bohre, A.K.: PV-wind hybrid system: a review with case study. Cogent Eng. 3(1), 1189305 (2016)
3. Ould Bilal, B., Sambou, V., Ndiaye, P.A., Kébé, C.M.F., Ndongo, M.: Study of the influence of load profile variation on the optimal sizing of a standalone hybrid PV/Wind/Battery/Diesel system. Energy Procedia 36, 1265–1275 (2013)
4. Upadhyay, S., Sharma, M.P.: A review on configurations, control and sizing methodologies of hybrid energy systems. Renew. Sustain. Energy Rev. 38, 47–63 (2014)
5. Ould Bilal, B., Sambou, V., Ndiaye, P.A., Kébé, C.M.F., Ndongo, M.: Multi-objective design of PV-wind-batteries hybrid systems by minimizing the annualized cost system and the loss of power supply probability (LPSP). In: Proceedings IEEE International Conference Industrial Technology, pp. 861–868 (2013)
6. Kolhe, M.L., Ranaweera, K.M.I.U., Gunawardana, A.G.B.S.: Techno-economic sizing of off-grid hybrid renewable energy system for rural electrification in Sri Lanka. Sustain. Energy Technol. Assess. 11, 53–64 (2015)
7. Ahmadi, S., Abdi, S.: Application of the hybrid big bang-big crunch algorithm for optimal sizing of a stand-alone hybrid PV/wind/battery system. Sol. Energy 134, 366–374 (2016)

8. Ramli, M.A.M., Bouchekara, H.R.E.H., Alghamdi, A.S.: Optimal sizing of PV/wind/diesel hybrid microgrid system using multi-objective self-adaptive differential evolution algorithm. Renew. Energy **121**, 400–411 (2018)
9. Amutha, W.M., Rajini, V.: Cost benefit and technical analysis of rural electrification alternatives in Southern India using HOMER. Renew. Sustain. Energy Rev. **62**, 236–246 (2016)
10. Rajbongshi, R., Borgohain, D., Mahapatra, S.: Optimization of PV-biomass-diesel and grid base hybrid energy systems for rural electrification by using HOMER. Energy **126**, 461–474 (2017)
11. https://eosweb.larc.nasa.gov/sse/RETScreen/

An Optimized, Low-Cost Off-grid Solar System: Design and Implementation

Pape Moussa Sonko[1], Diery Ngom[1], Mouhamed Ouesse[1], and Assane Gueye[1,2(✉)]

[1] Universite Alioune Diop de Bambey, Bambey, Senegal
assanel.gueye@uadb.edu.sn
[2] University of Maryland, College Park, USA

Abstract. This paper reports on the design and implementation of a low-cost off-grid solar installation system that maximizes the energy production for any given day. Our proposed solution consists of (1) a double axis solar tracker with electric actuators controlled by an Arduino board, (2) an MPPT (Maximum Power Point Tracking) power controller, with a capacity of 20 A, remotely accessible from a smartphone with a dedicated Android application that uses a Bluetooth connection and (3) a remote data logging system that periodically stores the installation data to an online database server using a Wifi connection. The overall cost of the system is about $215 ($72 for the regular and $143 for the solar tracker).

Keywords: MPPT regulator · Solar tracker · Connected regulator

1 Introduction

Energy has always been vital to the development of nations. It underpins all other sectors such as education, health, agriculture, and information systems. Consequently, when the energy sector is dysfunctional, the whole nation is impacted. This has been the case for Senegal where the population have witnessed a long period of frequent power outages between 2011 and 2016. According a study by the "Direction de la Prevision et des Etudes Economiques", these outages have had an economic impact of $16,500 per day [11].

As an alternative to unreliable grid power, the populations have turned to renewable energies, specifically solar, which presents many potentials in Senegal (it is free and available throughout the year). However, despite the opportunities it offers, there are several challenges that need to be overcome for an effective use of solar energy in Senegal (and in Africa in general). Two of the main challenges are *efficiency* and *cost*. In this paper, we report on a project that addresses these two issues by the design and implementation of a low-cost off-grid solar installation system that optimizes the production of energy for any given day.

1.1 The Current State of Electrification in Senegal (Africa)

In Africa, the overall electrification rate is quite low. According to the "Global Energy Architecture Performance Index" report (2017) [1], only five African countries

G. Bassioni et al. (Eds.): InterSol 2019, LNICST 296, pp. 38–49, 2019.
https://doi.org/10.1007/978-3-030-34863-2_4

(Morocco, Egypt, Tunisia, Algeria and Libya) have achieved a 100% electrification rate. The same report ranks Senegal at the eighth position among the 24 African countries in the study, with an electrification rate of 56.5%.

Access to electricity has always been an issue in Senegal. In addition, the existing and limited grid energy is unevenly distributed between rural and urban areas. While people in big cities are living with frequent power outages, the rural population is living in complete darkness; this, despite the many efforts deployed by the successive governments to significantly boost the energy sector. For instance, the PERACOD ("Programme de Promotion de l'Electrification Rurale et l'Approvisionnement durable en Combustibles Domestique") [2] program aims at expanding the electrical grid and increase the electrification rate to 60% by 2022. In the meantime, the majority of the Senegalese population is using oil lanterns and candles at night.

In the last decade, the populations have been increasingly turning towards renewable energies (in particular solar) because of the many potentials they offer. In fact, the amount of yearly solar radiation received in Senegal, could fill the energy deficit experienced by the SENELEC ("Société Nationale d'Electricité") and help remove the disparities in the energy distribution between urban and rural areas.

1.2 Solar Energy Potential in Senegal

Senegal has one of the highest solar potential in the world, with an average of 5.5 kWh/m^2/day raw energy (with some variations between the north and the south parts of the country: the average raw energy is equal to 5.8 kWh/m^2/day in the north, while it is equal to 4.03 kWh/m^2/day in the south) [3, 4]. This average raw solar energy is equivalent to 395 thousand billion of kWh per year, or 33.83 million PET (Petroleum Equivalent Tons). This is equivalent to 15 million times the total current energy consumption of the country [4]. If exploited with some minimal efficiency, the entire country can be powered solely by solar energy throughout the year.

In addition, sunshine is pretty stable throughout the year in Senegal. It is slightly less sunny during the rainy season, with August having the smallest sunshine rate. However, compared to March (which is the sunniest month of the year), the drop of the sunshine rate is less than 25%. As a contrast, in Europe, the drop between December and June can be as high as 250%.

Encouraged by this high solar potential, the government of Senegal has recently launched a campaign to motivate the population to adopt off-grid solar installations.

1.3 Architecture of an Off-grid (Autonomous) Photovoltaic System

One of the main characteristics of off-grid solar systems is that energy can be produced *only* during the day time. Therefore, there is a need to store (part of) the produced energy for night time consumption.

Figure 1 shows the architecture of an off-grid solar installation system. The energy production is done by the solar panels that use the photoelectric effect to produce a direct current. A solar charge controller is then used to control the associated voltage. Energy storage is performed by using this voltage to charge batteries. The controller also protects the batteries against overcharging which is known to dramatically reduce battery lifetime. At sunset, the panels stop producing current and the stored energy starts getting consumed for household needs. For that, an inverter is used to convert the direct current (DC) of the batteries to the alternative current (AC) needed to power most household apparels (TV, PC, Refrigerators, etc.).

Given that only the quantity of energy stored during the day is available for consumption at night, it is crucial for any solar installation to be able to charge the batteries at their maximal capacity before the sun goes down. That is one of the two objectives we have set in this project.

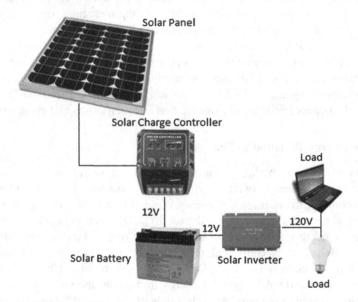

Fig. 1. Architecture of an autonomous photovoltaic system

2 Our Proposed Solution

In this section, we present our proposed solution. For recall, our goal is to design and implement a low-cost photovoltaic system with optimized efficiency. We start by relating some facts gathered from a survey conducted with solar installations professionals in Senegal and visits made to household installation units.

2.1 Observations from Field Visits

Because of the government's ongoing campaign to encourage populations to adopt off-grid solar energy, an increasing number of Senegalese households are acquiring solar installations. In December 2017, we surveyed installation and maintenance professionals and visited several households installations to study the performance of the installed units. At the end of our filed visits, our main observation was that most installations have a deficit of production. For instance, at the end of each day, the batteries are usually not fully charged. The main reasons found for this deficit in production are the following:

1. The panels are usually not well dimensioned, which leads to insufficient power production,
2. The charge controller is often of very low quality,
3. The batteries used are often inappropriate (most of the time car batteries are used).

Among these causes of inefficiency, the low-quality charge controller is the most widespread. This is principally due to the very high cost of the controller (in the Senegalese market), which makes people to turn toward cheaper but very *low-quality* controllers. Unfortunately, the quality of the controller is very crucial for the efficiency of the overall system.

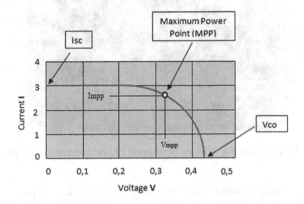

Fig. 2. Characteristics of an MPPT charge controller

The optimal charge controller has been known to be the MPPT, which sets the panels to produce at their optimal power, as shown in Fig. 2. Unfortunately, the MPPT controllers that are available in today's Senegalese market are very expensive. For instance, for a 30 A capacity, the Victron 100/30 controller that is the most available costs around $180. This is more than ten times the lower-quality PWM controller that is found in most installations in Senegal (costs around $15). With these low-quality charge controllers, the batteries are rarely fully charged before the sun goes down. This, combined with the inappropriate batteries, leads to unreliable systems with batteries that usually get discharged before the sun rises again. Not only this causes a deficit in energy, but it also can damage household apparels.

As a solution, we propose a low-cost implementation of the MPPT by using an Arduino board (which is quite cheap). To further enhance the production of the system, we build a solar tracker that maintains the panels oriented in the direction of the sun, at all times. With this, the maximum (possible) power production is guaranteed, whether it is very sunny or not.

2.2 The Automatic Solar Tracker

The solar tracker is built with two rotations axes, each equipped with a servomotor. The two axes guide the movement of the tracker in order to maintain a 90 degrees incidence angle at all times. The overall system is controlled by an Arduino microcontroller board on which we have implemented the "Perturb and Observe" (P&O) tracking algorithm. The algorithm dynamically re-computes the *average* position of the panels by making use of data gathered by four photoresistor sensors (Light Dependent Resistors—(LDR)) placed in the four corners of the support unit. Figure 3 shows a picture of the positioned LDRs.

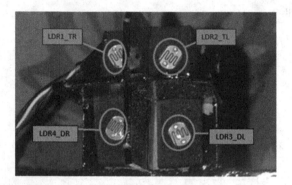

Fig. 3. Photoresistor sensors positioned on the support of the panel

The tracking algorithm continually executes the following steps:

- First, it computes the averages as follows:
  - Top average: *avgt = (LDR1_TR + LDR2_TL)/2*;
  - Down average: *avgd = (LDR4_DR + LDR3_DL)/2*;
  - Left average: *avgl = (LDR1_TR + LDR4_DR)/2*;
  - Right average: *avgr = (LDR2_TL + LDR3_DL)/2*.
- After that, the differences between averages are computed as follows:
  - *dv = (avgt − avgd)*,
  - *dh = (avgl − avgr)*.
- Finally, the algorithm compares the values of dv and dh to a tolerance level t and uses the result to update the position of the panel. The updates are done as follows:
  - *If (dv>t or dv < −t)*, then
      If (avgt > avgd), then, orient the support towards the top,
      Else, orient the support towards the bottom;
  - *If (dh>t or dh < −t)*, then
      If (avgl < avgr), then, orient the support towards the right,
      Else, if (avgl < avgr), then, orient the support towards the left;
      Else If (avgl == avgr), then, maintain current position.

It is possible to tune the sensitivity to the fluctuations of the luminosity by varying the tolerance value (**t**) using a potentiometer. This allows us to control the precision of the tracker.

Figure 4 shows the circuit diagram of the tracker, while Fig. 5 shows a picture of the panels mounted on top of the support of the tracker.

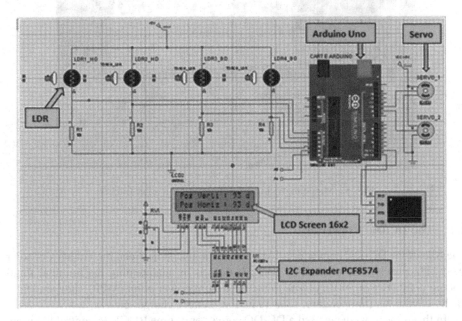

Fig. 4. Diagram of the solar tracker

2.3   The MPPT Charge Controller

MPPT is a technic used in off-grid solar installations to maximize the power extraction under all conditions [3, 4]. It is composed with an algorithm embedded into an electronic circuit [5–7]. In our case, we use an Arduino board as microcontroller on which we implement the MPPT algorithm as well as the P&O algorithm. The controller regulates the output voltage toward the batteries to protect them against overcharging but also against overvoltage (by use of a diode TVS at input and at output) and overcurrent (by use of a fuse). To allow remote access, the controller is also equipped with a Bluetooth module (HC-05) and a Wifi module (ESP-01). The Bluetooth module is used to communicated with a dedicated Android application that gives to the users the possibility to remotely access the installation data via a smartphone. The Wifi modules serves as a channel to periodically log the system data onto an online database server. These added functionalities enable the user to access the system data from anywhere and at any time.

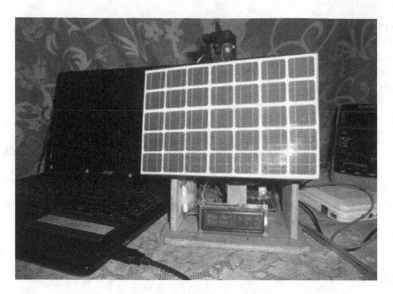

Fig. 5. Miniaturized implementation of the solar tracker

2.4 The DC/DC Converter

The role of the DC-DC converter is to optimize the match between the voltages of solar array (PV panels) and the battery bank. It does it by maintaining the nominal functioning point (FP) *on or very close to* the maximum power point (MPP), independently of the conditions (temperature, solar radiation, battery charge, etc…).

In this project, we have used a DC-DC converter of type BUCK to control the input voltage. On the other hand, the reference voltage is fixed or set by the P&O algorithm that varies the cyclic ratio (*D*) of the static converter.

The whole conversion process works as follows: The Arduino board generates a 5 V PMW signal. An associated embedded circuit (Half-Bridge Driver IR2014) then enables the switching of the MOSFET transistor (IRFZ44N) of the converter. This allows to vary the cyclic ratio which maximizes the power transfer towards the output of the controller. The BUCK controller always gives an output voltage that is lower than the input. The value of this output voltage is given by the following formula:

$$Vout = Vin * D,$$

where, **Vout** is the output voltage, **Vin** is the input voltage and **D** is a cyclic ratio.

The value of the inductance is an important parameter for the efficiency of the system. The optimal value is compute using the following formula:

$$L = (V_{in} - V_{out}) * D * \frac{1}{f} * \frac{1}{dl}$$

where, **L** is the inductance, *f* the switching frequency, and *dl* is the ripple current (*here dl is chosen between 30 and 40% of the output current*). The circuit diagrams of the converters are shown in Figs. 6 and 7.

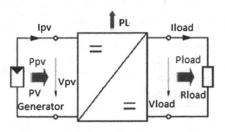

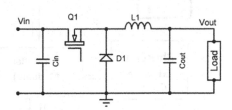

Fig. 6. Circuit of the DC-DC converter   **Fig. 7.** Circuit of the BUCK converter

2.5 The Arduino Board

The Arduino board represents the brain of the MPPT controller. For our implementation, we use an Arduino UNO model. Its reduced size and weight makes it suitable for usage in systems with limited space. It is equipped with a type B mini USB port that allows it to be programmed via a computer. It is also capable of performing Analog-Digital conversion. The table below shows the main characteristics of our Arduino board.

Table 1. Characteristics of the Arduino board

Arduino Card Name	Microcontroller	Flash memory (Ko) Boot	SRAM (Ko)	EEPROM (Ko)	Voltage (V)	Logical level (V)	Digital I/O	Analog I/O
Nano	Atmega168/328	16/32 (2)	1/2	0.5/1	7-12	5	14 (6)	9 (10bits)

We use the digital pins (D0 = RX and D1 = TX) for the serial communication with the Wifi model. Pins D4 and D7 are used as virtual serial interface to enable communication with the Bluetooth module.

2.6 Overview of MPPT Controller

Table 1 shows an overview of the different internal components of the MPPT controller. The solar panels produce the photovoltaic energy. The Arduino board generates the PWM signal to control the DC-DC controller. This signal permits to vary the cyclic ratio to adapt the output voltage towards the charges (batteries). The Arduino board also exchanges information with the outside world via the Bluetooth and the Wifi modules. Figure 8 shows a picture of the different components of the MPPT module.

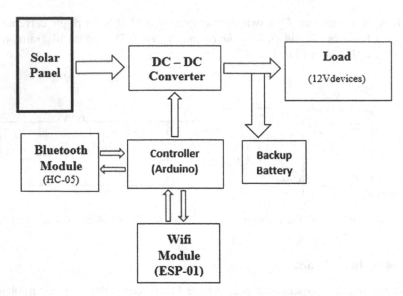

Fig. 8. Overview of the different components of the MPPT charge controller

2.7   The P&O (Perturb and Observe) Algorithm

To vary the cyclic ratio (which leads to the control of the output voltage), we use the P&O algorithm. It is a very simple and easy to implement algorithm. As its name suggests, it perturbs the system, then observes the power generated by the PV to then move the nominal functioning point toward the MPP according to the following dynamic equation:

$$V(k) = V(k-1) + \Delta V \cdot sign\left(\frac{dP}{dV}\bigg|_{V=V_{k-1}}\right)$$

A flow diagram of the algorithm is shown is Fig. 9, below.

At each step, after measuring the voltage and current and computing the corresponding power, the following verification tests are performed:

- *If (P(k) > P(k − 1), then:*
  - **If V(k) > V(k − 1), then** *increase the cyclic ration*
  - **Else,** *then decrease the cyclic ratio (V(k) becomes V(k − 1));*
- *If (P(k) < P(k − 1), then:*
  - **If V(k) > V(k − 1), then** *decrease the cyclic ratio,*
  - **Else,** *increase the cyclic ratio (V(k) becomes V(k − 1)).*

This procedure is periodically repeated until a maximum power point is reached.

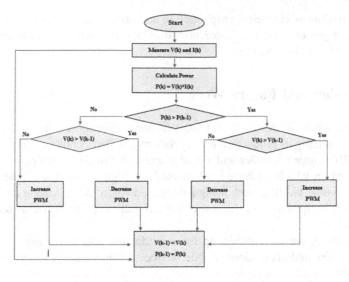

Fig. 9. Flow diagram of the P&O algorithm

3 Related Work

Solar tracking has long been used to increase the efficiency of photovoltaic systems. They have been implemented both with one and two axles. In [8] a double-axle solar tracking system has been used to gather the maximum sun radiation during the day and maximize the produced energy. Unlike our system though, the authors do not use an Arduino board to control the installation. Instead, an PID (proportional integral derivative) controller was implemented to adjust the position of the structure. Using the Arduino allowed us to build a system with similar functionalities at a much lower price.

In [9] a dual-axle solar tracker has been implemented with the additional functionalities of data logging, as in our system. However, the authors use an Atmega 328 microcontroller instead of an Arduino board. Their implementation is *passive* in in the sense that the position of the sun is pre-calculated and hard-coded in the system. Contrary, our implementation dynamically recomputes the position of the sun and hence, is more *active*. This is done using an algorithm that takes as input data acquired by a set of photoresistor sensors placed on the surface of the panels, giving accurate information about the position of the sun at any given time. Finally, our system is also more flexible, as it is able to orient the panels on both axles.

With respect to the implementation of the MPPT technic using an Arduino board, a work similar t ours is presented in [10]. Unlike this work though, ours is not limited to only the design/conception an MPPT controller. Our system is more complete and is embedded with additional functionalities such as remote access to the system data and state of the installation. This can be done via Bluetooth or Wifi. We have also developed a dedicated Android application that enable remote access through a smart phone. Hence, the operator can at any given time and from anywhere consult the system data (online or via their smartphone). In addition, the system data is periodically logged onto a server database, hence providing the possibility of different king of historic studies and data mining.

4 Conclusion and Future Work

In this work, we have designed and implemented a low-cost solar energy system capable of optimizing its production under arbitrary weather conditions. It is composed with an MPPT charge controller and a double axel solar tracker, both controlled by an Arduino board on which we have implemented our algorithms. The whole system is remotely accessible via Bluetooth using a dedicated Android application and via Wifi. Its overall cost is equal to ¼ of the cost of the currently available systems with similar performance.

In perspective, we are considering the manufacture and marketing of connected MPPT controllers and stand-alone mobile devices (solar trackers) for solar panels at very affordable prices in Senegal.

References

1. Global Energy Architecture Performance Index Report 2017: Forum économique mondial (WEF) et le cabinet de conseil en stratégie Accenture Strategy, 22 mars 2017
2. Wole-Osho, I., Bamisile, O., Adun, H., Yusuf, I.: Comparison of renewable energy potential in relation to renewable energy policy in ECOW AS countries. 978-1-5090-3784-1/16/ $31.00 ©2016 IEEE
3. Youm, I., Sarr, J., Sail, M., Kane, M.M.: Renewable energy activities in Senegal: a review. Renew. Sustain. Energy Rev. 4(l), 75–89 (2000)
4. Mboup, S.B.: Comment le projet d'énergie solaire au Sénégal affectera t-il le complexe énergétique du pays, compte tenu des tendances actuelles du marché de l'énergie. In: 9th multi-year expert meeting on commodities and development, 12–13 October 2017, Geneva (2017)
5. Vasant, L.G., Pawar, V.R.: Optimization of solar-wind energy system power for battery charging using MPPT. In: International Conference on Energy, Communication, Data Analytics and Soft Computing (ICECDS-2017) (2017)
6. Definition and explanations on the MPPT (Maximum Power Point Tracking). http://energie28.blogspot.com/2016/11/definition-and-explications-on-the-mppt.html. Accessed 17th September 2018
7. Srivastava, M., Agarwal, S., Sharma, E.: Design and simulation of disturbance and observe MPPT algorithm for 72 cell solar PV system. Int. J. Soft Comput. Eng. (IJSCE) 4(6) (2015). ISSN 2231-2307
8. Allamehzadeh, H.: Solar energy overview and maximizing power output of a solar array using sun trackers. In: 2016 IEEE Conference on Technologies for Sustainability (SusTech) (2016)
9. Makhija, S., Khatwani, A., Khan, M.F., Goel, V., Roja, M.M.: Design & implementation of an automated dual-axis solar tracker with data-logging. In: International Conference on Inventive Systems and Control (ICISC-2017) (2017)

10. Pathare, M., Datta, D., Valunjkar, R., Shetty, V., Sawant, A., Pai, S.: Designing and implementation of maximum power point tracking (MPPT) solar charge controller. In: 2017 International Conference on Nascent Technologies in the Engineering Field (ICNTE-2017) (2017)
11. Direction de la prévision et des études économiques (Dpee), Senegal: «Impact des délestages sur l'activité économique et le bien-être des populations». http://www.dpee.sn/Impact-des-Delestages-sur-l.html?lang=fr. Accessed 1st Nov 2018

Africa's Online Access: What Data Is Getting Accessed and Where It Is Hosted?

Babacar Mbaye[1], Assane Gueye[1,2(✉)], Desire Banse[3],
and Alassane Diop[4]

[1] Universite Alioune Diop de Bambey, Bambey, Sénégal
assanel.gueye@uadb.edu.sn
[2] University of Maryland, College Park, USA
[3] Prometheus Computing, LLC, New Market, USA
[4] Universite Virtuelle du Sénégal, Dakar, Sénégal

Abstract. Recent studies have shown that most of the web traffic going from one African country to another has to transit through ISP's in other continents before coming back to Africa. This phenomenon is known as boomerang routing and proposals are being made on how to correct it. However, there is a more fundamental question that needs to be addressed: what web content is of interest to Africans and where is it hosted? Indeed, if most of the data needed by Africans is within the continent and yet boomerang is still prevalent, then correcting it is of paramount importance. If, on the other hand, most the data accessed by Africans is hosted outside the continent, then data repatriation might be more beneficial than boomerang correction.

By using publicly available data, this paper attempts to shed some light to that question. Our study suggests that locally producing content and locally hosting it should be given priority to correcting boomerang. The data used as well as the analytical process that have led to such a conclusion are presented in the sequel.

Keywords: Boomerang routing · Africa web access content · Data content · Website hosting

1 Introduction

ICTs have brought a lot of hope for socio-economic development in Africa. Many World Bank indicators have already confirmed that Africa is the continent that is witnessing the most of benefits from ICT development [1]. Well aware of this, the African Union (AU) and member countries are now engaged on several projects to build ICT infrastructures within the continent. For instance, the AU has adopted in 2012 the Program for Infrastructure Development In Africa (PIDA) [2]. Another project initiated by the African Union Commission is the African Internet Exchange System (AXIS) project that supports the establishment of National and Regional IXPs in Africa [3]. The main goal of these projects is to improve user experience by reducing cost and delay. Cost and delay are however closely dependent to where the data that most users access is located/hosted (locally or remotely). As a consequence, for an optimal improvement of African users' experience it is necessary to know the nature of the data they access as well as its location.

© ICST Institute for Computer Sciences, Social Informatics and Telecommunications Engineering 2019
Published by Springer Nature Switzerland AG 2019. All Rights Reserved
G. Bassioni et al. (Eds.): InterSol 2019, LNICST 296, pp. 50–61, 2019.
https://doi.org/10.1007/978-3-030-34863-2_5

The main goal of this project is to study Africa's online access. More precisely, we are interested in understanding the nature of the data that is accessed by users within the continent, as well as the physical location of the servers where the data is hosted. For that, we make use of publicly available data sets.

We gathered data provided by the site Alexa [4]. The free version of the provided data is a list of the 50 most visited sites by users of each country in the world. We wrote a python script that crawls the Alexa website and downloads, for each African country, the 50 mostly visited websites. We then use the Maxmind (IP) [5] geolocation database to find the geolocation of the servers that host those websites. We also analyze the content of the websites to determine whether it is mainly destined for an African audience or it is for any user around the world. Finally, the results of our findings are discussed, and conclusions and guidance are provided.

Our study has shown that despite the high Internet penetration rate claimed in Africa (mostly boosted by mobile data), most of the data that Africans attempt to access is located outside the continent. In other terms, very few Africans make use of the existing website hosting services that are available in the continent. Furthermore, only one (1) in five (5) of the most visited sites by Africans carries "purely" African content and only a fifth of those purely African sites are hosted within the continent. When it comes to Africans' interest to site designed by/for another African country, the data indicates a lack of cross-country interest. Finally, the study shows that African sites are dominated by news (information) category and categories of sites such as health, science, e-government, education and sport are not popular in Africa.

In conclusion, despite the high Internet penetration rate in Africa and despite the many projects to developing internetworking infrastructures in the continent, most of the traffic generated by African must transit through international network (even though the requested content is primarily destined to Africans). Consequently, end users will continue to experience additional cost and delay. However, according to our data, the main cause of this is not "boomerang routing". Rather, the additional delay and cost is mainly due to the fact that data accessed by most Africans is overwhelmingly located outside of the continent. Thus, in additional to developing network infrastructures within the continent, we believe that Africa should encourage the production of local content that is hosted locally.

This paper is organized as follows. We first describe the data used in our study in Sect. 2. We present the data, discuss some of its known (and sometimes addressed) limitations, and present some of the pre-processing work done for the analysis. The data analysis is presented in Sect. 3. We provide a summary of related work in Sect. 4. Concluding remarks as well as perspectives are given in Sect. 5.

2   Data Acquisition and Pre-processing

2.1   Alexa Traffic Data

Alexa Internet, Inc. is an American web traffic analysis company based in San Francisco. It is a subsidiary of Amazon. The Alexa Top Sites web service provides ranked lists of the top sites on the Internet. The ranking is based on the anonymous usage patterns of a large and global sample of millions of Internet users using one of many different Alexa's browser extensions. In addition, Alexa gathers much of its traffic data from direct sources in the form of sites that have chosen to install the Alexa script on their site and certify their metrics [4].

The global traffic rank is a measure of how a website is doing relative to all other sites on the web over the past 3 months. The rank is calculated using a proprietary methodology that combines a site's estimated average of daily unique visitors and its estimated number of pageviews over the past 3 months. Alexa also provides a similar country-specific ranking, which is a measurement of how a website ranks in a particular country relative to other sites over the past month.

A site's ranking is based on a combined measure of reach and page views computed over a trailing 3-month period. Reach is determined by the number of unique Alexa users who visit a site on a given day. Page views are the total number of Alexa user page requests for a site. However, multiple requests for the same page (URL) on the same day by the same user are counted as a single page view. The site with the highest combination of users and page views is ranked #1.

Alexa provides a fraction of its ranking data for free (it also offers many other datasets and services with a subscription fee). This version includes a list of the 50 most visited sites by users of each country in the world. We gathered that data by writing a python script that crawls the Alexa website and downloads, for each African country, the 50 mostly visited websites. We then use the Maxmind (IP) geolocation database to find the geolocation of each of the websites and perform our data analysis presented in Sect. 3.

2.2 Alexa Data Limitations

Since its launch in 1998, there have been many concerns raised about the Alexa dataset. Originally, webpages were only ranked amongst users who had the Alexa Toolbar installed. Therefore, the data could be biased if a specific audience subgroup was reluctant to take part in the rankings. This caused some controversies over how representative Alexa's user base was of typical Internet behavior, especially for less-visited sites. In 2007, a study has provided examples of Alexa rankings known to contradict data from other web analytics services, including ranking YouTube ahead of Google [6].

This particular concern has however been addressed by Alexa in 2008, when they introduced [https://techcrunch.com/2008/04/16/alexa-overhauls-ranking-system/] new practices in which they would not only use data from their toolbar, but also from twenty five thousands of other widgets, plug-ins and services.

Alexa data has also been largely dubbed to be biased against sites with relatively low measured traffic, which tend to be inaccurately ranked by Alexa. For instance, it can be read from Alexa's website [4] that they "do not receive enough data from their sources to make rankings beyond 100,000 statistically meaningful. This means that, for example, the difference in traffic between a site ranked 1,000,000 and a site ranked 2,000,000 has low statistical significance." This limitation could have an impact in the study carried in this paper as many African sites are expected to, a priori, receive low traffic. However, our comparative studies have shown that Alexa rankings correlate well with other raking systems such as SimilarWeb [7] and SEMrush [8]. Furthermore, this study confirms Alexa's claim that the closer a site gets to number 1, the more reliable its rank is. For the present study, we have compared Alexa and SimilarWeb rankings for three African countries for which SimilarWeb has available data. The comparison shows a 75% similarity. Furthermore, this paper is mainly concerned with sites that Africans mostly visit, and we expect these "top" sites to receive relatively high traffic. Hence, the omission of sites that receive low traffic data should not impact our analysis.

Bearing these limitations in mind (as well as the many critics that Alexa has addressed since 2008), we believe that Alexa and its cousin sites (SimilarWeb and SEMrush) are valuable tools that provide "good enough" traffic estimates for any site. Some of the limitations are inherent to the indirect method used to collect the data. Indeed, no indirect method for traffic determination will ever be as exact as the direct tools such as Google Analytics, or log file analyzers. However, the problem with Google Analytics is that you can't get that data for other people's sites and the data is mostly private. Overall, we believe that the results of our study can be used as first order guidance, given the lack of traffic data, especially with respect to Africa.

2.3   Data Pre-processing

As mentioned earlier, we have written a python script that crawls the Alexa website to collect the 50 most visited sites in every African country. The second step was to determine the physical location of the servers that host the sites. For that, we use the Maxmind geolocation database [5] that gives the geolocation of most Internet servers/routers. Maxmind is known to have some limitations with fine-grained localization such as city geolocation coordinates. However, its country level localization is accepted to be fairly accurate. In this paper, we are concerned only with country level localization.

After the localization of all the sites (whenever possible), we categorized them into:

- **"purely African"** (sites with mainly African content and mainly targeting African audience, such as www.seneweb.com) and
- **"others"** (all other sites, such as www.google.com).

This site categorization required a manual process in which we took several steps.

First, we look at the extension of the site's url. If it corresponds to the code of an African country (e.g., www.irembo.goc.rw), we classify the site as "purely African". Otherwise, (the extension does not correspond to an African country code), we load the page into a browser and analyze a set of metadata fields. The title of the site is a first indicator for classification. For instance, the title of the site www.seneweb.com is "Seneweb: le Senegal dans le Web", which clearly suggests that the site is Senegalese. If the title is not very informative, we inspect (and combine) a list of other fields such as: the language, the videos, the type of information, the title of the tabs, the other sites that are referenced, the site footer, the address and phone number in the contact section (if any) etc.

Some ambiguities might arise with this classification method, in which case we make some arbitrage. For example, sites such as www.google.country-code are classified as "others", because they are considered to belong to google and do not necessarily carry "African content". When we cannot geo-localize a site or classify it (after using all the methods above), we just ignore it. We also ignore sites that generate error codes such as "http error code 404: page not found".

Using this procedure, we were able to gather geo-localized site information is **47** African countries with an average of **48.7** sites per country. In the next section, we present our findings.

3   Data Analysis

Before proceeding to the analysis, we would like to put the African online access into a global perspective. For that, we collected Akamai's HTTP[1] hits per second data for a period of five day (during the period of November 1st to November 5th, 2018). The data can be classified by region, as show in Fig. 1.

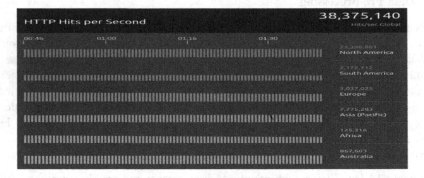

Fig. 1. HTTP Hits per Second (See footnote 1)

Considering the 5-day average, we found that the African traffic represents less than half percent of the global web traffic. Even though this is about requests received by Akamai servers, it can be fairly considered as proportionally representative. This means that our work is about a very small percentage of the global web traffic, despite the fact that African Internet users stands at 10.9%, as of December 2017 (according to InternetWorldStat [9]).

---

[1] Hits per Second Globally measures the number of raw requests received by Akamai servers from each major continental region. "Hits/sec. global", displayed at the top of the graph, is the cumulative number of hits, while the data points displayed vertically along the right are regional breakdowns. 24 h data patterns as well as 24 h peak data points are made available for each region. HTTP Hits per Second is measured in actual hits/sec [10].

After putting our working in a global perspective, we can proceed to the analysis. The analysis consisted in finding trends in website ranking, content consumption and finding probable explanation to the trends. We first consider the physical location of the servers that host the 50 mostly visited websites from any African country. To geo-locate a site, we query the Maxmind database by providing the site's url or IP address.

3.1 In-country Hosting

Figure 2 shows the percentage of sites that are hosted in each African country (among the 50 mostly visited sites in the country). Overall, we found that for any given African country, only less than 25% of the mostly visited sites are hosted in the country, with a continental average equal to 4.3% This indicates that overwhelming portion of the web traffic generated from the countries will transit internationally.

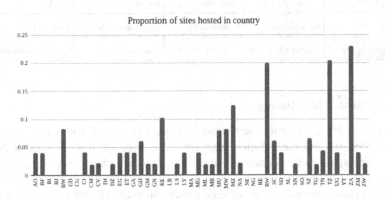

Fig. 2. Proportion of sites hosting in each African country

A closer look at the site hosting distribution shows that countries that have a solid number of sites hosted in country are those which have a good infrastructure. The top 5 of these countries are: South Africa, Tanzania, Rwanda, Mozambique and Kenya. Focusing on these five countries, we then look at the top 10 most visited websites per country (see Table 1).

We found that most of the top ten sites are foreign by content and hosting location (usually, they are Google, Facebook, Yahoo and Wikipedia). This is the trend that has been observed for almost all countries in the world (developed and developing). Indeed, it is well known that whose sites dominate the web. Our analysis is just a confirmation that the domination is occurs also in Africa.

We also found that each of these 5 countries has at least one site hosted in-country among the top 10, while none of the countries in the bottom half (with respect to number of in-country hosting) has a site hosted within the country among the 10 mostly visited sites. The world average of in-country hosted sites (US excluded) is equal 1.8.

Table 1. Ten (10) mostly visited site for the top 5 countries with in-country hosting

South Africa	Tanzania	Rwanda	Kenya	Botswana
0;google.com	0;google.com	0;google.com	0;google.com	0;google.com
1;google.co.za	1;youtube.com	1;youtube.com	1;youtube.com	1;youtube.com
2;youtube.com	2;yahoo.com_	2;igihe.com	2;standardmedia.co.ke	2;google.co.bw
3;facebook.com	3;facebook.com	3;google.rw	3;tuko.co.ke	3;yahoo.com_
4;yahoo.com_	4;jamiiforums.com	4;yahoo.com_	4;the-star.co.ke	4;facebook.com
5;wikipedia.org	5;ghafla.com	5;inyarwanda.com	5;facebook.com	5;wikipedia.org
6;dstv.com	6;instagram.com	6;facebook.com	6;yahoo.com_	6;gov.bw
7;gumtree.co.za	7;blogspot.com	7;umuryango.rw	7;sde.co.ke	7;ub.bw
8;fnb.co.za	8;wikipedia.org	8;umuseke.rw	8;sportpesa.co.ke	8;ask.com
9;instagram.com	9;meridianbet.co.tz	9;irembo.gov.rw	9;kenyans.co.ke	9;jobsbotswana.info

3.2   Continent-Wide Hosting

Having noticed that most of the sites viewed by users in a given country are not hosted in the country, we ask the question whether those sites are hosted in other African country. The answer to this question will inform about whether the African traffic will stay within the continent.

Figure 3 shows the proportion of sites viewed in each African country and hosted within the continent. We have mostly the same graph as for in-country hosted except for Soudan, Swaziland, Namibia, Mauritius and Lesotho. This suggests that hosting services that are available in some African countries (such as South Africa) are not used by other countries. The reasons behind this are not studied in the paper, however, understanding them could be key in developing Africa's internetworking infrastructures.

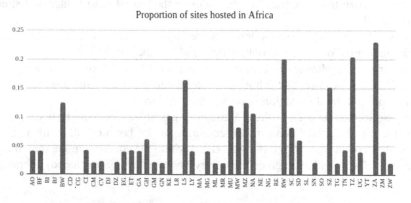

Fig. 3. Proportion of sites hosted within Africa

3.3 "Purely" African Sites

In this section, we are interested in figuring out which of the 50 mostly visited sites of each country carries a content that is mostly destined to an African audience. We use the procedure described in Sect. 2.3 to categorize the sites. Figure 4 shows the proportion of sites that were classified as "purely African".

The distribution of "purely" African sites is disproportionate and much lower compared to sites outside the continent. In average, only 20% of the mostly visited sites in the continent are considered as "purely" African. This indicates that even the traffic that is generated "by Africans and for Africans" has to transit through international link when accessed from within the continent.

It is to be noticed that the classification of a site as "purely African" is not correlated to the fact that the site is hosted within the continent or not. For instance, Mauritania is the country with the most sites classified as such (31 sites belonging to the country). However, only 1 of those sites is hosted within the country. This phenomenon is quite common across the continent, as shown in Fig. 4.

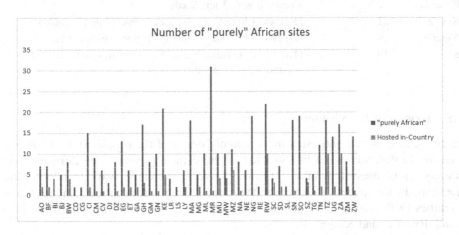

Fig. 4. Number of "purely" African sites

3.4 Content of the Sites

Having determined the most popular African sites as well as the "purely" African ones, we turn to the content in these sites.

We also found that each of these 5 countries has at least one site hosted in-country among the top 10, while none of the countries in the bottom half (with respect to number of in-country hosting) has a site hosted within the country among the 10 mostly visited sites. The world average of in-country hosted sites (US excluded) is equal 1.8.

Table 1 shows that social media sites are the most popular ones in the continent. As was mentioned earlier, this dominance is quite the same in other countries (developed and developing). Table 2 below summarizes the content of the top five African countries with the largest number of "purely" African sites. As can be seen, news information sites are the most dominant ones and represent 64% of the sites. According to the data, government sites (e-gov) are not very popular in the continent, except for Rwanda which has 36% of e-gov sites among the most popular. This is not surprising as Rwanda has dematerialized 80% of its government services and is the leader with respect to that aspect. Education sites are also not very popular, which correlates well with the lack of popular universities in the continent. Also, some categories such as health, science and sport are missing among the most popular sites. The lack of health and science sites reflects well general observations in those sectors in the continent. However, despite the popularity of sport in Africa, there are still not many sites that propose "sport" content in the continent.

Table 2. Classification of "purely" African sites

Country	# "purely" African	Content
Mauritania	31	29 news, 1 gov, 1 business
Rwanda	22	9 news, 8 gov, 3 job, 2 edu
Kenya	22	11 news, 4 lottery, 2 gov, 2 business, 2 edu, 1 employ
Nigeria	19	12 news, 3 business, 2 lottery, 1 gov, 1 e-commerce
SN	19	11 news, 2 business, 1 edu, 1 adult, 1 money transfer, 1 cinema, 1 gov, 1 phone

3.5   Origins of the Visitors

In this section, we are interested in the country origin of the people who visit Africa website. In that, we would like to know if the content generated by Africans (one country) is of interest to other Africans. There are multiple ways to address the question. In this paper, we consider the most "purely" African sites in the top 4 countries (with respect to the number of in-country hosted sites: South Africa, Tanzania, Rwanda, and Kenya.

In South Africa, dstv.com comes out at 77.8% of visitors originating from South Africa. Nigeria and Angola follow at respectively 6.9% and 5.1%. South Africa has 80% of African total internet hosts as of 2013.

In Tanzania, 83.7% of visitors to jamiiforums.com come from within the country. The USA, UK and India are the next top origin of the requests. There is a large immigration population from Tanzania in the UK.

In Rwanda, we have about 2/3 of the visitors to igihe.com originating within the country. The following top countries with requests are in order the USA, Belgium, and Canada. Only 9% of those total requests come from a search engine, which means the website has mostly regulars, hence native or interested in business.

In Kenya, only 46.6% of visitors to standardmedia.co.ke originate from Kenya. Japan at 7.8%, the USA at 7.7% and China at 6.2% are the next largest visitors. Up to a quarter of visitors are coming from search engines. This website is also a news media website.

These observations suggest that data generated in a country does not (so far) interest other African. In other terms, the idea of "pan-Africanism" is not yet perceived online.

4 Related Work

Because of the high hope that ICT infrastructures is raising in Africa, network connectivity within the continent has recently attracted a lot of interest. The International Telecommunication Union (ITU) publishes yearly data on access to telecommunication services [11]. Several other reports are available documenting various aspects of access to the Internet such as regulation [12] and infrastructure assessment [13]. The studies in [14–16] were interested in the evolution of the African connectivity of the years. While these papers are mostly interested in the development of communication infrastructures in the continent, our paper is focused on the data that is accessed by African. Authors in [14–16] consider the intra-Africa communication an quantify the fraction of traffic that leaves the continent when a communication takes place between two African users. This phenomenon, call boomerang routing, is very important because it raises many issues: cost, delay, and privacy. Our paper is interested in the same issues, but asks a more fundamental question: where is the data that most African access and what is its nature? Understanding this later question is key to addressing the boomerang phenomenon. The study in [17] is similar to ours. It considers the content use and hosting in Africa. The authors address the question by making use of three datasets: (1) user surveys gathering from a campaign on https://researchictafrica.net/ that included seven African countries, (2) a list of African news websites compiled from ABYZ News Links, and (3) Traceroute data collected by the authors. Although the authors tackle the same questions as in our papers, their datasets present a number of limitations. The data from https://researchictafrica.net/ just covers 7 countries in the continent. Also, the news website data is most likely not representative (for a typical African user). For instance, among the sites listed by ABYZ News Links (for Senegal and Burkina Fasso), very few are among the 50 mostly visited sites according to Alexa. On the other hand, our paper is based on the most visited sites in the continent. In that, we believe that our dataset is more representative and gives better answers to the questions raised. However, despite the difference of the dataset used, the two studies come to the same conclusions and thus confirm each other.

5 Conclusion and Perspective

In this paper we consider the content and the hosting of the data that Africans are mostly accessing on the web. We make use of publicly available dataset provided by the site Alexa. Our study has shown that despite the high Internet penetration rate claimed in Africa (mostly boosted by mobile data), most of the data that African attempt to access is located outside the continent. Furthermore, only 1 in 5 of the most visited sites by African carries "purely" African sites and only a fifth of those purely African sites are hosted within the continent. When it comes to African's interest to site design by/for another country, the data indicates a lack of cross interest. Finally, the study shows that African sites are dominated by news (information) category and categories of sites such as health, science, e-government, education and sport are not popular in Africa.

Our study suggests that despite the high Internet penetration rate in Africa and despite the many projects to developing internetworking infrastructures in the continent, most of the traffic generated by African must transit through international network (even though the requested content is primarily destined to Africans). Consequently, end users will continue to experience additional cost and delay. Thus, in additional to developing network infrastructures within the continent, we believe that Africa should encourage the production of local content that is hosted locally.

The main limitation of the paper is the lack of reliable data and this is very understandable: in fact, to date (and to the authors' knowledge) there is no good dataset on Internet communication in Africa. Alexa provides data on most visited websites but is largely criticized because of potential biases against small local websites. The measurement platforms such as CAIDA, RouteViews, RIPE Atlas, all focus on other parts of the world and lack representative data for Africa.

The authors would like to suggest to (and invite) the community to start thinking about a continent-wide data collection and measurement platform. Only this will enable the conclusive studies needed to understand the current African Internet communication ecosystem and provide guidance for building our future networks.

Acknowledgements. This work was partially accomplished under NIST Cooperative Agreement No. 70NANB16H024 with the University of Maryland.

References

1. World Bank (WB). Information and communications for development 2009: Extending reach and increasing impact. https://issuu.com/world.bank.publications/docs/9780821376 058. Accessed 15 Dec 2018
2. Program for Infrastructure Development In Africa. http://www.au-pida.org/. Accessed 02 Jan 2018
3. The African Internet Exchange System (AXIS) Project. https://au.int/en/african-internet-exchange-system-axis-project-overview. Accessed 24 Dec 2017
4. Alexa Top Sites. https://www.alexa.com/topsites. Accessed 01 Oct 2018
5. Maxmind geolocation service, December 2017. https://www.maxmind.com/en/home
6. Wikipedia: Critics on Alexa Data. https://en.wikipedia.org/wiki/Michael_Arrington. Accessed 12 Dec 2018
7. SimilarWeb: Website Traffic Statistics & Market Intelligence. https://www.similarweb.com/home. Accessed 01 Dec 2018
8. SemRush: Service for Competitor Search. https://www.semrush.com/. Accessed 01 Dec 2018
9. Internet World Stats: Usage and Population Statistics.. https://www.internetworldstats.com/stats1.htm. Accessed 15 Dec 2018
10. AKAMAI: HTTP Hits per Second. https://www.akamai.com/us/en/solutions/intelligent-platform/visualizing-akamai/real-time-web-metrics.jsp. Accessed 02 Nov 2018

11. ITU: White Paper on Broadband Regulation and Policy in Asia-Pacific Region: Facilitating faster Broadband Deployment, November 2016
12. ITU Regulatory and Market Environment: Study on International Internet Connectivity in Sub-Saharan Africa. https://www.itu.int/en/ITU-D/Regulatory-Market/Documents/IIC_Africa_Final-en.pdf. Accessed 13 July 2018
13. ITU: Assessment of Telecommunication and ICT Infrastructure in Africa. http://www.itu.int/ITU-D/afr/events/arusha-ITU-NEPAD/Documents/doc7(elotu-english).pdf
14. Fanou, R., Francois, P., Aben, E.: On the diversity of interdomain routing in Africa. In: Mirkovic, J., Liu, Y. (eds.) PAM 2015. LNCS, vol. 8995, pp. 41–54. Springer, Cham (2015). https://doi.org/10.1007/978-3-319-15509-8_4
15. Chavula, J., Feamster, N., Bagula, A., Suleman, H.: Quantifying the effects of circuitous routes on the latency of intra-Africa internet traffic: a study of research and education networks. In: Nungu, A., Pehrson, B., Sansa-Otim, J. (eds.) AFRICOMM 2014. LNICST, vol. 147, pp. 64–73. Springer, Cham (2015). https://doi.org/10.1007/978-3-319-16886-9_7
16. Gueye, A., Mbaye, B.: On the prevalence of boomerang routing in Africa: analysis and potential solutions. In: Kebe, C.M.F., Gueye, A., Ndiaye, A., Garba, A. (eds.) InterSol 2018. LNICST, vol. 249, pp. 3–12. Springer, Cham (2018). https://doi.org/10.1007/978-3-319-98878-8_1
17. Calandro, E., Chavula, J., Phokeer, A.: Internet development in Africa: a content use, hosting and distribution perspective. In: Mendy, G., Ouya, S., Dioum, I., Thiaré, O. (eds.) AFRICOMM 2018. LNICST, vol. 275, pp. 131–141. Springer, Cham (2019). https://doi.org/10.1007/978-3-030-16042-5_13

Distributed Network Slicing and User Association in Unequal STBC-SNR Branch

Mamadou Diallo Diouf$^{(\boxtimes)}$ and M. Ndong

Laboratory of Information Processing and Intelligence Systems (LTISI),
Ecole Polytechnique de Thies (EPT), Thies, Senegal
mddiouf@ept.sn, massa.ndong@uvs.edu.sn
http://www.ept.sn

Abstract. Virtualized Wireless Networks (VWN) strive to offer efficient power allocation and spectral efficiency to each user assigned to
a given slice at any time. We propose a user-slice association based on
the softmax of the probability of successful transmission using space-
time block code (STBC) to encode the data transmission in a wireless
channel. Each slice is defined by a set of Base stations (BS) or relays or
Access Points (APs) or Small cell Base Stations and their related physical resources or a combination of such stations. The slices constitute a
distributed-space-time block code which provides the data traffic for the
mobile terminals. A minimisation of the derived bit error rate (BER) is
used to find the optimal transmit power at each slice. The optimisation
is constrained by the outage at the small cell located near the cooperating transmit slices. Such constraint improves the initialisation of the
iterative algorithm compared to randomly choosing initial points. The
proposed optimisation yields a dynamic selection of the slices with power
control pertaining to the outdoor mobile terminal performance and the
outage. The simulations show that the selection of a slice based on the
softmax of the probability of successful transmissions ensures a better
probability of successful transmissions compared to a permutation based
selection.

Keywords: Virtualization Wireless Network (VWN) · Space-Time
Block Coding (STBC) · Softmax

1 Introduction

The next generation cellular wireless networks called 5G is expected to be
deployed around 2020. This technology is hailed to provide higher data rate,
lower end-to-end latency, improved spectrum/energy efficiency, and reduced cost
per bit. In general, addressing these requirements will require significantly larger
amount of spectrum, more aggressive frequency reuse, extreme densification of
small cells, and the wide use of several enabling technologies (e.g., full-duplex,

© ICST Institute for Computer Sciences, Social Informatics and Telecommunications Engineering 2019
Published by Springer Nature Switzerland AG 2019. All Rights Reserved
G. Bassioni et al. (Eds.): InterSol 2019, LNICST 296, pp. 62–69, 2019.
https://doi.org/10.1007/978-3-030-34863-2_6

massive MIMO, C-RAN, and wireless virtualization) [1]. Here, we will focus on the issue of wireless virtualization which has been receiving increasing attention from both academia and industry [2,3]. Virtualization enables the decoupling of infrastructure from the services it provides. In this case, Mobile Virtual Network Operators (MVNOs) lease the infrastructure of Mobile Operators (MOs) to offer services to their customers. Each MO or infrastructure providers (InPs) can make available for lease a certain number of slices. A slice is defined by a set of Base stations (BS) or relays or Access Points (APs) or Small cell Base Stations and their related physical resources or a combination of such stations along their radio resources. Considering an MVNO who has agreement with several MOs, the user equipment(UE) subscribed to such MVNO should be able to profit from the services of the MVNO which are provided through different physical infrastructures. Virtualization can offer several benefits. First, decoupling and sharing the network infrastructure can help reduce capital expenses (CapEx) and operation expenses (OpEx) [4]. Another benefit of this technique lies in the fact that the use of resources can be improved by moderating the dynamic demands of users of different MVNOs. This provides the benefits of statistical multiplexing. Reducing limits and problems with small service providers could enrich the services provided to users. Current mobile communication research endeavors to achieve cochannel deployment of MVNO slices and legacy macro-cell as a response to the ever-growing demand in wireless channel capacity. In such multi-tier cellular network, transmit power allocation with regard to out-age constraint is an issue due to cross-tier interference [6]. Power allocation for STBC transmit diversity can be achieved by selecting two antenna elements out of all transmitters which are optimal in the sense of a dynamic power allocation which minimizes the symbol error rate. Suboptimal and near-optimum transmit power allocations are derived in [12] and [13] respectively. In addition, Outage probability analysis of spatially distributed relaying based on STBC is provided for ergodic and non-ergodic channel. The performance of distributed STBC in the previously cited work is achieved by using channel state information (CSI) availability, in addition to being oblivious to the difference in signal-to-noise ratio (SNR) branch considering large scale fading environment of multi-tier cellular networks. Our proposal derives the two-slices transmit powers independently of CSI while considering path loss effect on unequal SNR branch. In [17], the output SNR of a selected diversity branches with unequal SNRs [16] is maximized through maximum ratio combining. The work in [18] differs from [17] by its application of unequal transmit power allocation to the Alamouti scheme. We propose a slice selection based on sofmax learning. Each slice has at least two antennas and the Alamouti STBC scheme is considered between a slice and a UE. The softmax is training over the bit-error rate of the link between slice and UE. The simulations show that the selection of a receiver based on the soft-max of the probability of successful transmissions ensures a better probability of successful transmissions compared to a permutation based selection.

2 System Model

We consider universal spectrum sharing between a UEs and randomly distributed MVNO slices. Each base slice serves at least one MVNO user. The downlink between the MBS and the MUEs is interfaced by a set of slices as illustrated in Fig. 1. The slices are equally distanced from the MBS. We assume a close access operation of the MVNO slices base stations, i.e. a MVNO slice base station is solely accessed by its registered MVNO slices users.

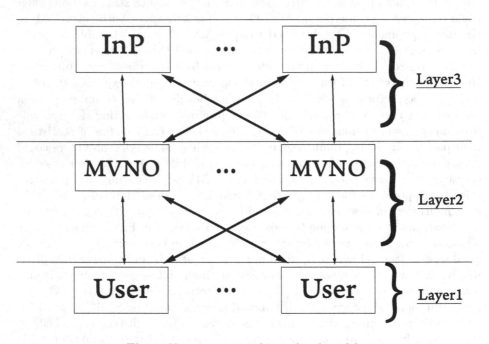

Fig. 1. User association hierarchical model.

We consider VWNs where a transmitter selects its receiver (slice) without knowing whether the transmission will be successful. We denote by Pa the probability of availability of a receiver. We express the probability of a successful transmission as:

$$perf(p,t,i) = \begin{cases} 1, if\ transmission\ successful \\ 0, otherwise. \end{cases} \quad (1)$$

where p, t, i are indexes for mobile user (transmitter), time and selected receiver respectively. A successful transmission can be defined as correctly receiving a certain portion of packets or bits. The reward function is defined to be

$$R(p,t,i) = t(perf(p,t,i)Pa - cost(i)), \quad (2)$$

where $cost(p,t,i)$ is the cost to select the ith receiver.

3   STBC Unequal Branch SNRs

Space-Time block Coding (STBC) is a wireless transmission scheme which exploits multiple antennas at the transmit side without channel state information (CSI) to provide maximum likelihood decoding based on linear processing at the receiver. The receiver can have one or more antenna elements. STBC for two transmit antennas has been discovered by Alamouti [7]. We assume that each station transmits with two antenna elements with the Alamouti encoding scheme and maximum likelihood detection is performed at the receiver. Such encoding and decoding schemes have low complexity [8]. A design a modern wireless system with adjustable transmit powers which minimise the bit error rate (BER) comparing equal and unequal signal-to-noise ratio in STBC wireless communications is presented in [6].

$$SNR = \frac{P_1 d_1^{-\alpha_{out}}}{N_0}|h_1|^2 + \frac{P_2 d_2^{-\alpha_{out}}}{N_0}|h_2|^2 \tag{3}$$

$$\lambda_i = \frac{P_i d_i^{-\alpha_{out}}}{N_0} \tag{4}$$

λ_i means the average SNR for the ith MUE transmitting with power Pi at a distance di to the receiver and α_{out} is the outdoor path loss exponent.

$$P_b = \frac{\sqrt{\lambda_1\lambda_2} + \sqrt{\lambda_2}(1+\lambda_1) + \sqrt{\lambda_1}(1+\lambda_2)}{2K_{BER}(\sqrt{\lambda_1} + \sqrt{1+\lambda_1})\sqrt{(1+\lambda_1)(1+\lambda_2)}(\sqrt{\lambda_2} + \sqrt{1+\lambda_2})} \tag{5}$$

where

$$K_{BER} = \sqrt{\lambda_2(1+\lambda_1)} + \sqrt{\lambda_1(1+\lambda_2)}$$

Each slice has at least two antennas; the STBC can be applied to determine the SNR. Each slice is characterized by its SNR. Considering Pb, we can evaluate the performance of each slice. So we can use the BER as parameters for selecting a slice. The softmax allows us to select a slice. The derivation of Pb is done in [6].

4   Proposed Slice Selection Methods

Softmax [5] regression or multinomial logistic regression is a generalization of logistic regression in case we want to treat several classes. The software softmax allows to build neural networks with several standardized outputs. This makes it particularly suitable for creating classifications by neural networks with probabilistic outputs. It is particularly useful for neural networks where it is desired to apply a non-binary classification. In this case, simple logistic regression is not enough. We propose to select a slice based on the highest successful packet transmission rate. Each MO proposes a set of slices to an MVNO. The MVNO selects the slices available to associate each slice or a set of selected slices to one or several of its UEs. Assuming the STBC scheme already described, we use the BER performance as the selective criterion to decide the mobile user(s) to slice association.

5 Numerical Investigation

To investigate the proposal, we set up as a benchmark a slice-user association based on a permutation of the slices, i.e. a UE is associated to a slice by permuting the set of the slices. We assume that the average SNR at each selected slice is chosen from 5.5 dB, 8.9 dB, 11 dB. For instance, if "Slice 1", "Slice 2" and "Slice 3" have the average SNRs "5.5 dB", "8.9 dB" and "11 dB" respectively, then a user is associated to "Slice 1" for the first time slot, to "Slice 2" for the second time slot and to "Slice 3" for the third time slot. For the 4th time slot, the user will be associated with "Slice 1" and so forth. Following such association scheme, the BER is computed and the probability of successful transmission for such user is given in Fig. 2.

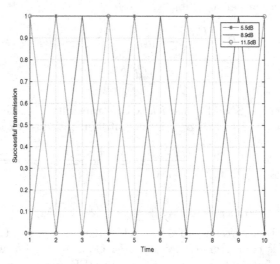

Fig. 2. Probability of successful transmissions per receiver by permutation of the receivers.

The proposed scheme uses the softmax to compute the parameter used to associate a mobile user to a slice. It assumes some training periods. The training consists of using the benchmark for a certain number of time slots and then compute the softmax value by using 6. If the softmax value output at the i_{th} slice is the highest at a given time slot, then the mobile user is associated with the i_{th} slice. We consider a transmitting device as a mobile user or UE. A mobile user can transmit to a any slice. The softmax is computed as:

$$Sfmax(p,i) = \frac{e^{-AvPerf(p,i)}}{\sum_{k=1}^{N} e^{-AvPerf(k,i)}},\tag{6}$$

where N is the number of mobiles users and

$$AvPerf(p,i) = \sum_{n=1}^{T} perf(p,t,i)\tag{7}$$

is the average of successful transmissions over a period of time T.

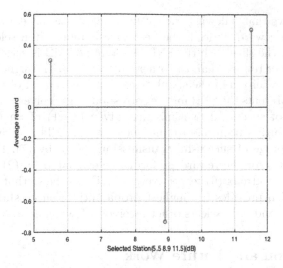

Fig. 3. Reward per receiver by receiver selection based on permutation of the receivers.

Figures 3 and 4 illustrate our proposal which consists of associating a mobile user to a slice if the latter has the highest softmax output. The softmax output is computed by (3). The reward performance illustrated Fig. 3 shows a shorter gap in reward between the slice with 5.5 dB and the one with 11 dB than the gap obtained with softmax-based selection criterion as illustrated in Fig. 4.

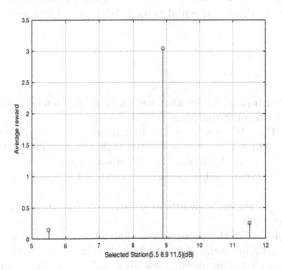

Fig. 4. Reward per receiver by receiver selection based on Softmax.

Figure 4 shows that following the softmax based user-slice association yields a better average reward. Indeed, the best slice is more often selected than the others. In Fig. 3, the slice with the SNR averaging 8.9 dB is selected more often and yields a higher reward than the other slices. We set the signal-to-noise ratio (SNR) for the 3 receivers in the simulations. On Fig. 2, each of the values {5.5, 8.9, 11.5 dB} represents the SNR for the corresponding receiver. Figure 2 presents the probability of successful transmissions given by (1) of an MS selecting a receiver by permuting from one to another each time. This allows the computation of the average of successful transmissions given by (7). Figure 3 can be compared to Fig. 4 for the reward performance evaluated by (2) using the permutation and the softmax (6) respectively. The Fig. 4 shows that the MS selects one receiver which provides the highest probability of successful transmissions most of the time and only selects other receiver a few times.

6   Conclusion and Future Work

The number of slices which can be made available by MOs for wireless virtualized networks can be high and can change adaptively. The mobile users subscribers to the MVNOs services will benefits greatly in an adaptive mobile user-slice association which can be managed by a virtual interface. Our proposal and computer simulation illustrate an implementation of a user-slice association for wireless virtualized networks and the better association it provides compared to a permutation-based one. We would like to extend this work by investigating deeper in the softmax usage in research, and apply more antennas (3 or 4) at the transmitter for the STBC schemes. Additionaly, transmit power allocation will be investigated regarding non equal branch SNR in STBC and MIMO channel uncertainty.

References

1. Hossain, E., Hasan, M.: 5G cellular: key enabling technologies and research challenges. IEEE Instrum. Meas. Mag. (2015). To appear
2. Liang, C., Yu, F.R.: Wireless network virtualization: a survey, some research issues and challenges. IEEE Commun. Surv. Tutorials **17**, 358–380 (2014)
3. Costa-Perez, X., Guo, T., Mahindra, R., Rangarajan, S.: Radio access network virtualization for future mobile carrier networks. IEEE Wirel. Commun. Mag. **517**, 27–35 (2013)
4. LNCS Homepage. http://www.artizanetworks.com/resources/tutorials/cran.html. Accessed 1 Nov 2018
5. Gao, B., Pavel, L.: On the properties of the softmax function with application in game theory and reinforcement learning. arXiv:1704.00805 (2018)
6. Ndong, M., Fujii, T.: Joint antenna selection and power allocation for distributed-STBC cognitive small cell networks. In: Symposium on Wireless Personal Multimedia Communications (WPMC), pp. 439–444 (2014)
7. Alamouti, S.: A simple transmit diversity technique for wireless communications. IEEE J. Sel. Areas Commun. **16**(8), 1451–1458 (1998)

8. Tarokh, V., Jafarkhani, H., Calderbank, A.R.: Space-time block coding for wireless communications: performance results. IEEE J. Sel. Areas Commun. **17**(3), 451–460 (1999)
9. Wang, J.C., Jiang, H., Zhang, X., Leung, V.C.M., Hanzo, L.: Learning-aided network association for hybrid indoor LiFi-WiFi systems. IEEE Trans. Veh. Technol. **67**, 3561–3574 (2018)
10. Zhu, K., Hossain, E.: Virtualization of 5G cellular networks as a hierarchical combinatorial auction. IEEE Trans. Mob. Comput. **15**(10), 2640–2654 (2016)
11. Wildemeersch, M., Quek, T.S., Slump, C.H., Rabbachin, A.: Cognitive small cell networks: energy efficiency and trade-Offs. IEEE Trans. Wirel. Commun. **61**(9), 4016–4029 (2013)
12. Lu, Z., Cimini, L.J.: Efficient power allocation for decentralized distributed space-time block coding. IEEE Trans. Wirel. Commun. **8**(3), 1102–1106 (2009)
13. Dohler, M., Aghvami, A.H., Zhou, Z., Li, Y., Vucetic, B.: Near-optimum transmit power allocation for space-time block encoded wireless communication systems. IEE Proc. Commun. **153**(3), 459–463 (2006)
14. Khan, F.A., Yunfei, C., Alouini, M.-S.: Novel receivers for AF re-laying with distributed STBC using cascaded and disintegrated channel estimation. IEEE Trans. Wirel. Commun. **11**(4), 1370–1379 (2012)
15. Razi, A., Afghah, F., Abedi, A.: Power optimized DSTBC assisted DMF relaying in wireless sensor networks with redundant super nodes. IEEE Trans. Wirel. Commun. **12**(2), 636–645 (2013)
16. Proakis, J.G., Salehi, M.: Digital Communications, 5th edn. McGraw Hill, New York (2008)
17. Win, M.Z., Winters, J.H.: Analysis of hybrid selection/maximal-ratio combining of diversity branches with unequal SNR in Rayleigh fading. In: Vehicular Technology Conference (VTC), pp. 215–220 (1999)
18. Jian, C., Haifeng, W., Lilleberg, J., Shixin, C.: Unequally powered STBC for slow flat Rayleigh fading channel. In: Wireless Communications and Networking Conference (WCNC), pp. 291–295 (2002)

Follow Africa: Building an African News Recommender Systems

Moustapha Diouf Fall and Modou Gueye[✉]

Université Cheikh Anta Diop, Dakar, Senegal
moustaphad.fall@gmail.com, modou2.gueye@ucad.edu.sn

Abstract. Recommender systems have become an important component of Web media. From VoD providers (Netflix, Amazon Video) (https://goo.gl/g3G1ys) to news websites (Yahoo! News, CNN) (https://goo.gl/yA2NB6), users have become accustomed to personalized content. However, news recommendation differs from traditional recommendation due to the short lifetime of news. Indeed, News is particularly characterized by a short time span during which they are relevant. Therefore, in addition, to suggest suited news to users, news recommender systems (NRS) have to deal with news recency in order to avoid recommending already read content somewhere else.

In most of the cases, NRS implicitly collect users' click history and readings to build topic-based user profiles. News websites generally integrate some keywords into the news articles which sum up their content. But this is not always the case for African news websites.

In this paper, we present *Follow Africa*, an African news recommender system. We introduce a recency-based recommendation model which also takes account of users' previous readings. We show the effectiveness of our proposal through the results we obtain in a month-lasted online experiment with more than one hundred users.

Keywords: News recommendation · Recency-based algorithm · Keyword assignment

1 Introduction

The news is an important aspect in modern society, they are the best resources to know what happens around us. However, the abundance of new information that is daily published online through different channels and portals can make it challenging for users to find the content they are interested to read, consequently, they can be overwhelmed and may miss some important news.

News recommender systems (NRS) aim to recommend suited news articles to readers instead of leaving them spending a long time searching content which may be interesting.

NRS is different from the other kinds of recommender systems (RS) as they have to work with a continuous stream of short-lived items. Indeed, the news is

© ICST Institute for Computer Sciences, Social Informatics and Telecommunications Engineering 2019
Published by Springer Nature Switzerland AG 2019. All Rights Reserved
G. Bassioni et al. (Eds.): InterSol 2019, LNICST 296, pp. 70–81, 2019.
https://doi.org/10.1007/978-3-030-34863-2_7

particularly characterized by a short time span during which they are relevant, after this time their relevance can decrease very quickly. Therefore, in addition, to suggest suited news to users based on the history of what they read, NRS have to deal with their recency in order to avoid recommending already read content somewhere else.

In the context of African news, making some recommendations is more difficult. News articles from many African news websites are not well structured and do not integrate keywords which describe the topics of their articles. This makes the crawling of their content more difficult.

We have also to take account of user privacy when computing his recommendations. Thus in this work, we propose a privacy-heeded NRS which handles the challenge of helping readers to be aware of fresh Africa-related news articles which might suit them.

In our knowledge there is no news recommender system build specially for African news. The ones like Flipboard, Google News, Yahoo! News and so on show Africa in overhaul but not in deep. Furthermore, they only rely on international news websites and do not use African regional ones which can give some local useful news. International news websites are well structured. It is easy to get a summary of news articles as they generally give some keywords inside their articles which sum up them. But for regional African news websites that is not the case. There is a real challenge in crawling and summarizing their articles.

The aim of *Follow Africa* is to propose news recommendations related to Africa. Its architecture is organized into two components. A back-end component which makes all the tasks of news crawling and summarizing into topics, and a Front-end component which heeds privacy and locally computes news recommendations to show to readers. We present in this work these two components. We detail how we make recommendations and point out the effectiveness of our proposal through some results that we get from a month-lasted online experiment over many readers[1].

The sequel of this paper is organized as follows. In Sect. 2 we present some related works in news recommendation. In Sect. 3 we provide a detailed presentation of *Follow Africa*. We expose its architecture and explain how we recommend suited news articles. Then in Sect. 4.2 we show our experimental results. Finally, in Sect. 5 we conclude this paper and present some future works.

2   Related Works

Two different approaches are commonly used in news recommendation: content-based and collaborative filtering. Each of them presents some drawbacks and advantages [12]. The collaborative filtering approach considers the opinions of peer users to generate news recommendations. In [6] , the authors use collaborative methods to make new recommendations. However, this approach presents

---

[1] One can install *Follow Africa*'s Android mobile application from https://goo.gl/t8nahh.

two majors drawbacks as cited by [11]. First, collaborative methods do not recommend an article that many users have not yet read. Second, the trend to recommend "buzz" articles while some people have no interest in this kind of articles. For these reasons and some security and privacy aspects, content-based approaches are better suited for news recommendation [3]. In content-based approaches, keywords are used to describe a news article and a user profile is built to indicate the type of news this user likes. We take this approach and use the keywords of news articles to understand what topics are of interest to the user.

In the literature, many authors have proposed topics-based news recommendations like in [14]. However, in this work, we combine the interest of users on news topics by the recency of news articles in order to recommend fresh and suited news content. Moreover, we take into account users' reading privacy, therefore we propose a news recommender system which even runs on the reader's mobile. Recommender systems retrieve users' feedback in various forms. They can explicitly ask the user to give feedback by rating the articles [2] or collect implicit feedback based on user clicks and readings. Even if the second method is less accurate than the first, it allows to gets more feedback as users do not give any ratings. Furthermore, it is not bothering. Our proposal only uses implicit, positive feedback.

3   Follow Africa

As said above, the purpose of *Follow Africa* is to find news articles related to Africa that may be of interest to a particular user. It continuously aggregates articles from several African news websites and other ones that publish some topics related to Africa in order to build personalized content for its readers.

In this section, we show the architectural system of *Follow Africa*, then we discuss its functioning and some issues we have faced with unstructured or mistaken data from some new websites. Finally, we present the recommendation model behind our mobile application and the algorithm to compute recommendations.

3.1   Architecture and Functioning

The architecture of *Follow Africa* has two parts: a back-end side and a front-end one. The first is responsible for harvesting articles from news websites and providing them to the front-end side. The latter computes locally on the mobile the recommendations to make to a user and displays the selected articles. Figure 1 shows the architecture of the overall system of *Follow Africa*.

The back-end side represents all the background works we do to gather news articles to give to users. Its different elements are listed below.

- Web: this element corresponds to the web sources from which we extract news, ranging from several popular and well-known websites to nameless ones.

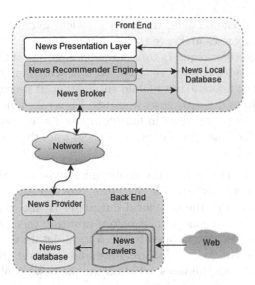

Fig. 1. Architecture of *Follow Africa*

Hence let us notice that our content is not confined to news, we also add some fashion or cooking magazines to bring more diversity in our content. Currently, we have more than forty websites as news sources. They provide news in French language and cover almost all the categories of news like politic, sport, health and so on. Obviously, they have not the same page structure, some of them are well organized while the others are messy.

- News Crawlers: we use different scripts to harvest articles from the news websites. For each website and depending on its page structure, we assign a custom news crawler.

  Periodically, each news crawler browses its target website and search for newly published articles. It retrieves the main content of each new article like the title, the lead paragraph, the publication date and time, the illustrative image and, when they are available, the keywords which give the related topics of the article. In the case where any keyword is not available, the crawler uses a topic assignment method to fill the missing data. In Sect. 3.2, we explain the topic assignment method we used. Furthermore, we compress the illustrative image in a smaller size in order to optimize the communication cost with the front-end side which is implemented in readers' mobiles.

- News Database: The news database stores all the crawled articles. As news is ephemeral, every day we delete from the database all articles which are older than seven days. By doing this, we make sure to only consider news over a period of one week.

- News Provider: The news provider is one of the most important components of our architecture as it handles all the requests from the front-end side (*i.e.*, the mobile app) and prevents the user to have an article more than once.

To summarize the back-end side, the news crawlers harvest periodically fresh news articles from websites and save their main content on the database. When the news provider receives requests from a reader's mobile application, it selects all the articles the reader has not yet received and sent them to him.

The front-end side refers to our mobile application. It presents to the readers the collected data from different news websites. Figure 2(a) gives an overview of its interface. This site is organized in four components to ensure that the users see first the news which may be of interest to them from the multitude of articles he has in his disposition.

- News Broker: it carries out all the communications with the back-end side. Especially, it communicates with the news provider and collects the latest news that it records in the new local database. It also verifies that all the collected items are in a good format before inserting them into the database.
- News Local Database: We decided to use a local database because in Africa, Internet access is not so easy for everyone and we want to be able to work offline. As a result, all the news article from the news broker are saved and used when the news presentation layer requests them. News articles do not always stay in the database. Of course, they are deleted after a specified period.
- News Recommender Engine: the task of the recommender engine is to compute and save scores of interest a reader might have for yet unread news articles. Each time the reader reads or clicks on an article or some new articles are added on the news local database by the news broker, it recomputes the scores of articles.
  Section 3.3 details the recommendation model behind the news we suggest to users for reading.
- News Presentation Layer: it implements all the IHM of the mobile app. Figure 2 shows an overview of it's Home's page and the recommendation's one. When the reader clicks on a news article, the news presentation layer updates his profile by adding the topics of the article. Then the recommender engine recomputes the scores of interest of articles and ranks them in decreasing order. Finally, the presentation layer refreshes its display with these ranked articles.

3.2   Topics Assignment

Most news websites sum up in their articles the topics they cover through some keywords. More formally, let be $\mathcal{A}$ and $\mathcal{T}$ respectively the set of news articles and one of possible topics that describe news. We consider for a news article $a \in \mathcal{A}$ the set $\mathcal{T}_a$ defined by

$$\mathcal{T}_a = \{t \mid t \in \mathcal{T}\} \tag{1}$$

as the set of topics t that sum up the article a. From this definition, we set the description D_a of a news article a by a triplet of information as follows

$$D_a = (c_a, s_a, \mathcal{T}_a), s_a \in \mathbb{R}^+ \tag{2}$$

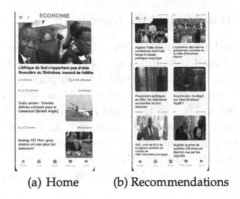

(a) Home   (b) Recommendations

Fig. 2. Overviews of the news presentation layer

where c_a merges the title, image and lead paragraph of the news article and s_a represents the staleness of the article. We consider the staleness of an article as the number of elapsed days since the article was published online. Through the staleness of articles we consider their recency.

Despite the fact that many news websites summarize their articles with keywords representing their topics, some websites do not. In this case, we use a custom taxonomy database for assigning some topics to news articles. We explain our approach.

First, our taxonomy database is organized as a key-value table where the values are sets of words: $[k \Rightarrow \{t \mid t \in \mathcal{T}\}]$. For instance, we can find in the following key-value instances:

$$\left[\text{``sadio mane''} \Rightarrow \{\text{``football''}, \text{``sport''}, \text{``senegal''}\}, \text{``election''} \Rightarrow \{\text{``politic''}\} \right]$$

Therefore when a news crawler finds a news article without topics that describe it, the crawler breaks its content into several parts through string tokenization [5]. Then the crawler browses the taxonomy database with the tokens and retrieves related topics. The retrieved topics are associated with the article and the all is saved in the database.

Topics assignment is also called keywords assignment. Many assignment methods are suggested in the literature [4] with some that use advanced natural processing language libraries but they are especially dedicated to English language and are not so useful for other languages like French [9].

Once news articles are harvested and topics assignment is done for those we have not yet established topics, the articles are saved on the news database. They are sent to readers by the news provider when they ask new content. Our recommender system takes the relay on the readers' mobiles and makes personalized recommendations to show to them. In the next section, we present the recommendation model we use.

3.3   Recommendation Model and Algorithm

We use a content-based recommendation model under our news presentation pages. Indeed content-based techniques are more robust to face cold start problem than collaborative filtering [13]. In order to simplify the rest of this section, let us consider int the following the sets $\mathcal{U}$ and $\mathcal{D}$ as respectively the set of all users (*i.e.*, our readers) and one of the valid calendar dates.

The recommendation task can be summarized as to find the top-K highest interesting news articles for a user $u \in \mathcal{U}$ and recommend them to him. Let be a utility function which computes the score of interest a reader might have for some news articles., i.e., $score : \mathcal{U} \times \mathcal{A} \rightarrow \mathbb{R}$. We can formalize the task of recommendation as follows:

$$Top_u^K = \underset{a \in \mathcal{A}}{argmax}^K \; score(u, a) \tag{3}$$

The basic assumption of personalizing content is that users reasonably have consistent interests that may change over time [11]. Thus each user can be followed up by a profile which is a representation of all his interests and properties like age, gender, occupation and so on.

In the case of news recommendation, a user profile usually corresponds to a data structure which sums up his preferences on news topics. With *Follow Africa* we set the profile P_u of a given user $u \in \mathcal{U}$ by

$$P_u = \{(t, w_t, d_t) \mid t \in \mathcal{T}, w_t \in \mathbb{R}^+, d_t \in \mathcal{D}\} \tag{4}$$

where each triplet (t, w_t, d_t) represents a news topic t which interests the user with an interest-valued weight w_t and the last date d_t when the user read an article related to that topic.

The user profile helps us to predict what he may like or not. To build the profile we assume a click on an article means he is interested in the subject of the article, so we update his profile by adding the topics of the article to it. In addition to adding a topic t to the user profile, we set its interest-valued weight w_t to one. In case that is not the first time that the topic is added, we increase its interest-valued weight by a unit.

To prevent the cold start problem which refers to new users (their profiles are empty), we ask users to choose a least three main topics that interest them at the first time they start to use the app.

From the Eq. 4, we define all the topics of interest to a user u as

$$\mathcal{T}_u = \{t \mid \exists \, w_t \in \mathbb{R}^+ \wedge d_t \in \mathcal{D} : (t, w_t, d_t) \in P_u\} \tag{5}$$

and we compute the interest-valued weight of a news article a for a user u by the following score function

$$score(u, a) = e^{-s_a} \times \left(\sum_{t \in \{\mathcal{T}_u \cap \mathcal{T}_a\}} w_t \right) \tag{6}$$

By this interest-valued function we take account of the user's favorite topics and the staleness of news articles. The first part e^{-s_a} takes account of the stale-ness of articles (*i.e.*, their recency). We decided to represent the evolution of a news article's staleness by the exponential function as the probability a user has already read an article on somewhat website greatly increases day after day. The second part of our function represents the intrinsic interest of the article for the user.

Since the user's favourite topics may change over time depending on several contextual elements, his profile must be updated each time he expresses a par-ticular interest in some topics by reading a new article or just click on it. In this work, we build the profiles of users based only on their clicks on articles. In other words, we just consider the implicit positive feedback of users. In addition, for some privacy concerns, we store each user's profile on his mobile as the data belongs to him. Moreover, as the recommendations are carried out on the user mobile, we alleviate our server which runs the back-end tasks.

Once we computed the interest-valued weights that a user may have on news articles, we sort them in decreasing order. Let us notice that all articles that do not have topics are ignored. The articles that a user has already read are ignored too. We do not recommend an article that a user has already read. However, an article that has been recommended can be recommended again because it is difficult to interpret why a user has not yet clicked on. Algorithm 1 details more our recommendation process.

Algorithm 1. *Follow Africa*'s recommendation algorithm

Data: $\{D_a \mid a \in \mathcal{A}\}$, P_u
Result: $S = [(a, score(u,a)) \mid a \in \mathcal{A}]$
1 **begin**
2    $S \longleftarrow [\,]$;
3   **foreach** $a \in \mathcal{A}$ **do**
4      $S.add(a, score(u,a))$;
5   **end**
6   Sort S by decreasing $score(u,a)$;
7   **return** S
8 **end**

---

4 Experimentation

We present in this section the effectiveness of our recommendation model. We led an online experiment on a population of 113 real readers. In the next two subsections, we shortly describe how we did the experiment by the evaluation measures and methodology we used. Then we present the results we obtained.

4.1 Evaluation Measures and Methodology

One can evaluate RS by using three approaches: offline analysis, user studies or online experiments. Furthermore, a combination of these approaches is also possible [1].

Offline analysis is typically easy to conduct, as they require no interaction with real users. However, it is hard to find publicly available datasets for news recommendation. The one we know is the Plista dataset [7], but all its contained news are in German. User studies is an alternative. In this case, a small group of persons will use the mobile app in a controlled environment and then their experience will be reported. However, we may have to consider various biases in the experimental design of such studies. Therefore we decide to carry out an online evaluation where a pool of real users who are unaware of the experiment are used. As some authors said, this is perhaps the most trustworthy approach [8]. However, it can only collect certain types of data.

So we conducted an online experiment for a month with the recourse of a week-based size-increasing pool of real users. Table 1 details the increasing of the pool size. By weekly increasing the pool of users, we want to take into account the evolution of the users' profiles.

Table 1. Week-based size-increasing pool of users

Week	Dec. 16–22	Dec. 23–29	Dec. 30–Janv. 5	Janv. 6–12
# New users	38	23	19	33
# Total	38	61	80	113

We did the experiment from December 16, 2018, to January 12, 2019, with a total of 113 users at the end whose 58.8% of male and 41.2% of female ranging from 18 to 54 years old.

To measure the effectiveness of our news recommender system, we mainly measure changes in the retention rate of new users to determine the extent to which our recommendation is keeping users engagement. We did two things.

1. we first track the increase in overall users retention by measuring the evolution of the number of established active users,
2. then we divide users into four week-based cohorts depending on the first time they used the mobile app. For each cohort, we measure the retention rate of its users during the next weeks.

4.2   Experimental Results

We present in this part the results of our online experiment.

Active Users Evolution. Active users refer to those who frequently use the app. Note that by "frequently" we do not necessarily say every day. An active user can skip a day and do not use the app, but not two days.

We log monthly (28-day), weekly (7-day), and daily (1-day) active users percentage evolution in the range from December 16, 2018, to January 12, 2019. Figure 3 displays the evolution of active users.

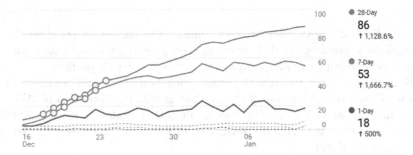

Fig. 3. Active users evolution

We can see that the number of active users is increasing. At the date of January 12, 2019, we count 86 active users among all our 113 users. Either 76% of our users actively use the app and access to recommended news articles. However, active users do not use the app in the same manner. Some of them discovered the app during the last week of the experiment while some other users began to use it in previous weeks. Therefore we led the evaluation below where we take into consideration this fact.

New Users Retention. To measure the ability of our recommendations to retain new users over time, we measure the percentage of active users who use the mobile app every day since the first time they opened it. Let us note that we do not consider here users which remained at least one day without using the app. We divided users into four week-based cohorts. Each cohort is a set of users who started using our application during the same week. Table 1 gives the number of users into each cohort.

Figure 4 shows the extent to which our recommendations retain new users. It indicates whether users acquired a week ago continue to use the app. Each row represents a cohort. The bottom row represents the most recent cohort while the top one corresponds to the earliest cohort.

As we can see, the retention rate of each group decreases after the first week of use of the application, but increases slightly from the Week 2. This is an

	Week 0	Week 1	Week 2	Week 3
	100%	38.8%	42.6%	39.5%
Dec 16 - Dec 22 38 Users	100%	36.8%	42.1%	39.5%
Dec 23 - Dec 29 23 Users	100%	39.1%	43.5%	
Dec 30 - Jan 5 19 Users	100%	42.1%		
Jan 6 - Jan 12 33 Users	100%			

Fig. 4. New users retention

expected effect of the well known issue named the cold start problem. Indeed recommender systems meet difficulties to recommend items to a user who has not yet read enough news articles and then who is not well profiled.

RS need some time to learn the users click behaviour and understand the topics which are in the interest of them. That is why the retention of Week 2 is greater than the one of Week 1. Our recommendation model seems to work better after one week of usage. This demonstrates in a certain extent the effectiveness of our recommendations.

We remark also that the user retention rate of last cohorts is higher than the one of first cohorts. When we investigate the kind of users of each cohort, we discovered that the first cohort is almost composed by friends whom we gave the app while the rest are some unknown people who have installed *Follow Africa* from the Google's play store (maybe they know the app from the Facebook page we dedicated to it). The latter seem to have more engagement than our friends who would just accept to install the app due to our friendship.

5   Conclusion

In this paper, we presented a news recommender system we called *Follow Africa*. We detailed its architecture and discussed how it carries out recommendations. The experiment we led online points out the effectiveness of its recommendation.

As future works, we target to collect and create a news dataset from our current readers. Thus we will be able to compare in the same baseline our news recommendation model to some others in the literature [10].

Currently, some redundant news articles often occur in our recommendations despite they are provided by different websites. By redundancy, we refer to the similarity of their information and not of their content in terms of expressions or sentences. Thus we want to investigate article de-duplication methods which allow eliminating redundant news articles.

References

1. Abel, F., Deldjoo, Y., Elahi, M., Kohlsdorf, D.: Recsys challenge 2017: offline and online evaluation. In: Proceedings of the Eleventh ACM Conference on Recommender Systems, RecSys 2017, pp. 372–373. ACM, New York (2017)
2. Billsus, D., Pazzani, M.J.: A hybrid user model for news story classification. In: Kay, J. (ed.) UM99 User Modeling. CICMS, vol. 407, pp. 99–108. Springer, Vienna (1999). https://doi.org/10.1007/978-3-7091-2490-1_10
3. Calandrino, J.A., Kilzer, A., Narayanan, A., Felten, E.W., Shmatikov, V.: "you might also like:" privacy risks of collaborative filtering. In: 2011 IEEE Symposium on Security and Privacy, pp. 231–246, May 2011
4. Dakka, W., Gravano, L.: Efficient summarization-aware search for online news articles. In: JCDL, pp. 63–72. ACM (2007)
5. Dridan, R., Oepen, S.: Tokenization: returning to a long solved problem a survey, contrastive experiment, recommendations, and toolkit. In: Proceedings of the 50th Annual Meeting of the Association for Computational Linguistics: Short Papers - Volume 2, ACL 2012, pp. 378–382. Association for Computational Linguistics, Stroudsburg (2012)
6. Garcin, F., Zhou, K., Faltings, B., Schickel, V.: Personalized news recommendation based on collaborative filtering. In: Proceedings of the The 2012 IEEE/WIC/ACM International Joint Conferences on Web Intelligence and Intelligent Agent Technology - Volume 01, WI-IAT 2012, pp. 437–441. IEEE Computer Society, Washington (2012)
7. Kille, B., Hopfgartner, F., Brodt, T., Heintz, T.: The plista dataset. In: Proceedings of the 2013 International News Recommender Systems Workshop and Challenge, NRS 2013, pp. 16–23. ACM, New York (2013)
8. Kohavi, R., Longbotham, R., Sommerfield, D., Henne, R.: Controlled experiments on the web: survey and practical guide. Data Min. Knowl. Disc. 18(1), 140–181 (2009)
9. Kompan, M., Bieliková, M.: Content-based news recommendation. In: Buccafurri, F., Semeraro, G. (eds.) EC-Web 2010. LNBIP, vol. 61, pp. 61–72. Springer, Heidelberg (2010). https://doi.org/10.1007/978-3-642-15208-5_6
10. Li, L., Wang, D.-D., Zhu, S.-Z., Li, T.: Personalized news recommendation: a review and an experimental investigation. J. Comput. Sci. Technol. 26(5), 754–766 (2011)
11. Liu, J., Dolan, P., Pedersen, E.R.: Personalized news recommendation based on click behavior. In: Proceedings of the 15th International Conference on Intelligent User Interfaces, IUI 2010, pp. 31–40. ACM, New York (2010)
12. Shah, L., Gaudani, H., Balani, P.: Article: survey on recommendation system. Int. J. Comput. Appl. 137(7), 43–49 (2016). Published by Foundation of Computer Science (FCS), NY, USA
13. Volkovs, M., Yu, G.W., Poutanen, T.: Content-based neighbor models for cold start in recommender systems. In: Proceedings of the Recommender Systems Challenge 2017, RecSys Challenge 2017, pp. 7:1–7:6. ACM, New York (2017)
14. Wang, Z., Hahn, K., Kim, Y., Song, S., Seo, J.-M.: A news-topic recommender system based on keywords extraction. Multimedia Tools Appl. 77(4), 4339–4353 (2018)

An Ontological Model for the Annotation of Infectious Disease Simulation Models

Papa Alioune Cisse[1(✉)], Gaoussou Camara[2], Jean Marie Dembele[1,3], and Moussa Lo[1,3]

[1] LANI, UFR SAT, Université Gaston Berger, B.P. 234, Saint-Louis, Sénégal
papaaliounecisse@yahoo.fr,
jean-marie.dembele@ugb.edu.sn, moussa.lo@uvs.edu.sn
[2] Université Alioune Diop, B.P. 30, Bambey, Sénégal
gaoussou.camara@uadb.edu.sn
[3] Sorbonne Université, IRD, UMMISCO, 93143 Bondy, France

Abstract. In this paper, we propose a conceptualization of knowledge of infectious disease simulation models. This model is intended to annotate a set of qualitative and quantitative simulation models to automate their composition in a process of simulation of the spread of infectious diseases. We propose a use case illustrating the use of the ontological model for the annotation of two schistosomiasis simulation models.

Keywords: Ontology · Annotation · Composition · Simulation model · Infectious disease · Schistosomiasis

1 Introduction

In the study of complex social and natural phenomena, it is sometimes necessary to combine several dynamics or several points of view of a system to correctly understand its functioning and its evolution [1, 2]. Thus, the modelers of these systems are more and more confronted with the difficulties of representing them with a single model. In addition, they generally rely on multidisciplinary theories and use different modeling approaches to represent these subsystems. This often results on the one hand, in having several heterogeneous models for the same system; and on the other hand, the necessity to compose these different models in order to better understand this system [3].

In addition, the process of simulating a behavior of these multi-model systems is in itself a delicate exercise that requires the ability to identify, compare, and select models that can answer the question behind a simulation; then, if several models are selected, to assemble them and to integrate data and applications needed to perform the simulations.

In this work, we are interested in the field of infectious diseases and in simulation models of their underlying dynamics. It's a work that aims to set up an ontology-based platform to automate the simulation process of infectious disease models. The purpose of this article is therefore to propose a conceptualization of the knowledge of these models. The resulting ontology will serve as a basis for annotating a set of qualitative and quantitative simulation models for infectious diseases.

G. Bassioni et al. (Eds.): InterSol 2019, LNICST 296, pp. 82–91, 2019.
https://doi.org/10.1007/978-3-030-34863-2_8

After presenting the context of our work in Sect. 2 of this paper, we present in Sect. 3 some related works. Section 4 proposes a taxonomy of knowledge of infectious disease simulation models on which the ontology we propose in Sect. 5 is based. Section 6 presents a use case of two simulation models of schistosomiasis annotated with this ontology.

2 Context

The field of an infectious disease spread can be divided into two subdomains: the sub-domain of the disease (its transmission mechanism within a population, the various entities included in it and their relationships) and the sub-domain of risk factors (the set of socio-economic, environmental, biological and behavioral elements, that may influence the spread of the disease) [3, 4]. In each of these subdomains, we can identify a set of underlying dynamics. For example, concerning schistosomiasis, its transmission mechanism is often described according to two dynamics: intra-host dynamics (which gives the evolution of the pathogen inside the host organism) and extra-host dynamics or infection dynamics (which ensures the passage of the pathogen from one host to another). The dynamics of access to infectious water, based on a set of socio-economic factors, is also crucial [5]. Each of these dynamics is in itself a complex phenomenon involving several heterogeneous entities of different natures and sizes, also evolving in different environments.

Conceptually, we can see the propagation of an infectious disease as a system with several levels of interactions, which can be located at different spatial and temporal scales (see Fig. 1).

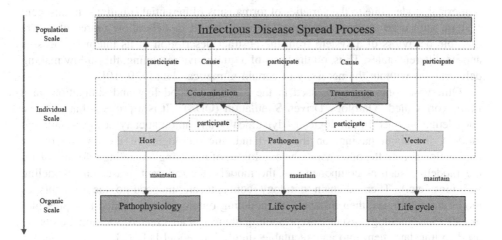

Fig. 1. Scales of infectious disease spread process

This point of view reveals two important things: the difficulty (see the impossibility) of having a single model that represents all these levels of interaction and the possibility to model a level or a set of levels while ignoring the others [3, 5].

The specific problem that interests us in this work is that of the spread of schistosomiasis in Senegal. In recent years, it has been studied by several teams of researchers working in different fields of research: biology, epidemiology, biomathematics, bioinformatics... For this, there is currently a variety of models on schistosomiasis. These models are established on the basis of different modeling approaches and multiple objectives, targeting particular levels of interaction, manipulating heterogeneous data and simulated in dedicated platforms. The ontology we propose allows annotating these different models and their associated simulation platforms.

3 Ontology and Simulation Models

Ontologies are interested in representing the knowledge of a domain. They consist more precisely in the identification of concepts and their relations, and in proposing their formal representation for resource annotation and semantic reasoning [6–8]. Based on these representations, an autonomous agent will have the ability to understand and effectively manage a system, reason and make deliberations.

In recent years, the modeling and simulation community has been using ontologies to improve and facilitate the framework of his work.

Ontologies are used in modeling and simulation as a qualitative approach to represent complex systems. This ontology-based modeling approach is often used to overcome the limitations of numerical modeling approaches: difficulties in obtaining numerical data to conduct simulations; difficult to compose or integrate a set of numerical models due to the varieties of formalisms (differential equations, multi-agent system, etc.) used to represent them. Ontology-based models allow representing the possible behaviors of a system from the abstract description of its internal processes and its different states. Thus, on the basis of a qualitative reasoning, they allow making deliberations without the necessity of certain numerical data [4, 9, 10].

Otherwise, ontologies are used in the process of modeling and simulation, in a framework called "Ontology Driven Simulation (ODS)". It is a process that uses the knowledge encoded in ontologies to dynamically and automatically design simulation models. It's about having, on the one hand, the ontologies of the domain or the application and on the other hand, the ontologies of modeling (encoding information on the modeling such as components of the models, the different phases and modeling activities, etc.). Then, domain ontology concepts are mapped to the concepts of modeling ontologies, then instances of modeling ontologies are created to represent a model. Once ontology instances representing the model are created, additional tools are used to translate them into an executable simulation model [11, 12].

Other works go further in the use of ontologies in modeling and simulation. This is the case of works that use ontologies to drive the integration of models and interoperable simulation applications. In the process of application integration, there are two main difficulties that have been until now technical limitations for the modeling community: semantic accessibility, caused by the inability to explicitly specify the semantics of information contained in different applications; and logical disconnection, caused by the inability to explicitly represent constraints related to the information contained in different applications [12, 13]. In these latest articles, the authors show how to use ontologies to overcome these technical limitations and facilitate the integration of interoperable applications.

In [14], authors use ontologies to assemble semi-automatically, simulation models of an industrial installation composed of a set of hardware devices. Indeed, in this industrial system, each device (composed of a set of devices) is simulated by selecting one or more models. To automate this task, the authors propose an ontology of the industrial plant and its various hardware devices, an ontology of the library of simulation models used to simulate the devices of the industry, a mapping ontology between devices and simulation models and a semantic engine that, from a given hardware device, selects and assembles (if necessary) the models necessary for its simulation.

4 Taxonomy of Simulation Models of Infectious Diseases

In the study of infectious disease simulation models, we identified different types of model categories. This typing is due to the fact that one can consider different points of view, considering them as "keys of determination", to categorize the simulation models of diseases. A useful way of constructing taxonomy of models is to establish subsumption relations between the elements of these different viewpoints.

> **First point of view** – the models are categorized according to the three dimensions (scales) considered in the spread of infectious diseases (organic scale-lower scale, individual scale and population scale-higher scale). It is the **dimensional categorization** of simulation models of infectious diseases.
> **Second point of view** – the models are categorized according to their objective functions (modeling objectives). It is the **functional categorization** of simulation models of infectious diseases.
> **Third point of view** – the models are categorized according to the modeling techniques and formalisms used. It is the **technical categorization** of simulation models of infectious diseases.

Thus, any simulation model of an infectious disease must be identified according to these different types of categories. We give below the details of each categorization.

4.1 Dimensional Categorization

A description of infectious disease models is given by considering three dimensions (scales):

- Population scale: in this dimension, models focus on the spread of diseases, on the populations of actors included (populations of final hosts, intermediate hosts, populations of pathogens, vector populations, etc.) and on the factors involved. We found here models of transmission dynamics or epidemiological models. They are two categories: epidemiological models of transmission and geographical models.

Epidemiological Models of Transmission (**EMT**) relate to variations in infection rates in human hosts and vectors. There are several types of epidemiological models of transmission: **SI, SIR, SIER**, etc. Geographic Models (**GEM**) are epidemiological models that incorporate environmental factors and describe the spatial distribution of diseases or vectors [15].

- Scale of individuals: in this dimension, models focus on individuals in a particular population and consider their actions and interactions with, sometimes, components of other populations or other influential factors. We found here models of population dynamics (population of pathogens - **MPP**, vector population - **MVP**) which mainly deal with genetic aspects of pathogen dynamics with sometime, human and vector host components and/or an epidemiological component (i.e. the level of transmission) [16]. One found here also models of host-to-host contamination or pathogen transmission (**MC**) [3, 4].
- Organic scale: in this dimension, models look at pathophysiological processes. One found here Intra-host models (**MIH**) that generally describe the dynamics of parasite larval stages and its interactions with body organs and the immune system [17]. They also study their interactions with drugs and the effects of medicinal treatments in pest biology [18].

4.2   Functional Categorization

A categorization of models is given considering the problems posed or the modeling objectives (their objective functions). Generally, simulation models of infectious disease can be classified into two broad categories: predictive models, also called behavioral models and understanding models, also called models of knowledge [16].

Predictive models (Prediction function) are models of "black box" types, built on the basis of quantitative and/or qualitative data only, expressed as input and output parameters. There are several types of predictive models depending on the possible objectives: simulation models (**Simulate**: simulate the spread of a disease in a given population, simulate the behavior of a pathogen, etc.), prediction models (**Predict**: predict the spread of an epidemic after the occurrence of an event, etc.), evaluation models (**Assess**: evaluate or estimate the impact of a control strategy, assess the role of the geographic dimension in the distribution of a disease, etc.).

Knowledge models (**Comprehension** function) are constructed on the basis of assumptions that are often sought to confirm or refute, or that are used to understand certain aspects of diseases.

4.3   Technical Categorization

A categorization of models is given here by considering the techniques and formalisms used to model the dynamics of infectious diseases. Mainly, we can consider two broad categories of simulation models: numerical models (or quantitative models) and analytical models (or qualitative models).

Numerical models (**Quantitative**) are built on the basis of quantified numerical data. Among these types of models, there are mathematical models based on equations (**EBM**) and agent-based models (**ABM**).

Qualitative models (**Qualitative**) attempt to explain in a qualitative way, without certain numerical data, the phenomena. Among this type of models, there are ontology-based models (**OBM**), cellular automaton-based models (**CABM**), and so on.

5 An Ontology of Infectious Diseases Simulation Models

The ontology that we propose here will allow annotating simulation models of infectious diseases. It is based on the taxonomy proposed in the previous section (illustrated in Fig. 2) and includes other elements related to parameters (**Parameter**), hypothesis (**Hypothesis**), actors (**Actor**), objects (**Object**) and activities (**Activity**) taken into account in the model, as well as the implementation language (**Language**) and simulation platform (**Platform**) used. Other elements related to the identification of models are also added: model ID (**ID**), authors of the model (**Author**), its publication journal (**Journal**), the publication title of the article (**Title**) and a short description of the model (**Description**).

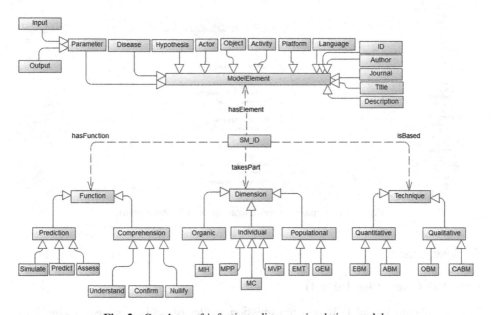

Fig. 2. Ontology of infectious diseases simulation models

This ontology allows describing, in a generic way, any simulation model of an infectious disease by specifying its scale (intra-host, epidemiological, etc.), its objective function (prediction, comprehension, etc.), formalism used (Equations, Agents, Ontology, etc.), elements included (parameters, assumptions, actors, objects of the environment, activities or dynamics implemented, etc.), implementation language and execution platform.

The Fig. 3 is a preliminary OWL formalization of the ontology through Protégé.

To use this ontology for a particular infectious disease (Schistosomiasis, for example), it is necessary to make the mapping between it (**SM-ID**) and the domain ontology of schistosomiasis (*IDOSCHISTO*) [10]. This mapping is ensured by a coupling between these two ontologies which results in the establishment of links between, for example, concepts as **Disease**, **Actor**, **Activity**, **Object**, **Dimension**, etc. in **SM-ID** and the corresponding elements in **IDOSCHISTO**. The resulting ontology (Ontology of Schistosomiasis Simulation Models - **OSM-Schisto**) will thus be able to annotate all Simulation Models of Schistosomiasis.

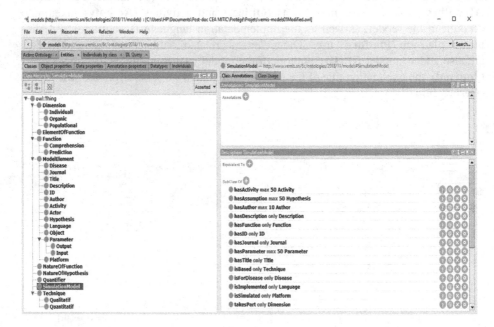

Fig. 3. The ontology formalization with Protégé editor

6   Use Cases

6.1   Use Case 1 (See Table 1)

This simulation model [19] is a transmission model of schistosomiasis taking into account heterogeneities. The authors calculate the basic reproductive rate R_0 in order to pronounce on the disease-free equilibrium which is globally asymptotically stable if $R_0 < 1$; and on the disease-endemic equilibrium which is globally asymptotically stable if $R_0 > 1$.

Table 1. First simulation model annotated.

Concept	Instance
Function	Simulate
Dimension	Epidemiological model of transmission
Technique	Numerical: based-Equation
Language	ODE
Platform	Scilab
Actor	Human Population; population of mollusk
Object	Geographical sites: residential (village), water points (pond, river, pond)
Activity	Agriculture, travel
Input parameter	Human population, number of pools, number of dwellings (villages)
Output parameter	Basic reproduction rate

6.2 Use Case 2 (See Table 2)

This simulation model [20] is a transmission model that aims to assess the spatial impact on schistosomiasis control policies. Three control policies are considered: treatment of infected individuals, elimination of cercariae and elimination of mollusks. The authors calculate the evolution of infections by applying different spatial configurations with each of these three control policies with.

Table 2. Second simulation model annotated.

Concept	Instance
Function	Assess
Dimension	Epidemiological model of transmission
Technique	Numerical: Agent-based
Language	GAML
Platform	GAMA
Actor	Human population (man, woman, child); mollusc population; pathogen
Object	Geographical sites: residential (village), water points (pond, river, pond), roads, schools
Activity	Fun, housewives, and professionals activities; treatment of individuals, elimination of mollusks, elimination of cercariae
Input parameter	GIS of the studied area (dwellings, water points, roads, schools), human populations, mollusks and pathogens
Output parameter	Evolutions of the spread of the disease

7 Conclusion and Perspectives

In this paper, we have proposed a core ontological model for annotating quantitative and qualitative simulation models for infectious diseases. We highlighted the main concepts and there relations. Use cases are presented for illustrating how the onto-logical model could be used for annotating existing simulation model for schistoso-miasis disease.

Our future work will first focus on finalizing the formalization and the validation of the ontology. Second, we will implement the ontology-based library, a web platform, for hosting infectious diseases simulation models and their metadata. Then, we will set up a semantic engine that, based a user request, will autonomously orchestrate the simulation process. The orchestration of the simulations consists first of choosing the type of model (numerical or qualitative), then selecting the simulation models to compose and finally integrating the data and the applications necessary for the real-ization of a simulation.

Acknowledgements. This work is supported by the African Center of Excellence in Mathe-matics Computer Science and ICT (CEA-MITIC) through a postdoctoral contract within the VEMIS project (Infectious Disease Epidemiological Monitoring in Senegal).

References

1. Fianyo, Y.E.: Couplage de modèles à l'aide d'agents : le système OSIRIS. Paris 9 (2001)
2. Gaud, N.A.: Systèmes multi–agents holoniques : de l'analyse à l'implantation : méta-modèle, méthodologie, et simulation multi-niveaux. Besançon (2007)
3. Cissé, P.A.: Simulation à base d'agents de la propagation de la Schistosomiase : une approche de composition et de déploiement de modèles (2016). https://tel.archives-ouvertes.fr/tel-01538809/document
4. Camara, G.: Conception d'un système de veille épidémiologique à base d'ontologies : application à la schistosomiase au Sénégal (2013)
5. Cisse, P.A., Dembele, J.M., Lo, M., Cambier, C.: Multi-agent Systems for Epidemiology: example of an agent-based simulation platform for schistosomiasis. In: Bajo, J., et al. (eds.) Highlights of Practical Applications of Cyber-Physical Multi-Agent Systems, pp. 157–168. Springer, Heidelberg (2017). https://doi.org/10.1007/978-3-319-60285-1_13
6. Durak, U., Ören, T.: Towards an ontology for simulation systems engineering. In: Proceedings of the 49th Annual Simulation Symposium, pp. 13:1–13:8. Society for Computer Simulation International, San Diego, CA, USA (2016)
7. Fishwick, P.A., Miller, J.A.: Ontologies for modeling and simulation: issues and approaches. In: Proceedings of the 2004 Winter Simulation Conference 2004, p. 264 (2004)
8. Miller, J.A., Baramidze, G.T., Sheth, A.P., Fishwick, P.A.: Investigating ontologies for simulation modeling. In: Proceedings of the 37th Annual Simulation Symposium 2004, pp. 55–63 (2004)
9. Camara, G., Després, S., Lo, M., Djedidi, R.: Construction d'une ontologie de domaine et d'une ontologie des processus de la propagation des maladies infectieuses. Revue d'Intelligence Artificielle. **28**, 167–190 (2014)

10. Camara, G., Despres, S., Lo, M.: IDOSCHISTO : une extension de l'ontologie noyau des maladies infectieuses (IDO-Core) pour la schistosomiase. In: Faron-Zucker, C. (ed.) Actes des 25èmes Journées francophones d'Ingénierie des Connaissances (IC2014), pp. 39–50. Clermont-Ferrand, France (2014)

11. Silver, G.A., Hassan, O.A.-H., Miller, J.A.: From domain ontologies to modeling ontologies to executable simulation models. In: Proceedings of the 39th Conference on Winter Simulation: 40 Years! The Best is Yet to Come, pp. 1108–1117. IEEE Press, Piscataway, NJ, USA (2007)

12. Benjamin, P., Patki, M., Mayer, R.: Using ontologies for simulation modeling. In: Proceedings of the 38th Conference on Winter Simulation, pp. 1151–1159. Winter Simulation Conference (2006)

13. Benjamin, P., Akella, K.: Towards ontology-driven interoperability for simulation-based applications. In: Winter Simulation Conference, pp. 1375–1386. Winter Simulation Conference (2009)

14. Novák, P., Šindelář, R.: Applications of ontologies for assembling simulation models of industrial systems. In: Meersman, R., Dillon, T., Herrero, P. (eds.) OTM 2011. LNCS, vol. 7046, pp. 148–157. Springer, Heidelberg (2011). https://doi.org/10.1007/978-3-642-25126-9_24

15. Tran, A., Biteau-Coroller, F., Guis, H., Roger, F.: Modélisation des maladies vectorielles. Épidémiologie et santé animale. **47**, 35–51 (2005)

16. Rogier, C., Sallet, G.: Modélisation du paludisme. Med. Trop. **64**, 89–97 (2004)

17. Anderson, R.M., May, R.M.: Regulation and stability of host-parasite population interactions: I regulatory processes. J. Anim. Ecol. **47**, 219–247 (1978)

18. Xu, D., Curtis, J., Feng, Z., Minchella, D.J.: On the role of schistosome mating structure in the maintenance of drug-resistant strains. Bull. Math. Biol. **68**, 209–229 (2006)

19. Gilles, R., Gauthier, S., Lena, T.: A transmission model of Bilharzia: a mathematical analysis of an heterogeneous model. Revue Africaine de la Recherche en Informatique et Mathématiques Appliquées. **14**, 1–13 (2010)

20. Cisse, P.A., Dembele, J.M., Lo, M., Cambier, C.: Assessing the spatial impact on an agent-based modeling of epidemic control: case of schistosomiasis. In: Glass, K., Colbaugh, R., Ormerod, P., Tsao, J. (eds.) Complex 2012. LNICST, vol. 126, pp. 58–69. Springer, Cham (2013). https://doi.org/10.1007/978-3-319-03473-7_6

S-SDS: A Framework for Security Deployment as Service in Software Defined Networks

Adama Coly[✉] and Maïssa Mbaye

Laboratoire D'Analyse Numérique et Informatique, Gaston Berger University,
Saint-Louis, Senegal
{coly.adama,maissa.mbaye}@ugb.edu.sn

Abstract. Software Defined Networking (SDN) is an emerging networking paradigm that addresses current network design limitations. It promotes centralized control of the network by clearly separating *Control Plane* and *Data Plane*. In one hand, Security in SDN is one of the most challenging research topics. In the other hand, deployment of security as service is one of the most cutting-edge topic. In this paper, we propose a general framework for security deployment as a service in SDN networks. As a case study we proposed extension of OpenFlow protocol for IPsec VPN set. We have evaluated this proposal using a real world testbed based on Mininet and Floodlight. Preliminary results show that our proposal can enable security service without drastically degrading performance in comparison to deploy security on endpoints of communications.

Keywords: SDS · SDN · Control plane · Data plane · IPsec ·
OpenFlow · Security service deployment · Network Security ·
Floodlight · Mininet

1 Introduction

Traditional networking appears to be reaching its limits during the late of 2010s decade. Firstly, classical network design views networks as composed of specialized devices (router, switch, firewall, etc.) which have proprietary firmwares that include hard coded functions and forwarding logic. This is a big limitation to network evolution since it is almost impossible to implement a new non-standard functionality (e.g. new routing protocol or firewall extension ...) without the agreement of the device manufacturers. Deployment of new innovative network features depends on the speed with which network equipment vendors implement them in their firmwares. To overcome this limitation, network devices should be programmable. Secondly, current network devices make forwarding decision according to their local configuration set by administrator. If the device is replaced, the same tedious configuration may be done again. To overcome this

G. Bassioni et al. (Eds.): InterSol 2019, LNICST 296, pp. 92–103, 2019.
https://doi.org/10.1007/978-3-030-34863-2_9

limitation, the operating logic of network device should be separated from the forwarding function.

Software Defined Networking is an emerging networking paradigm that addresses, among others, these limitations to overcome network evolution. SDN, clearly separates *Control Plane* and *Data Plane*. *Control Plane* manages how and where to forward packets, and can be hosted by a physical server or in the cloud. *Data Plane* that manages packet forwarding based on flow tables (routing table + access control list), is implanted inside network switches [2].

This separation of Control Plane from Data Plane and centralisation in an equipement called Controller, bring new threats like Single Point of Failure and make difficult the deployment of security services on equipements. However, providing security services in SDN is one of the most challenging topics in this area [1]. It covers two aspects: security for SDN infrastructure itself and deployment of security services for the end-users using a SDN core network. Securing SDN infrastructure is a fairly well-known problem now and is addressed by several works [2–7]. However, deployment of security services provided by SDN for customers is less addressed by research community. Among problems of communications' security of end-users, SDN do not yet support efficiently security services such as confidentiality, on-demand secured tunnel establishment, etc.

In this paper, we propose a framework that enables security services (e.g. IPsec Tunnels) deployment in SDN network. Main outcomes of our work are: proposition of an architecture for security service deployment in SDN, a new extension of the OpenFlow protocol for secured tunnels management, and, finally integration of an IPsec-based tunnel mechanism in SDN as use case.

The remainder of this paper is organized as follows. The second section is focused on related works while third section presents background concepts of our proposal namely SDN architecture and IPsec Protocol. On fourth part we present our approach of security services deployment architecture and present the case of an OpenFlow's IPsec extension. The fifth part is dedicated to performance evaluation. Finally, we finish by conclusion and future works.

2   Related Works

Security in SDN covers two different aspects: security for SDN infrastructure itself and deployment of security as service in SDN.

Most of prior research efforts address SDN security threats identification and SDN security solutions [1]. As proof, there are many surveys about this topic [2–7]. SDN Security threats can be different kinds such as:

- Man-in-the middle attack because of optional use of TLS [2,3];
- DDoS attacks because of single point of failure in centralized environment around the controller [2–6];
- Lack of authentication and authorization due to no compelling authentication and authorization mechanisms for applications and more threatening in case of large number of third-party applications [2].

Solutions for these threats have been proposed such as DDoS Detection (for DDoS attacks), SE-Floodlight for lack of authentication & authorization. In the case of Man-in-the- middle attack when malicious node is between the controller and the switch, TLS can be an efficient solution. When it is between different switches, solutions based on tunnels have been proposed [3].

We also have in literature design-oriented security service based on SDN/NFV for end-users. In [8], authors use firewalling for an SDN infrastructure to secure network device from suspicious and malicious traffic. In [9] authors proposed a new architecture of security service based on network virtualization functions. Their proposition offers a security service function chain that enables ICT (Information and Communication Technology) service providers to provision a dynamic and flexible secure service on the SDN network for customers. Authors in [10] propose a solution which introduces of a third plane, the security plane, in addition to the data plane and control plane. They present an SDN security design approach, which strikes a good balance between network performance and security features. This proposed approach can prevent DDoS attacks targeting either the controller or the different hosts in the network, and how to trace back the source of the attack. Proposal in [11] use SDN based IPsec authentication to secure client application. Solution in [12] consists of an architecture that combines IDS with programmable features of SDN for detection and mitigation of malicious traffic. In [3] they used IPsec as a security application to secure a communication between two endpoints against Man-in-the-Middle attacks.

We can see that researches about security services for end-users, use externals components to acheive their goal. As far as we know, there is no proposition using only the SDN infrastructure. With our approach a security service can be deployed to secure communication of two end-users using SDN core Network. The security service is provided using an extension of the OpenFlow protocol or any other Southbound API. We will present a use of IPsec as case study for OpenFlow extension. This evaluation will permit us to determine which is beneficial between deploying IPsec, using SDN approach, between End-Points and between BGS. This will lead to see if it's relevant to apply our approach.

3   Background Concepts

3.1   Software Defined Networking Architecture

Commonly adopted SDN architecture is presented in Fig. 1. Which is composed of 3 layers: Application Layer where network applications are deployed (e.g. Routing protocols; Firewall ...); Control Layer that manages the network forwarding logic and is implemented by a node called SDN Controller; finally, Infrastructure Layer where we have physical equipment and forwarding.

Communication between two layers in SDN architecture is done by using an API: NorthBound API between Application Layer and Control Layer; South-Bound API between Control Layer and Infrastructure Layer. An example of SouthBound API and the most famous is OpenFlow [13].

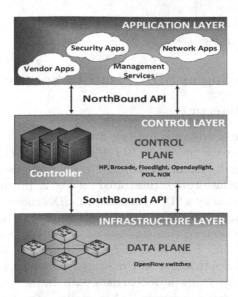

Fig. 1. Architecture SDN

SDN Security is a real challenge. Indeed, SDN should have internal security and provide security as a service for customer networks. Our main goal is to provide dynamic and extensible security service deployment architecture. With our approach a security service can be deployed to secure end-to-end communication through SDN Network in a transparent manner. We give as example the deployment of IPsec Tunnel as SDN network service. In next section will introduce the IPsec protocol.

3.2 IPsec

IPsec (Internet Protocol Security) [14] is a suite of protocols that provides security at Internet Layer of TCP/IP model. It can be used to provide a Virtual Private Network (VPN) or establish secured tunnels between two locations. The deployment of IPSec can be done between two End-Points, between two Gateways to serve different networks and between an End-Point and a Gateway. This protocol uses Internet Key Exchange (IKE) protocol for keys negotiation and management.

IPsec has two sub-protocols: The Encapsulation Security Payload (ESP) [15] and the Authentication Header (AH) [16]. A "Security Association" (SA) is a one-way (inbound or outbound) agreement between two communicating peers that specifies the IPsec protections to be provided to their communications. This includes the specific security protections, cryptographic algorithms, and secret keys to be applied, as well as specific types of traffic to be protected [17]. IPsec also uses two databases: Security Association Database (SAD) and Security Policy Database (SPD). SAD is a database for SA repository of different peers while SPD is a database that expresses the security protections to be provided to different types of traffic [17].

4 IPsec Tunneling as SDN Security Service

4.1 General Architecture

Our proposal aims to provide secure IPsec Tunnel between two legacy networks using bump in the wire configuration (BITW). With this architecture, endpoints of communication can communicate securely by delegating security to SDN network. The general architecture is illustrated on Fig. 2. In this architecture non SDN networks are linked by a SDN core network. SDN core network is composed of Border Gateway Switches (BGS) and Core Internal Switches (CIS). BGS are ingress and egress of secured communications. They can establish on demand tunnels with instructions from controller. SDN controller communicates with BGS using extended Southbound API messages to deploy the service in Data Plane. Service is deployed only in BGS in data path. In the two cases, all switches are ready to activate security service if they receive corresponding instructions from Controller via Southbound API. An extension of OpenFlow southbound API is used for these instructions.

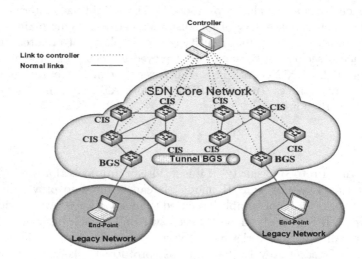

Fig. 2. Architecture of SDN based IPsec

When a client subscribes to an SLA (Service Level Agreement) including a security service, controller is configured according to this contract. If a flow matches to corresponding client traffic, controller deploys the service by sending a "SecTrans" message with security policies to the Border Gateways Switches involved in this communication. The remaining transaction is managed by South-Bound Extension. As a use case that illustrates how our proposal operates, we deploy secure tunneling service based IPsec as SDN Security Service. To achieve this, we extended OpenFlow protocol for IPsec tunnel establishment and we define an extended structure for Flow Tables inside Switches.

4.2 Secure Communication Service Deployment

Our first proposal is an extension of OpenFlow standard protocol, by adding "SecTrans" message. It is a controller-to-switch message which is used to allow the IPsec tunnel to be used between involved switches.

Our second proposal is to add a new column on the Flow Table named"IPsec" which can be set to "Yes" to allow the use of IPsec between two BGS or "No" if we don't. The new structure of our new Flow Table is represented by the Fig. 3. With these proposals, the controller is responsible for generating and transmitting IKE credentials. It is also responsible for the control and application of IPsec SPDs. It therefore has a centralized view of the network and security policies. The IKE implemented in the network resource runs to create the IPsec

Fig. 3. New structure of our new Flow Table

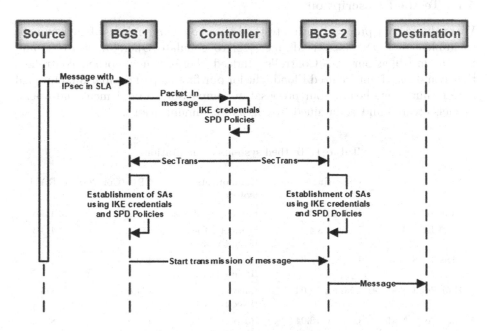

Fig. 4. Flow chart of IPsec service deployment

security associations by using these policies and credentials. Figure 4 illustrates a typical communication in SDN including deployment of IPsec tunnel.

If a source end-point sends a traffic to another client using IPsec tunnel, the following procedure will take place:

1. The Border Gateway Switch connected to the source will send a"Packet_In" message (an OpenFlow message) to the controller to ask what to do with these packets.
2. If there is matching with a service subscriber's traffic, the controller will generate IKE credentials and SPD Policies and sends them to the two switches (ingress and egress) involved BGS in addition to the SecTrans message to allow transmission in IPsec tunnel. The message will add/modify a flow with "yes" on IPsec field.
3. The border routers use the IKE credentials and SPD Policies to establish SAs before starting transmission.

When this procedure is executed, all the messages between these two endpoints are transmitted using the tunnel. In fact security is bumped in the wire in this architecture. Main benefit of this is security is deployed on BGS and used on demand by endpoint clients.

5   Implementation and Performance Evaluation

5.1   Testbed Description

We evaluated our proposal with a testbed based on commonly used environment to implement SDN, namely Mininet [18] to simulate Openflow switches and Floodlight [19] as our SDN Controller. Indeed, there are many others controllers that can be used but we used Floodlight for our first step of evaluation. Our goal is to evaluate overhead of our proposal in comparison to implement end-to-end tunnels created and maintained by edges of communications.

Table 1. Testbed systems configurations.

Hosts	Operating system	Components (software)	CPU (Core/GHz)	RAM
Controller	Debian 8.4	Floodlight master	4/3.2	4 GB
SDN BGS A	Debian 8.4	Mininet , Racoon, IPsec-tools	4/3.2	4 GB
SDN BGS B	Ubuntu 18.04	Mininet , Racoon, IPsec-tools	4/2.4	4 GB
End-Point Node A	Ubuntu 18.04	Racoon, IPsec-tools	8/4.0	8 GB
End-Point Node B	Ubuntu 18.04	Racoon, IPsec-tools	4/3.2	8 GB

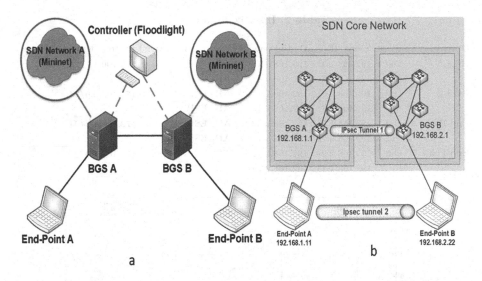

Fig. 5. a. Physical topology of testbed. **b.** Logical topology of testbed

We build a topology with five physical computers/server interconnected as illustrated in Fig. 5a and with configurations as in Table 1.

We use Mininet to run an SDN core networks by combining two networks located on different servers. We also use Floodlight as the SDN controller. Table 1 summarizes node system configurations.

On each BGS of each network is connected two End-Points illustrated as computer laptop in Fig. 5b.

For this testbed, we have two scenarios : One with an IPsec tunnel between End-Points ; and a second one with an IPsec tunnel between Border Gateway Switches (BGS). The first scenario corresponds to a normal situation in which SDN network does not play any role in IPsec Tunnel management. The second scenario corresponds to our proposal with establishment of tunnels between BGS. Comparison of these two will enable us to evaluate the overhead of our proposal.

SAs keys are managed by the Racoon daemon [20] on the different entities (see Table 1). Table 2 is a summary of IPsec SA configuration in both scenarios.

5.2 Performance Results and Analysis

We want to evaluate the impact of our proposal in the Quality of Service of the Network. We use standard QoS parameters for each scenario: Data transmission delay; Throughput; Jitters; CPU load for cryptography overhead.

Using iperf tool [21], we evaluate delay for three cases : the case of an SDN Network Without IPsec; the case of an SDN Network with an IPsec Tunnel between End-Points and finally in the case of an SDN Network with an IPsec Tunnel between Border Gateway Switches (BGS). For this evaluation, iperf will send packets in high speed then we can evaluate difference between differents cases.

Table 2. IPsec configuration.

Gateways	Flow	Source IP	Destination IP	SAs encapsulation	Secured network address
BGS A	Out	192.168.1.1	192.168.2.1	AH, ESP	172.100.1.0/24
	In	192.168.2.1	192.168.1.1	AH, ESP	
BGS B	Out	192.168.2.1	192.168.1.1	AH, ESP	172.100.2.0/24
	In	192.168.1.1	192.168.2.1	AH, ESP	
End-Point A	Out	192.168.1.11	192.168.2.22	AH, ESP	172.100.1.0/24
	In	192.168.2.22	192.168.1.11	AH, ESP	
End-Point B	Out	192.168.2.22	192.168.1.11	AH, ESP	172.100.2.0/24
	In	192.168.1.11	192.168.2.22	AH, ESP	

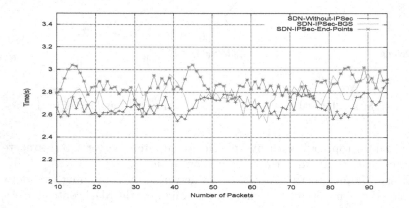

Fig. 6. Performance of SDN security service in term of Delay

Figure 6 illustrates the data transmission delay for 100 packets in related cases. We can notive that the delay is more important when the IPsec tunnel is implemented between End-Points than between Border Gateway Switches. This result can be an argument that have a security bumped in the wire as we proposed does not affect as much performance of the network in term of delay.

Figures 7, 8 and 9 represent respectively the variation of the average throughput, the jitter and CPU Load during the transmission of data in the cases as tests in Fig. 6.

We can see that the throughput when IPsec is located between BGS is more important than between End-Points. We can relate this result to the previous.

Figure 9 shows CPU variation during data transmission through the IPsec tunnel, for the Border Gateway Switch of the mininet network A (when the tunnel is implemented at the BGS) and for the End-Point A (when the tunnel is implemented at the End-Points).

We can see that the data transfer over the IPsec tunnel doesn't really affect the CPU Load of End-Point A. However, in the BGS, there is a variation of at most 4% of CPU LOAD. This is because the BGS does not have a pretty powerful CPU.

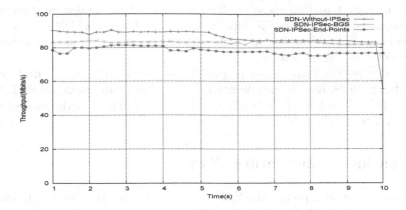

Fig. 7. Performance of SDN security service in term of Throughput

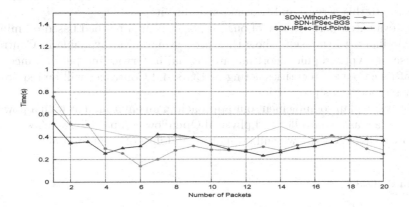

Fig. 8. Performance of SDN security service in term of jitters

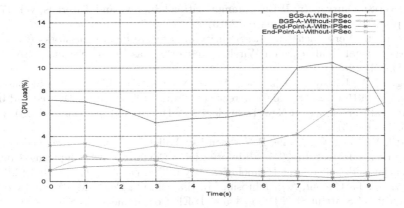

Fig. 9. Performance of SDN security service in term of CPU Load

In summary based on these results we can say that implementation of an IPsec tunnel at the BGS for the data transmission through a SDN core network does not significatively affect network performance as much in comparison to implement it at the end-Points.

Nevertheless the limits of our proposition is that we only have 2 End-Points connected to BGS. Results may be different if we have more than one End-Point on each BGS. In addition, BGS requires power of calculus in the case of they provide confidentiality.

6   Conclusion and Future Works

In this paper we have proposed a SDN architecture that enables deployment of IPsec tunnelling as SDN service. To achieve this we proposed an extension of Openflow protocol by adding a message and a security field on the flow table. Our solution moves complexity of IPsec to the controller. Customers can then subscribe to this service and transparently use it.

We evaluated performance of our proposal using a testbed based on mininet and floodlight. First results show that processing power available in Controller and use of cryptographic algorithm are crucial in forwarding performance. The uses of much powerful entities acting as BGS and Controller will be required to better supports this proposition.

Fistly, we plan to implement our approach in an environment with a powerful server, to act as a controller and physical Openflow compatible switches to build our core SDN. Secondly we will evaluate scalability of our proposal.

References

1. Bakhshi, T.: State of the art and recent research advances in software defined networking. Wirel. Commun. Mob. Comput. **2017**, 35 (2017). Article ID 7191647
2. Ahmad, I., Namal, S., Ylianttila, M., Gurtov, A.: Security in software defined networks: a survey. In: IEEE Communications Surveys and Tutorials, vol. 17, no. 4, pp. 2317–2346 (Fourthquarter 2015)
3. Ertaul, L., Venkatachalam, K.: Security of software defined networks (SDN). In: International Conference on Wireless Networks, Las Vegas, Nevada, USA, 17–20 July 2017 (2017)
4. Feghali, A., Kilany, R., Chamoun, M.: SDN security problems and solutions analysis. In: 2015 International Conference on Protocol Engineering (ICPE) and International Conference on New Technologies of Distributed Systems (NTDS), Paris, pp. 1–5 (2015)
5. Patil, V., Patil, C., Awale, R.N.: Security challenges in software defined network and their solutions. In: 2017 8th International Conference on Computing, Communication and Networking Technologies (ICCCNT), Delhi, India, pp. 1–5 (2017)
6. Dargahi, T., Caponi, A., Ambrosin, M., Bianchi, G., Conti, M.: A Survey on the Security of Stateful SDN Data Planes. IEEE Communications Surveys and Tutorials **19**(3), 1701–1725 (2017)

7. Shin, S., Xu, L., Hong, S., Gu, G.: Enhancing network security through software dened networking (SDN). In: 2016 25th International Conference on Computer Communication and Networks (ICCCN), Waikoloa, HI, pp. 1–9 (2016)
8. Satasiya, D., Raviya, R., Kumar, H.: Enhanced SDN security using firewall in a distributed scenario. In: 2016 International Conference on Advanced Communication Control and Computing Technologies (ICACCCT), Ramanathapuram, pp. 588–592 (2016)
9. Chou, L.D., Tseng, C.W., Huang, Y.K., Chen, K.C., Ou, T.F., Yen, C.K.: A security service on-demand architecture in SDN. In: 2016 International Conference on Information and Communication Technology Convergence (ICTC), Jeju, pp. 287–291 (2016)
10. Hussein, A., Elhajj, I.H., Chehab, A., Kayssi, A.: SDN security plane an architecture for resilient security services. In: 2016 IEEE International Conference on Cloud Engineering Workshop (IC2EW), Berlin, pp. 54–59 (2016)
11. Li, Y., Mao, J.: SDN-based access authentication and automatic configuration for IPsec. In: 2015 4th International Conference on Computer Science and Network Technology (ICCSNT), Harbin, pp. 996–999 (2015)
12. Monshizadeh, M., Khatri, V., Kantola, R.: Detection as a service: an SDN application. In: 2017 19th International Conference on Advanced Communication Technology (ICACT), Bongpyeong, pp. 285–290 (2017)
13. Software-Defined Networking (SDN) Definition. https://www.opennetworking.org/sdn-definition. Accessed 13 Jan 2018
14. Seo, K., Seo, K.: Security architecture for the internet protocol. RFC 4301 (Standard), Obsoletes 2401, December 2005
15. Seo, K.: IP Encapsulating Security Payload (ESP). RFC 4303 (Standard), Obsoletes 2406, December 2005
16. Seo, K.: IP Authentication Header. RFC 4302 (Standard), Obsoletes 2402, December 2005
17. Frankel, S., Krishnan, S.: IP Security (IPsec) and Internet Key Exchange (IKE) Document Roadmap. RFC 6071 (Informational), Obsoletes 2411, February 2011
18. Official website of Mininet. http://mininet.org. Accessed 11 Dec 2017
19. Official website of Floodlight. http://www.projectfloodlight.org/floodlight/. Accessed 2 Dec 2017
20. Official website of Racoon. https://packages.debian.org/fr/sid/racoon. Accessed 14 Mar 2019
21. Official website of Iperf. https://iperf.fr/. Accessed 13 Jan 2018

Enrichment of Medical Ontologies from Textual Clinical Reports: Towards Improving Linking Human Diseases and Signs

Adama Sow, Abdoulaye Guissé[(✉)], and Oumar Niang

Information Processing and Intelligent Systems Lab (LTISI),
Computer Science and Telecommunications Engineering Department,
Polytechnic School of Thiès, Thies, Senegal
{asow,aguisse,oniang}@ept.sn

Abstract. Healing a sick patient requires a medical diagnosis before proposing appropriate treatment. With the explosion of medical knowledges, we are interested in their exploitation to help clinician in collecting informations during diagnostic process. This article focuses on the development of a data model targeting knowledges available in both formal and non-formal resources. Our goal is to merge the strengths of all these resources to provide access to a variety of shared knowledges facilitating the identification and association of human diseases and to all of their available relevant characteristic signs such as symptoms and clinical signs.

On one side, we propose an ontology produced from a merging of several existing and open medical ontologies and terminologies. On another side, we exploit real cases of patients whose diagnosis has already been confirmed by clinicians. They are transcribed in textual reports in natural language, and we show that their analysis improves the list of signs of each disease. This work results in a knowledges base loaded from the known target ontologies on the bioportal platform such as DOID, MESH and SNOMED for diseases and, SYMP and CSSO ontologies for all existing signs.

Keywords: Medical diagnosis · Medical ontologies · Ontologies integration · Knowledge engineering · E-health system

1 Introduction

Medical diagnosis, as described in the [2] book, is a patient-centered cognitive activity whose quintessential competence belongs to the clinician. It's a process that consists of a continuous collection of the medical informations that the clinician makes before integrating and interpreting it for the management of his patient's health problems. The diagnosis usually includes four iterative steps: (i)

© ICST Institute for Computer Sciences, Social Informatics and Telecommunications Engineering 2019
Published by Springer Nature Switzerland AG 2019. All Rights Reserved
G. Bassioni et al. (Eds.): InterSol 2019, LNICST 296, pp. 104–115, 2019.
https://doi.org/10.1007/978-3-030-34863-2_10

the acquisition of contextual informations that takes into account antecedents, first physical examinations, and advanced examinations or clinical analysis, (ii) the formulation of hypothesis of potential diagnosis into a list of one or more diseases, (iii) the consistency collected informations with each hypothesis, (iv) and finally the evaluation of each hypothesis to identify and confirm the most certain diagnosis, otherwise the entire process must be taken up by expanding the collection.

This first collection step is as important as it's complex for the clinician, especially when it necessitates quickly recourse to masses of medical knowledge that are constantly exploding on an international scale. It's into the perspective of assisting clinicians in the exploitation of this knowledge, that our research is located. Our goal is more generally to develop a search engine (Fig. 1) that guides access to relevant medical informations at each of diagnostic process step. This engine would make it possible to navigate a knowledge base consisting of a medical ontology and a cases database of clinical diagnosis that have already been validated by clinicians.

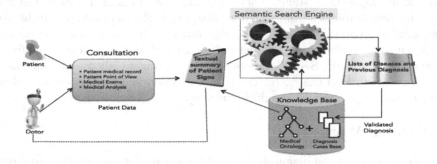

Fig. 1. Description of the medical diagnostic helping process

This article focuses on modeling this knowledge base (KB). It's about producting a data model targeting knowledge available in both formal and non-formal resources. The goal is to merge the strengths of all these resources to provide access to a variety of shared knowledge facilitating identification and association of human diseases to of their available relevant characteristic signs such as symptoms and symptoms and clinical signs.

The core of this KB is an ontology produced from a federation of several existing and open medical ontologies and terminologies. The obtained ontology covers a multitude of descriptive informations of human diseases but also describes the typology and the semantic of signs collected from a patient. Indeed, in existing ontologies we find on the one hand ontologies of diseases associated for each to a list of symptoms whose exhaustiveness is to be clarified, and on the other hand ontologies which conceptualize all the signs that can be appeared in a patient but without no link with diseases. These last ontologies include clinical signs whose values are obtained from in-depth examinations. Ontologies of diseases aiming at a generic conception do not take into account clinical signs which are nevertheless known into sign ontologies.

We propose to enrich our ontology associating each disease with their clinical signs. This is made possible by exploiting clinical reports for real cases of patients. These reports are usually transcribed into textual format in natural language by clinician. This one systematically archive all data of any patient in his medical folder (MF). Although the MFs are confidential, we have been able to obtain, in collaboration with local hospitals, anonymous descriptive case reports. The analysis of their content makes it possible to identify all the symptoms observed on a patient, as well as the clinical signs that made it possible to confirm an accurate diagnosis. However, these last signs being specific to a given patient, they are associated with a disease by the case that carries them. Cases are stored in the knowledge base. Each disease of our ontology is described by all the signs observed and verified in all the patients carrying this same disease. The association of sickness and its signs is thus continuously nourished as there are new cases of diagnosis.

Thus, in the Sect. 2, we perform a state study on medical ontologies and their use in diagnostic systems. Then, in Sect. 3, we present a selection of reference medical ontologies from which we begin to build an ontology suitable for diagnosis. In the Sects. 4 and 5, we describe our modeling approach to build and enrich our ontology from these target ontologies but also from textual cliniacal reports. Finally, in the Sect. 6, before the conclusion, we show our implementation process to load the extracted data, corresponding to diseases and their characteristic signs, into our resulting ontology.

2   Related Works

In order to establish the diagnosis [2], it is important for the clinician to cross-check all informations on the patient's state of health. It's precisely of the patient's opinion about his condition to identify his pains, physical examinations made by the clinician during consultations, and in-depth examinations (clinics and paraclinical), allow the identification of the most complex and implicit signs.

In medical diagnostic support systems [7], this collection phase is a cognitive activity where the semantics of information is controlled through knowledge known in medical jargon. It's for this very purpose medical ontologies have been conceived [1,4]. These are common medical vocabularies based on shared concepts facilitate the interoperability of documents between stakeholders in the field and especially the development of knowledge. Medical ontologies represent an evolution of medical thesauri; they do not limit themselves to defining terminologies but it goes further by clearly modeling medical entities such as diseases, their characteristic signs, their known treatments, or the hospital processes of patient care.

We are interested here in the medical ontologies of human diseases. The list is long and each ontology has its own specificities. But overall most of the known diseases are covered and each refers to a concept grouping its various nominative terms and synonyms, its different definitions and textual axioms and its characteristic signs. These include, among others, clinical signs and symptoms, but also possibly the causative agent of the disease, the mode of transmission, and localization in human anatomy. Also, taxonomic (or hierarchical) links are defined from among disease concepts to classify them into disease categories. This is facilitated by the fact that these ontologies are implemented in formal languages, such as OWL (Ontology Web Language), based on the principle of conceptual graphs, object-oriented concept and description logic.

Medical diagnostic support aids are expert systems where medical ontologies can be used as a knowledge base [5,7,8]. They are exploited globally for decision support: either to facilitate the comprehension of the terms present in the documents and the medical reports, or to allow the reasoning and the search for information in particular, in the diagnostic process, when it comes to identifying diseases associated with a given symptom or the characteristic symptoms of a specific disease. They have also been used to alert clinicians about the effects of chemicals on the treatment of certain diseases.

Thus, since the diagnostic process is based on the reasoning around diseases and their characteristic signs, the current difficulty, with regard to existing disease ontologies, lies in the fact that these signs are listed in a non-exhaustive manner [5] and not very formal [6]. Only the most common symptoms are stated in these ontologies and their presence varies from one patient to another. Moreover, the clinical signs take values at a patient are not even taken into account. There are, however, ontologies specific to the conceptualization of the signs [1,5] but they are not associated with diseases.

We are not aiming here to build an ontology from non-formal resources [3] but our goal is to merge the strengths of several existing ontologies in order to have an ontology sufficiently provided in terms of diseases and to associate with each of them all of its relevant signs and appearing in most of the patients who have been affected by the same diseases. This association has already been the subject of research. Indeed, [6], propose in their ontology project Disy, to give to the clinicians latitude to cite for each disease all its signs. The work of [5] offers an integration of ontologies in order to group together for each disease all of its signs present in these target resources. For our part, our proposal is similar to that of the latter authors in that we are also looking for a federation of ontologies of human diseases and signs in order to constitute a news that is adapted for medical diagnosis. However, despite this desire for federation, current ontologies are still not large enough to describe in detail the diseases with all of their characteristic signs. To overcome this, we try to focus on the analysis of real cases of patients who have already been diagnosed and whose clinicians have transcribed the entire process in textual reports. This analysis then makes it possible to list new signs, hitherto not yet taken into account in existing medical ontologies.

3   Ontologies for Medical Diagnosis

Constitution of our ontology consists of a federation of a set of ontologies around a structure unifying all human diseases as well as their characteristic signs. The diseases correspond to the possible diagnosis. The signs are those can be identified on a patient in order to conclude on a specific diagnosis that can refer to one or more diseases. Diseases are organized in a hierarchical way. They and their derived forms are grouped into categories, which may themselves be subcategories of diseases. The diseases are lexicalized in order to have for each disease the set of the most known nominative terms and their synonyms. For each disease, it will be important to keep all definitions in order to have the most shared semantics. Most of the known signs of each disease are formally listed from those available in the target medical ontologies.

We analyze and exploite here medical ontologies made available to the public via the BioPortal platform. We chose DOID[1], MESH[2], SNOMED[3] as disease ontologies, as well as SYMP[4], and CSSO[5] as ontologies of signs.

DOID ontology (Disease Ontology) serves us as a reference ontology. It proposes a hierarchy of *10389* human diseases and disease categories. With the Fig. 2, we can see each disease has a unique identifier (*rdf:about*), and is classified in one or more categories (*rdfs:subClassOf*). The disease of *Hepatitis A* belongs to the category "*DOID_37*" of ("*skin diseases*") and to the category "*DOID_934*" of ("*viral infectious diseases*"). However, from one identifier to another, there is no description to say that a given identifier refers to a disease or a category of diseases. But, considering the hierarchical graph, all the leaf concepts correspond to the diseases and those who have threads constitute categories.

```
<owl:Class rdf:about="http://purl.obolibrary.org/obo/DOID_12549">
    <rdfs:label rdf:datatype="http://www.w3.org/2001/XMLSchema#string">hepatitis A</rdfs:label>
    <rdfs:subClassOf rdf:resource="http://purl.obolibrary.org/obo/DOID_37"/>
    <rdfs:subClassOf rdf:resource="http://purl.obolibrary.org/obo/DOID_934"/>
    <obo:IAO_0000115 rdf:datatype="http://www.w3.org/2001/XMLSchema#string">A viral infectious disease that
    results_in inflammation located_in liver, has_material_basis_in Hepatitis A virus,
    which is transmitted_by ingestion of contaminated food or water,
    or transmitted_by direct contact with an infected person.
    The infection has_symptom fever, has_symptom fatigue, has_symptom loss of appetite, has_symptom nausea,
    has_symptom vomiting, has_symptom abdominal pain, has_symptom clay-colored bowel movements,
    has_symptom joint pain, and has_symptom jaundice.</obo:IAO_0000115>
    <oboInOwl:hasAlternativeId rdf:datatype="http://www.w3.org/2001/XMLSchema#string">DOID:12547</oboInOwl:hasAlternativeId>
    <oboInOwl:id rdf:datatype="http://www.w3.org/2001/XMLSchema#string">DOID:12549</oboInOwl:id>
    <oboInOwl:hasDbXref rdf:datatype="http://www.w3.org/2001/XMLSchema#string">MESH:D006506</oboInOwl:hasDbXref>
    <oboInOwl:hasDbXref rdf:datatype="http://www.w3.org/2001/XMLSchema#string">NCI:C3096</oboInOwl:hasDbXref>
    <oboInOwl:hasDbXref rdf:datatype="http://www.w3.org/2001/XMLSchema#string">SNOMEDCT_US_2016_03_01:154347003</oboInOwl:hasDbXref>
    <oboInOwl:hasDbXref rdf:datatype="http://www.w3.org/2001/XMLSchema#string">SNOMEDCT_US_2016_03_01:40468003</oboInOwl:hasDbXref>
    <oboInOwl:hasDbXref rdf:datatype="http://www.w3.org/2001/XMLSchema#string">UMLS_CUI:C0019159</oboInOwl:hasDbXref>
    <oboInOwl:hasRelatedSynonym rdf:datatype="http://www.w3.org/2001/XMLSchema#string">Viral hepatitis A</oboInOwl:hasRelatedSynonym>
    <oboInOwl:hasExactSynonym rdf:datatype="http://www.w3.org/2001/XMLSchema#string">Viral hepatitis, type A (disorder)</oboInOwl:hasExactSynonym>
    <oboInOwl:hasOBONamespace rdf:datatype="http://www.w3.org/2001/XMLSchema#string">disease_ontology</oboInOwl:hasOBONamespace>
</owl:Class>
```

Fig. 2. *Hepatitis A* disease description in DOID

Each disease in DOID refers (*oboInOwl:hasDbXref*) to the same disease in other ontological bases such as that of the Medical Subject Headings (MESH) terminological resource. It's one of the reference thesauri in the biomedical field.

---

[1] http://purl.bioontology.org/ontology/DOID.
[2] https://www.nlm.nih.gov/mesh/.
[3] http://purl.bioontology.org/ontology/SNOMEDCT.
[4] http://purl.bioontology.org/ontology/SYMP.
[5] http://purl.bioontology.org/ontology/CSSO.

It's known for the multitudes of synonymous terms proposed as denominations of a disease. Each of the diseases has a preferential term (*prefLabel:hepatitis A*) which is the most used denomination, but also of several synonymous terms (*altLabel:Viral hepatitis A, Viral hepatitis type A, Hepatitis Infectious, Hepatitides Infectious, Infectious Hepatitis, Infectious Hepatitides*). These terms correspond to different hepatitis A nominations around the world. Definitions disease available in MESH will be conserved in our ontology result. Otherwise, the DOID proposes also one tag as definition (*obo:IAO_*) in a semi-formalized language goes a little further in the description of the disease. It's easy to decompose this description from groups of verbal words such as *results_in, located_in, caused_by (or has_material_basis_in), transmitted_by* or *has_symptom* which refer to the characteristic signs of a disease, corresponding respectively to the manifestation of the disease, to its location in the human anatomy, to the agent at the origin of the disease, to its modes of transmission, and to his symptoms. This list of features is very variant from one disease to another in the DOID, it's always informed.

To overcome this lack of information, we use SNOMED (also referenced with *oboInOwl:hasDbXref*) which is one of the most successful ontologies in the medical field. SNOMED proposes a categorization of the different characteristics of a disease. It offers a rich and varied panorama of seven signs categories: Physical agents, Living organisms, Morphological properties (Symptoms), Biological functions (Clinical Signs), Chemical compounds, Social conditions, Topographic properties.

It is with this in mind that we have to consider the SYPM and CSSO ontologies. The first one is developed in the same project as the DOID, and in the same way as this one for the diseases, SYMP proposes a hierarchical structure complete of all the clinical signs and symptoms, which are also classified in categories of signs. SYMP affixes to each sign a definition referring to how it manifests itself in the patient. The second also brandishes the same goal as the SYMP but it is a little less accomplished. Only the third of SYMP signs are taken into account in CSSO. However, the latter brings a plus, a terminology for each sign. However, none of these two ontologies makes the difference between a clinical sign and a symptom, it's necessary to make the mapping with the categorization of the SNOMED signs.

4   Data Model Stucture

The different data formats of the ontologies we have selected are implemented with the W3C standards of the Semantic Web around the RDF, RDFS and OWL languages. So to facilitate the recovery of targeted data on each of these resources, we propose a structure (Fig. 3) using the same technologies and which inherits from them the same conceptual formalisms.

The structure is disease-centric (*Disease Class*) with all informations classes necessary for understanding the disease as well as the recommendation of potential diagnosis. Each disease is identified (*categorized_in*) in one or more categories (*SetOfDiseases Class*). Each disease is associated (*named*) with a set of

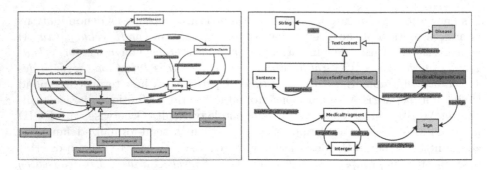

Fig. 3. Overall view data structure of our medical ontology combining diseases and signs

nominative terms (*NominativeTerms*) synonyms, from the preferred term (skos: prefLabel), to alternative terms (skos:altLabel, skos:hiddenLabel). Each disease is associated (characterized_by) with a set of semantic characteristics (Semantic-Characteristics Class) and through the relations *has_symptom, transmitted_by, located_in, caused_by, results_in* refer respectively to different types of signs such as Symptom or ClinicalSign, PhysicalAgent, TopographicalLocate, PhysicalAgent, ChimicalAgent or Symptom (morphological elements) or MedicalProcedure (Medical Procedure).

Each sign has a name and possibly a value, especially in the case of measurable clinical signs. Each of the signs classes, identifiable in SNOMED, group and list all the possible signs, but a given disease is associated only with the most common signs, the other signs are attached on a specific patient case for same diagnosis, and varie from one case to another. Moreover, in the overall data structure (Fig. 3) of the diagnostic recommendation engine, we can see that the patient is materialized by the textual description of his state of health (*SourceTextForPatientState*), and is associated with a medical diagnostic case (*MedicalDiagnosisCase*). The latter is linked (*associatedDisease*) to a disease based on a set of signs (*hasSign*). As a result the data structure implemented here, stores both an ontology of diseases and signs, but also the case base of validated diagnoses and especially links between diseases and their descriptive signs through these latter cases.

5   Contributions of Clinical Reports

After having established our federation of ontologies, we are discovering to what extent we can enrich this ontology from the analysis of medical reports of diagnostic cases that have already been validated by clinicians. We consider here a case of a patient diagnosed with Hepatitis A[6]. This disease is of viral ori-

---

[6] Example from http://www.immunologyclinic.com/.

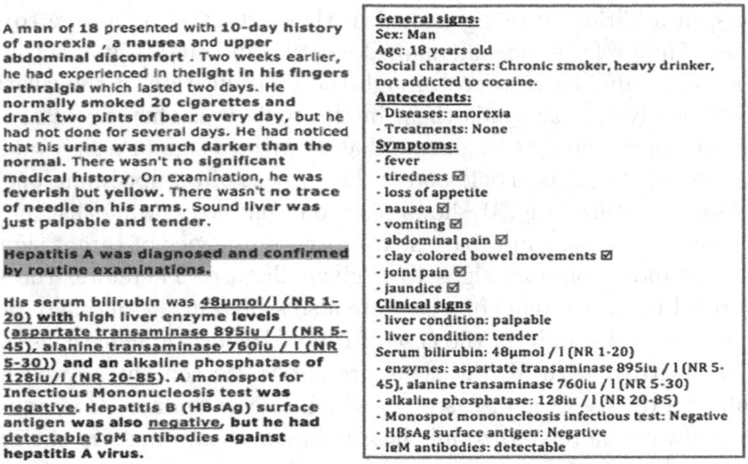

A man of 18 presented with 10-day history of anorexia , a nausea and upper abdominal discomfort . Two weeks earlier, he had experienced in thelight in his fingers arthralgia which lasted two days. He normally smoked 20 cigarettes and drank two pints of beer every day, but he had not done for several days. He had noticed that his urine was much darker than the normal. There wasn't no significant medical history. On examination, he was feverish but yellow. There wasn't no trace of needle on his arms. Sound liver was just palpable and tender.

Hepatitis A was diagnosed and confirmed by routine examinations.

His serum bilirubin was 48μmol/l (NR 1-20) with high liver enzyme levels (aspartate transaminase 895iu / l (NR 5-45), alanine transaminase 760iu / l (NR 5-30)) and an alkaline phosphatase of 128iu/l (NR 20-85). A monospot for Infectious Mononucleosis test was negative. Hepatitis B (HBsAg) surface antigen was also negative, but he had detectable IgM antibodies against hepatitis A virus.

General signs:
Sex: Man
Age: 18 years old
Social characters: Chronic smoker, heavy drinker, not addicted to cocaine.
Antecedents:
- Diseases: anorexia
- Treatments: None
Symptoms:
- fever
- tiredness ☑
- loss of appetite
- nausea ☑
- vomiting ☑
- abdominal pain ☑
- clay colored bowel movements ☑
- joint pain ☑
- jaundice ☑
Clinical signs
- liver condition: palpable
- liver condition: tender
Serum bilirubin: 48μmol / l (NR 1-20)
- enzymes: aspartate transaminase 895iu / l (NR 5-45), alanine transaminase 760iu / l (NR 5-30)
- alkaline phosphatase: 128iu / l (NR 20-85)
- Monospot mononucleosis infectious test: Negative
- HBsAg surface antigen: Negative
- IgM antibodies: detectable

Fig. 4. Textual report of real case of Hepatitis A

gin designating inflammation of the liver. It's listed among sexually transmitted infections is in the top ten (10) of most dangerous diseases in Senegal[7].

The case, taken as an example (Fig. 4), is transcribed in a textual report which includes the symptomatic description of the state of health of a patient whose diagnosis is then confirmed after a set of in-depth examinations. These types of reports explode in the registers (digital or not) of clinicians and gives a visibility on the signs necessary for diagnosis confirmation. Indeed, this report crosses all the characteristic signs allowing to conclude on Hepatitis A disease, and we will discover that its analysis extends our ontology because it makes it possible to associate a given disease with the set of relevant signs.

First, several types of signs present in this report. For Hepatitis A, only 9 general symptoms appear in the ontology. These are fever, fatigue, loss of appetite, nausea, vomiting, abdominal pain, clay colored bowel movements, joint pain, and jaundice. And only 7/9 are therefore identifiable for this case and correspond to the first observable signs in the patient. Other signs, although listed in the ontology (from SYMP and CSSO) and not associated with Hepatitis A, correspond to the general signs indicating its sex, age, and excesses, but also to antecedents and clinicals signs. These result from in-depth examinations and refer to nominative terms and values. In the end, more than 16 signs are added to those who describe Hepatitis A in the ontology.

Extraction of the signs from this textual report poses two problems: the identification of the known general symptoms of the ontology for Hepatitis A, and specific signs to the patient and not listed for this same disease. In both cases, there is a problem of NLP especially since the text is transcribed in natural language. The terms referring to symptoms are not difficult to detect according to detailed lexicons (preferential terms and synonyms) affixed to each sign. For

---

[7] http://www.who.int/countries/sen/en/.

other signs, in addition to being named in the text, it's imperative to extract their values. They refer to specific named entities and the assignment of one of these signs to a value have to go through the identification of the relationship (verbal or adjectival) that binds them in the text. It is then necessary to use NLP tools to identify all text fragments that describe a sign or a sign value. This part is not detailed in this article and is the subject of an upcoming one.

The data structure (Fig. 3) shows that our ontology, while listing all the signs that may be present in a patient from the ontologies of target signs, only associates the most common signs to a given disease. Therefore, the specific signs described in the contents of a case are also stored in the ontology but their values can be recorded only in the case of type *"MedicalDiagnosisCase"*, which is associated with it with all the signs present in its content as well as their values, and the diseases (or diseases) to which it corresponds. Consequently, a disease will always be related to all these common symptoms via the ontology of diseases, and to a set of specific signs according to the number of real cases already diagnosed.

6   Results

6.1   Data Selection from Target Medical Ontologies

Data structure (Fig. 3) is loaded by querying the different target ontological resources with the SPARQL query language. These are directly executed on SPARQL EndPoint, open query interfaces for browsing RDF graphs. Here we use BioPortal's. In total we have five (5) SPARQL query patterns that recovery:

- all the diseases which constitute the leaves of the classes starting from the DOID, as well as their definitions starting from MESH;
- all disease categories from the DOID where we select their name, description, and parent categories;
- all nominative terms synonyms of diseases from the DOID, but especially from MESH, are the preferred label, as well as alternative labels for each disease;
- all the basic characteristic signs for each disease from semi-formalized descriptions of the DOID;
- all the nominal terms synonymous of signs: the preferential labels are extracted from SYMP, the alternative labels are extracted from the ontologies CSSO, and SNOMED.

Thus in the Table 1, we show statical description of the ontology resulting from this loading of data. Only the human diseases available in DOID are taken into account, as well as their respective categories. For each disease, about 4 registered nominative terms are listed, which facilitates the identification of diagnosis in the exploited textual clinical reports. As for the signs, each is associated with about 5 nominative terms on average but only the general signs directly index diseases in the ontology, the clinical signs are associated with a disease only through the real cases where they take value. Knowing that a case as described in a textual clinical report always concludes on a disease and under the condition of the appearance of a precise list of symptoms and clinical signs.

Table 1. Description of resulting diseases and signs ontology

Element types	Ontological object	Target ontologies	Number of elements
Diagnosis			
Maladies	Diseases Class	DOID	6442
Categories	SetOfDiseases Class	DOID	3947
Synonyms diagnosis terms	AnnotationProperty (prefLabel, altLabel, hiddenLabel)	DOID, MESH	27586
Signs			
Symptoms and Clinical Signs	Symptom Class and CinicalSign Class - subClassOf Sign Class	SYMP	942
Other Signs	PhysicalAgent Class, ChemicalAgent Class, TopographicalLocate Class, MedicalProcedure Class:subClassOf Class Sign	DOID, SNOMED	6020
Synonyms signs terms	AnnotationProperty (prefLabel, altLabel)	CSSO, SNOMED	4710

6.2   Data Selection from Clinical Reports

Selection of data from the clinical reports involves their loading into the case base as described in the data structure. This process is based on the extraction of the signs present on each report. The cases are then formalized as RIF rules[8] that are compatibles with the ontology manipulation languages we use here such as RDF and OWL. Each case is described in two sides: the premise that refers to identified signs for the case and the conclusion corresponds to the diagnosed disease. Thus, for the extraction of signs, textual clinical reports are annotated with NLP tools such as NooJ[9] and Clamp[10] with regard to the ontology of diseases and signs. This work is the subject of another paper.

In the experimental setting of this work, we use on the one hand, ten (10) real cases of patients who have already been diagnosed. The examples chosen are different cases on tropical diseases[11] and allow us to visualize the contribution of cases. Indeed, on the Table 2 we can notice that for each disease, there is a precise number of general symptoms indicated by the ontology but the totality of them are not present in this patient. In addition, new symptoms identified in the ontology and not associated with the disease are emerging, as well as clinical

---

[8] https://www.w3.org/TR/rif-overview/.
[9] http://www.nooj-association.org/.
[10] https://clamp.uth.edu/.
[11] Examples in http://medecinetropicale.free.fr/.

Table 2. Symptoms and clinical signs into sample clinical reports

Disease	Symptoms linking with diseasee	Symptoms present in example case	New added symptoms	Clinical signs
Hepatitis A	9	7	7	9
Cholera	5	3	10	2
Rougeaole	6	4	11	3
Dengue	10	5	11	20
Tetanus	4	3	12	4
Malaria	6	4	8	24
Syphilis	5	2	12	14
Chikungunya	9	5	7	29
Typhoid fever	8	5	8	3
Meningitis	9	4	5	7

signs specific to each patient. For example, for the case that refers to Hepatitis A, of the 9 symptoms that appear in the ontology and associated with this disease, only 7 are identified, and in addition 7 other new symptoms are detected as well as the clinical signs.

On the other hand, we used a larger sample of 156 cases of the same Hepatitis A disease. The Table 3 shows symptom appetition rates and test intervals measuring clinical signs. This shows the importance of clinical reports, especially in the context of medical diagnostic assistance. It's possible to classify the characteristic features of each disease by order of appearance in most patients who have already been diagnosed. For clinical signs, the intervals indicate, as reports are added in the case base, what are the most frequent minimum and maximum values.

Table 3. Rate appearance of some symptoms and clinical signs on Hepatitis A clinical reports dataset

Symptoms	Fever	Fatigue	Loss-of-appetite	Vomiting	Abdo-pain	c-c-b-movs	Joint-pain
% appearance	39.1	64.1	20.5	50.0	12.8	11.5	19.2
Clinical signs	Liver-big	Liver-firm	Bilirubin	Aspartate	Alk-phos	Albumin	Protime
% or interval appearance	76.9	38,5	0.3 to 8	14 to 648	26 to 296	2.1 to 6.4	0 to 100

7   Conclusion

In this article, the problem is focused on the establishment of a medical diagnostic support system based on open and shared ontology resources. It's a question here of the constitution of a central ontology federating a set of ontologies and medical terminologies targets, which answer the need for information in order to facilitate the task of the clinician in the identification of the potential diagnosis, among which he will have the latitude of choose or validate the most reliable knowingly. This type of system does not replace the clinician.

We have therefore proposed a federation methodology around a data structure of RDF graph type facilitating the recovery of human diseases and their most relevant characteristic signs, from targeted ontologies but also from an analysis of real cases of confirmed diagnosis. In the end, we have an ontology of diseases and signs should serve as a knowledge base in the search engine we aim for. The work in perspective would be to validate this ontology by the actors in the field but this will only be done to assess its relevance and consistency in its role for the engine, which is to identify present signs at a patient, and find relevant diseases as diagnosis.

References

1. Anbarasi, M., Naveen, P., Selvaganapathi, S., Nowsath, M.: Ontology based medical diagnosis decision support system. Int. J. Eng. Res. Technol. (2013)
2. Balogh, E.P., Miller, B.T., Ball, J.R.: Improving diagnosis in health care. In: National Academies of Sciences, Engineering, and Medicine. The National Academies Press, Washington, DC (2015)
3. Charlet, J., Declerck, G., Dhombres, F., Gayet, P., Miroux, P., Vandenbussche, P.: Construire une ontologie médicale pour la recherche d'information: problématiques terminologiques et de modélisation (2012)
4. Hoehndorf, R., Schofield, P., Gkoutos, G.: The role of ontologies in biological and biomedical research: a functional perspective. Brief. Bioinf. J. **16**, 1069–1080 (2015)
5. Mohammed, O., Benlamri, R., Fong, S.: Building a diseases symptoms ontology for medical diagnosis: an integrative approach. In: IEEE International Conference on Future Generation Commnication Technology (FGCT 2012), Dcembre 2012
6. Oberkampf, H., Zillner, S., Bauer, B.: Interpreting patient data using medical background knowledge. In: 3rd International Conference on Biomedical Ontology (ICB0), 21–25 July 2012, Austria (2012)
7. S-Ortiz, J.A.R., Jimenez, A.L., Cater, J., Malends, C.A.: Ontology-based knowledge representation for supporting medical decisions. Rech. Comput. Sci. **68**, 127–136 (2013)
8. Valencia-García, R., Lagos-Ortiz, K., Medina-Moreira, J., Paredes-Valverde, M.A., Espinoza-Morán, W.: An ontology-based decision support system for the diagnosis of plant diseases. J. Inf. Technol. Res. **10**(4), 45–55 (2017)

Design of a Low-Cost Wind Turbine Controller for Decentralized Rural Electrification Through the Small Wind Turbine

Ababacar Ndiaye[1,2(✉)], Mohamed El Ali[3], Salif Sow[2],
Cheikh M. F. Kébé[2], Vincent Sambou[2], and Papa A. Ndiaye[2]

[1] Département de Physique, Université Assane Seck de Ziguinchor,
UFR – Sciences et Technologies, BP 523, Ziguinchor, Sénégal
`ab.ndiaye@univ-zig.sn`
[2] Centre International de Formation et de Recherche en Energie Solaire
(CIFRES), Ecole Supérieure Polytechnique – UCAD,
BP 5085 Dakar-Fann, Sénégal
[3] Département Génie Electrique et Informatique Industrielle,
IUT 'A' Paul Sabatier, 31400 Toulouse, France

Abstract. This paper present the development of a low-cost wind turbine controller for decentralized rural electrification through the small wind turbine. This controller allows on the one hand protecting the battery against overcharging and deep discharge. On the other hand, it helps to protect the turbine against strong winds. It is controlled by PIC microcontroller 16F877A. This control function is performed using an algorithm that continuously compares the battery voltage to the charge and discharge thresholds, and tilting towards dissipation resistors. The control signals generated by the microcontroller are PWM (Pulse Width Modulation) type. The validation of the main functions of the controller is presented. The main advantages of this controller are the robustness, the simplicity and especially the low cost.

Keywords: Controller · Wind turbine · Microcontroller

1 Introduction

As in photovoltaic systems, wind energy applications include most often batteries for storing excess energy and feed loads low and medium powers. The batteries are weak with the phenomena of overloading and deep discharge. This adversely affects the life of the batteries and is a weak point for renewable energies. To protect the batteries and prolong their lives, a controller should be used. For photovoltaic systems, the controller can only protect the batteries. The principle often used for photovoltaic controller consists in disconnecting the PV generator from the batteries. This disconnection occurs when the batteries are fully charged or deeply discharged (Amin et al. 2008). For wind turbine applications, the same principle cannot be used. Indeed, we cannot afford to disconnect the turbine from the batteries and keep it in a vacuum which will increase the risk of its destruction by overspeed. The principle adopted for the control

G. Bassioni et al. (Eds.): InterSol 2019, LNICST 296, pp. 116–127, 2019.
https://doi.org/10.1007/978-3-030-34863-2_11

of the batteries charge/discharge for wind systems must take into account this constraint. The wind turbine must always be loaded by the batteries and/or other charges (use, discharge resistors). In addition to the batteries, the controller protects the wind turbine.

The importance of a charging/discharging controller in an autonomous system such as a photovoltaic system or wind turbine needs no more to be discussed. However, it must be done very carefully in order to meet the requirements for reliability, simplicity, portability and cost. As in the embodiment of any system, the controller also poses a number of problems related to the existence of several possible architectures for load control (Usher and Ross 1998; Koutroulis and Kalaitzakis 2004; Thiringer and Petersson 2005) (maximum charging current with control battery voltage, constant voltage charging with control current battery, charging with adjustable intensity together with control of the battery voltage, etc.) and battery discharge (Usher and Ross 1998) (direct control of the battery voltage, check the battery voltage compensated or not the discharge current, discharge control across the state of battery charge. Several solutions are possible: analog, digital or mixed.

Additional constraints imposed on the controller such as the possibility of varying the parameters of the control algorithm and display the battery charge level, increase its complexity and lead us to opt for a smart solution based on microcontrollers.

This paper presents the different development steps of a battery controller for wind turbine applications, operating under the control of the microcontroller PIC16F877A.

2 Presentation of Wind Turbine and Regulation System

2.1 Characteristics of Wind the Turbine

The wind turbine used in this work was designed specifically for the African rural context, unlike wind turbines on the market. The electromechanical conversion is ensured by a permanent magnet three-phase alternator. The characteristics of this wind turbine are as:

- Starting speed: 2 m/s
- Stall speed: 10 m/s
- Nominal Power: 500 W
- Diameter of the helix: 3 m
- Type of mast: 18 m cable-stayed
- Control mode: Erasing gravitational lateral of the rotor

The figure below (Fig. 1) shows photo of the wind turbine.

Fig. 1. Photo of the wind turbine.

2.2 Performance of the Wind-Turbine

It is necessary to know precisely the behaviour of the wind turbine according to different parameters. The figure below (Fig. 2) shows, the characteristic curves of power and efficiency according to the wind speed of the wind-turbine.

The first of the figures shows the power curve of the wind turbine as a function of the wind speed. No power is delivered for a wind speed less than 2 m/s, we are in zone 1. The higher the wind speed, the more power the wind turbine develops; this is zone 2. The nominal power of the turbine is 500 W, which corresponds to a wind speed of 9 m/s. Beyond the stall speed of 10 m/s, the nominal power is exceeded, the turbine must be stopped. The second figure shows the efficiency of the wind turbine as a function of the wind speed. The ideal wind speed is between 3 m/s and 5 m/s for a maximum yield between 25% and 27.5%.

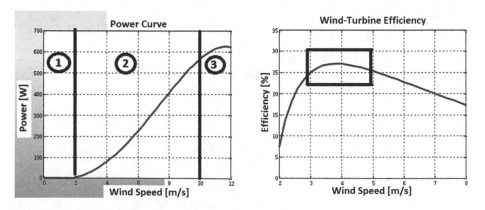

Fig. 2. Power curve and wind-turbine efficiency.

2.3   Problematic and Principle of Regulation

The voltage delivered by the turbine is three-phase, a diode bridge rectifies to provide a DC voltage at its output. This voltage will be used for battery charging. However, the wind never blows at a constant speed, so the mechanics of the wind turbine are subject to the constraints of the climate.

It is necessary to protect the battery from too high or low voltages at its terminals. Too high a voltage could cause irreversible battery destruction due to overcharging, and too low voltage could also cause irreversible destruction due to deep discharge. It will therefore be necessary to determine a high threshold and a low voltage threshold, their values are given by the manufacturer of the battery. Outside these thresholds for a long time, this can lead to the destruction of the battery.

This diagram below (Fig. 3) illustrates the configuration of the wind turbine with its regulation.

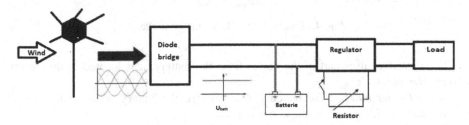

Fig. 3. Wind turbine/controller/battery/load.

The controller is placed parallel to the battery. It is accompanied by two external resistors: a resistance of use and a variable resistance of dissipation. The battery voltage will be measured permanently.

The role of the controller will be to control the connection of the control board to the two external resistors in order to protect the battery.

3   Presentation of the Regulation

This section first presents the basic block diagram of the charge controller. Then the electric diagram of the controller is presented. Finally, the flowchart that reflects the operation is presented.

3.1 Functional Blocks of the Controller

The diagram (Fig. 4) below illustrates the general operation of the controller.

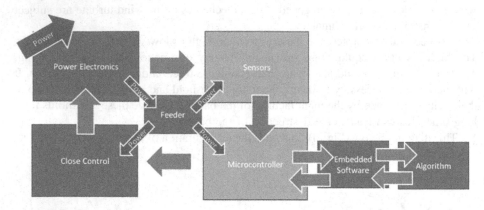

Fig. 4. Functional blocks of the controller.

The régalateur uses part of the power from the battery, it is located in the **Power Electronics block**.

In the **Feeder block**, a voltage controller converts the battery voltage into a lower voltage suitable for powering the controller.

The **Sensors block** has a voltage divider bridge. Its purpose is to adapt the voltage read at the terminals of the battery, in a voltage that can be read and interpreted by the microcontroller. This will permanently read the voltage across the battery. This is why this block is assimilated to a sensor.

The **microcontroll**er reads a voltage adapted at the input of its analog-digital converter. It contains a program (**Algorithm & Embedded Sof**tware) and will give output instructions.

The Close Control receives instructions from the microcontroller. It keeps the battery voltage between the two thresholds, it will decide whether or not it connects the battery to the external resistors.

3.2 Electrical Diagram of the Controller

The different blocks (Power Electronics, Feeder, Sensors, Microcontroller, Close Control) have been highlighted in the electrical diagram of the controller shown in Fig. 5.

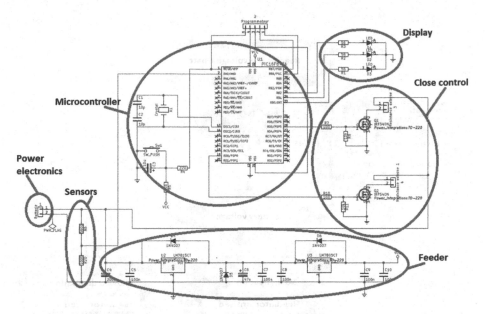

Fig. 5. Electrical diagram of the controller.

The microcontroller part contains a PIC 16F877A. It will therefore be necessary to study in detail the PIC datasheet in order to better adapt the functional blocks that surround it. In addition, this controller has a display of the status of the battery that has been called Display, via three LEDs of different colors.

3.3 Flow Chart of the Controller

The flowchart of the controller is shown in Fig. 6. It highlights the control of charge and discharge of the battery, and the visualization of the state of the battery. Note that the thresholds were determined for a 24 V battery.

The voltage (Ubatt) at the battery terminals is read continuously. Control of the charging/discharging of the battery and the display of its voltage will be a function of Ubatt.

The voltage thresholds defined for the 24 V battery are as follows:

- High threshold at 28 : Battery voltage should not rise above this threshold
- Low threshold at 24 V: Battery voltage should not drop below this threshold

Two external resistors are connected to the control board: load resistance and overflow resistance. These two resistors will be used depending on the voltage read at the terminals of the battery.

In addition, the control board allows to visualize the voltage at the battery terminals, through three LEDs. The full charge voltage is 26 V.

122   A. Ndiaye et al.

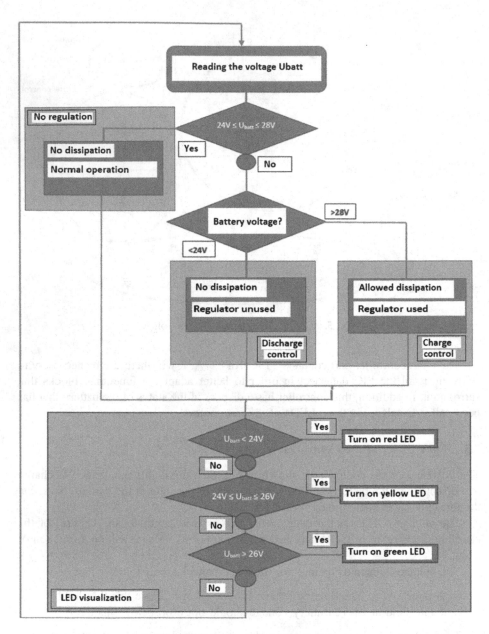

Fig. 6. Flow chart of the controller.

4 Presentation of Hardware Blocks

4.1 Power Supply Block

The input voltage of the controller is that read across the battery. The card requires a 5 V supply voltage, imposed by the microcontroller (PIC 16F877A). The purpose of the power supply is therefore to regulate the input voltage to a voltage of 5 V. The electrical diagram of the power supply unit of the control board is shown in Fig. 7.

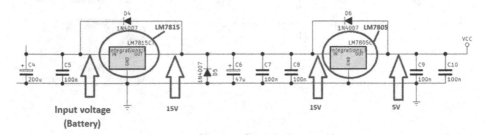

Fig. 7. Electrical diagram of the power supply.

The power supply unit consists of two series-connected voltage controllers, LM7815 and LM7805 respectively. These controllers have a maximum input voltage threshold and have fixed output voltages imposed by the manufacturer. These are linear type controllers, their disadvantage is that their efficiency is very low.

4.2 Analog to Digital Conversion

The voltage read at the terminals of the resistor R20 is connected to one of the analog inputs of the PIC. The PIC 16F877A has an 8-bit analog-to-digital converter, so $2^8 - 1 = 255$ values are possible. It can read only voltages between 0 V and 5 V, so it will read the voltage from the upstream divider bridge with a ratio of 6.6.

The following table (Table 1) shows the correspondence between the voltage at the terminals of the Ubatt battery, the voltage read at the analog input of the PIC and its digital image Vbat.

Table 1. Analog-digital conversion table.

Battery Volage U$_{batt}$	Voltage read after the divider bridge - at the analog input of the PIC	V$_{batt}$, Digital image of the battery voltage
33 V	$\dfrac{33V}{6.6} = 5.0V$	255
0 V	$\dfrac{0V}{6.6} = 0V$	0
24 V	$\dfrac{24V}{6.6} = 3.64V$	175
28 V	$\dfrac{28V}{6.6} = 4.24V$	204

Maximum value that can be read by the PIC

Minimum value that can be read by the PIC

Respectively the high threshold and the low threshold of the battery

5   Presentation and Test of the Controller

5.1   Presentation of Controller

The realization of wind turbine controller took place at the International Center for Training and Research in Solar Energy (ICTRSE) of Dakar University. As mentioned earlier, this controller consists of a power unit, a display unit of battery charge level and a control block around the PIC microcontroller.

Figure 8 shows the two sides of the controller board.

Fig. 8. Front (a) and rear (b) faces of the controller board.

5.2   Test Results

5.2.1   Visualization of the Battery Charge Level

The test validated this block. Indeed, the red LED lights for a voltage lower than 24 V, the green lights for a voltage greater than or equal to 26 V; the yellow LED lights up between 24 V and 26 V. We also verify that only one LED is active at a time. Figure 9 shows the results.

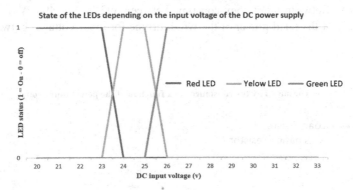

Fig. 9. State of the LEDs depending on the input voltage of the DC power supply.

5.2.2   Charge/Discharge Control

Now, the load and discharge control is tested. A DC voltage is applied at the input. Following the flowchart presented in Sect. 3.3, the voltage VGS of the transistor is checked; then the connection of the board to the external resistors, by raising the voltage at their terminals as shown in Fig. 10.

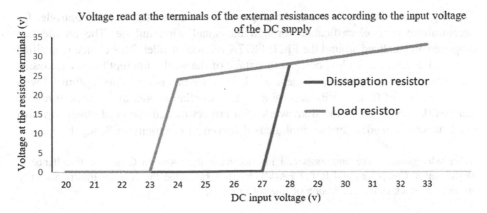

Fig. 10. Voltage read at the terminals of the external resistances according to the input voltage of the DC supply.

5.2.3   Power Budget

The characteristic curve of the power consumed by the resistors as a function of the input voltage of the DC supply is shown in Fig. 11. Remember that the nominal power of the wind turbine is 500 W. We observe that when a resistor is connected, we find the voltage of the battery at its terminals. First the utilization resistance is connected for a voltage across the battery between 24 V and 28 V, dissipating between 168 W and 196 W, i.e. between 34% and 40% of the rated power of the battery. Then the two resistors are connected simultaneously for a voltage across the battery greater than or equal to 28 V. Between them, they consume between 392 W and 490 W, or between 79% and 92% of the rated power of the wind turbine for input voltages between 28 V and 33 V.

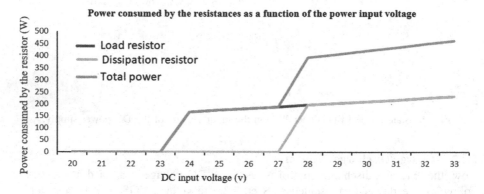

Fig. 11. Power consumed by the resistances as a function of the power input voltage.

6   Conclusion

The objective of this work was to develop a of a low-cost wind turbine controller for decentralized rural electrification through the small wind turbine. The architecture proposed and realized around the PIC16F877A microcontroller. This choice is justified by its robustness and its low cost. At this stage of the work, different blocks are tested and validated. A first prototype is developed. This will be improved and optimized with the integration of functionality according to the installation area of the wind turbines. This work comes within the framework of a project of realization of small low-cost wind turbines intended for the rural areas deprived of electricity in Senegal.

Acknowledgments. The authors would like to thank the "African Center of Excellence in Mathematics, Computing and ICT, CEA-MITIC" has supported the costs of transportation to present this work in the 3rd edition of Intersol in Cairo.

References

Amin, N., Azim, M.A., Sopian, K. Development of cost effective charge controller with data acquisition options for PV powered sensor nodes. In: 33rd IEEE Photovoltaic Specialists Conference, 2008. PVSC 2008 (2008)

Datasheet PIC 16F877A: Microchip Technology Inc. (2012)

Huet, F.: A review of impedance measurements for determination of the state-of charge. J. Power Sources **70**, 59–68 (1998)

Kirchev, M.A.: Studies of the pulse charge of lead-acid batteries for PV applications, part II. Impedance of the positive plate revisited (2007)

Koutroulis, E., Kalaitzakis, K.: Novel battery charging regulation system for photovoltaic applications. IEEE Proc. Electr. Power Appl. **151**(2), 191–197 (2004)

Mayeux, P.: Apprendre la Programmation des PIC par l'Expérimentation et la Simulation. ETSF 2nd edn. 2002 (2002)

Ndiaye, A., Dzahini, D., Ndiaye, P.A., Kébé, C.M.F., Sambou, V.: Impact of injected charges, clock noise and operational amplifier imperfections on the sample and hold (SH) overall performance. Appl. Phys. Res. **4**(4), 18–25 (2012). https://doi.org/10.5539/apr.v4n4p18

Ndiaye, A., Judalet, V., Kébé, C.M.F., Ndiaye, P.A.: Développement d'un régulateur de charge/décharge de batterie à seuils configurables pour des applications éoliennes. J. des Sciences Pour l'Ingénieur **1**(12), 57–62 (2010). http://www.ajol.info/index.php/jspi/article/view/67976

Usher, E.P., Ross, M.M.D.: Recommended Practices for Charge Controllers. Report IEA PVPS T3-05 (1998)

Thiringer, T., Petersson, a.: Control of a Variable-Speed Pitch-Regulated Wind Turbine, Chalmers University of Technology (2005)

Heier, S.: Wind Energy Conversion systems, pp. 39–41, Wiley (2006)

Ingram, G.: Wind Turbine Blade Analysis Using the Blade Element Momentum Method, Durham University, October 2011

The Circular Relationship Between Poverty, Environment, and Economic Development: The Case of Shakshouk Village, Fayoum

Nada Tewfik[(✉)] , Marwa Abdel Latif , and Mohamed Salheen

Ain Shams University, Cairo, Egypt
{nada.samir,m.abdellatif,
Mohamed.salheen}@eng.asu.edu.eg

Abstract. Rural Communities living within Protected Areas (PAs) depend mainly on the natural environment for their livelihoods and tend to be among the poorest in the country; since the degradation of the environment jeopardizes their economic-resource base. Moreover, economic development pressures cause changes in PAs' contexts leading to negative and positive impacts on the environment and people, which then affect the long-term benefits of development. In this regard, an integration between the different themes of Poverty, Environment and Economic Development is crucial – especially when challenges and practices intertwine on ground. With notions of integration starting in the Egyptian context; the case study of Shakshouk village within Qaroun Protected Area in Fayoum is investigated- where the majority of the community is rural poor who live in degraded environments and face continuous development pressures. This paper explores the mutual positive and negative influence existing between Poverty- Environment- Economic Development in order to map the system's dynamics of Shakshouk; using on-site semi structured interviews, observation and building on previous secondary data. It ends by shedding light on a circular relationship existing between Poverty, Environment and Economic Development which has to be considered by decision makers in future sectoral interventions.

Keywords: Poverty · Environment · Economic Development · Shakshouk · Qaroun · Fayoum

1 Introduction

The recent National Biodiversity Strategy and Action Plan of Egypt (NBSAP) envisions that "By 2030, biodiversity in Egypt is valued, mainstreamed, maintained for the good livelihoods and conserved for the sustainable use of future generations" (Ministry of Environment 2016, p. 2). In this vision, Egyptian authorities highlight a shared responsibility among the environment and people. This could be understood since on the one hand, PAs help communities living within or nearby them to maintain their traditional lifestyles, while offering them means to improve their standards of living; in terms of fisheries, water, and other ecosystem services for their consumption or income generation (Fisher et al. 2005; USAID 2006; Ministry of Environment 2016; Allam

© ICST Institute for Computer Sciences, Social Informatics and Telecommunications Engineering 2019
Published by Springer Nature Switzerland AG 2019. All Rights Reserved
G. Bassioni et al. (Eds.): InterSol 2019, LNICST 296, pp. 128–143, 2019.
https://doi.org/10.1007/978-3-030-34863-2_12

2018). On the other hand, people –themselves- should preserve the environment richness to balance between current and future needs (Howarth 1972; Ministry of Environment 2016).

However, despite the great efforts of managing PAs; biodiversity crises still exist and many fragile environments of PAs are threatened and degraded (Carey, Dudley and Stolton 2000; Dudley et al. 2008). Furthermore, it is in such environmentally fragile contexts that rural communities are particularly dependent on natural resources for their livelihoods (Fisher et al. 2005). Lacking access to resources and/or legal control, communities within or near PAs tend to be among the poorest and most marginalized people in the nation (UNESCO 2001; DFID et al. 2002; Barbier 2010). As an action of survival, sometimes these rural poor people worsen the environmental degradation (Fisher et al. 2005). What makes the situation more critical is that places rich in biodiversity with poor communities tend to face economic development pressures as part of modernization trends (EEAA/NCS 2006). These kinds of developments benefit from the place assets and usually pose positive and negative impacts on the environment and people (UNESCO 2001; Fisher et al. 2005). In similar situations, literature shows that achieving sustainability requires the integration of economic, social and environmental aspects (Rosendo and Brown 2004). Accordingly, multidisciplinary approaches need to be incorporated in which concepts of environmental conservation, local community development work hand in hand with economic development objectives (ibid).

2 Methodology

This paper is based on studying the case of Shakshouk Village; a human settlement within Qaroun Protected Area, located directly on Lake Qaroun where direct interaction between human and nature exists. The area of Shakshouk includes different forms of economic development such as tourism-based development, fish and shrimps-based development, and salt extraction industry. This makes it a good case study to understand economic development, environment and poverty linkages.

The research is based on primary and secondary sources. The field work took place between January 2017 and October 2018 where primary data was collected through observation, structured and semi-structured interviews with a range of Fayoum stakeholders. This included conservationists from EEAA, ministry of Environment, and Qaroun protectorate; as well as, developers from industrial companies, touristic resorts, and private companies. The viewpoints of civil society were clarified during on-site meetings, with the fishermen syndicate and Shakshouk local NGO. The secondary sources included online reportages, textual data and maps from national agencies such as the General Organization for Physical Planning (GOPP), Egyptian Environmental Affairs Agency (EEAA), Tourism Development Agency (TDA), General Authority for Fish Resources Development (GAFRD), Fayoum governorate and Shakshouk Local Authority; as well as, international bodies such as Bird Life Inter-national, International Union for Conservation of Nature (IUCN), and United Nations Development Programme (UNDP). It is important to note that results of this study are context specific;

since they are affected by the unique context of place in terms of spatial, political, and socio-economic variations.

3   Shakshouk Village Context: Exploring Community Poverty, Natural Environment and Economic Development

Shakshouk is a village of Ibshway center in Fayoum governorate, 90 km away from Cairo (see Fig. 1) The village lies in the North West of Fayoum Depression, within the boundaries of Qaroun Protected Area (QPA) (Heiba 2012). The population of Shakshouk is estimated to be around 33267 in 2017 (CAPMAS 2017) varying between fishermen, farmers, and other jobs. The village of Shakshouk has a medical unit, two schools, the local authority office, a water stream intersecting the urban fabric, the protectorate management unit, and it is surrounded by agriculture lands.

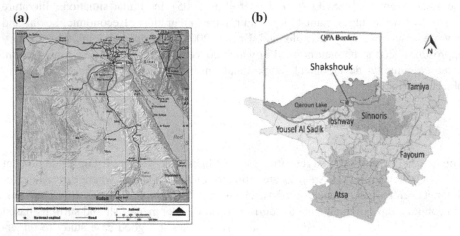

Fig. 1. Maps showing (a) Fayoum Governorate within Egypt, (b) Shakshouk in Ibshway center. Source: (State Information Service 2004)

In order to understand the interrelationships among the three themes of poverty of the local community, natural environment and economic development in the context of Shakshouk Village (see Fig. 2) this section begins by describing each theme separately with regard to the others. Afterwards in the discussion section, mapping the mutual influences among them is pinpointed. In this framework, the environment is explored first; since it is the place hosting the community and development. Other than that, the other themes are explored with no specific order of importance.

Fig. 2. Diagram illustrating the relationship between poverty, environment and economic development. Source: Authors

3.1   The Status of the Environment in Shakshouk

Shakshouk settlement is located in one of the lowest points of Fayoum depression on the edge of the closed basin of Lake Qaroun (EEAA/NCS 2006; 2007). The village gets water for agriculture from highlands of Fayoum through a number of drains and watercourses. The village receives a small share from the limited amount of irrigation water of Fayoum region (EEAA/NCS 2006; 2007; El-shabrawy and Dumont 2009; AbdelMaaboud 2018). Due to its topography, water that reaches the village is already polluted and highly saline (Shahid et al. 2013; EMISAL 2018). Furthermore, the village suffers from bad quality of water in lake Qaroun. The lake receives around 86% of a mix between untreated domestic, agricultural, and industrial drainage from the whole Fayoum governorate. Since the lake is a closed system, water leaves the lake only through evaporation, hence its water is full of high levels of heavy metals, pesticides and chemicals (EEAA 2008; Hussein et al. 2008; El-Serafy et al. 2014; GAFRD 2016; Heiba 2016; 2018; AbdelMaaboud 2018; EMISAL 2018; Youssef 2018).

As for fauna, Shakshouk is part of Qaroun Protected Area, which was declared in 1989 as a wetland for its importance as a resting place for migratory birds during winter (EEAA/NCS 2006; Shahid et al. 2013). In this regard, QPA is considered an "Important Bird Area" and a part of RAMSAR Convention[1] for its regional and international importance after spotting rare birds species (Hussein *et al.* 2008; AbdelLatib 2009; Heiba 2012; RAMSAR 2012; Heiba 2016; Bird Life 2018). Unfortunately, in winter 1998, numbers of birds' population counted plummeted after the increase of water salinity (EEAA/NCS 2007). Occasionally, hunting violations happen threatening the environment leading to a loss of biodiversity. In 1998 for example, 3000 birds were found dead on the lake's shores victims of poison probably by fish farmers (Afrol 2018; Bird Life 2018); such acts highlight the nature of tension arising between conservationists and rural communities in Fayoum.

---

[1] "The Convention on Wetlands, called the RAMSAR Convention, is an intergovernmental treaty providing the framework for national and international cooperation to conserve wetlands". (RAMSAR 2012).

Additionally, the lake had hosted a variety of marine life including more than 10 types of fish and shrimps. The fish from the lake contributed to 65% of fish production in Fayoum governorate in 2009 (Hussein *et al.* 2008; El-shabrawy and Dumont 2009). However, the fish population and fish industry suffered from a dramatic decline (EEAA/NCS 2007; GAFRD 2018; Ramadan 2018) (see Fig. 3). This could be attributed to three main reasons. First is the over exploiting practices of over-fishing and early harvesting of fish fry. Second is the high levels of pollution above permissible limits for fish to exist (Abou El-Gheit et al. 2012; Heiba 2016; Youssef 2018). Third is the presence of the 'Isopoda' parasite that was transported to the lake with fish fry since five years. This parasite caused the death of more than 90% of fish in the lake (GAFRD 2018). The only living species are currently low quality shrimps which are not affected by this parasite and survive the high levels of pollution. These shrimps are usually used for feeding poultry and animals (Youssef 2018).

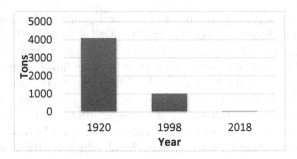

Fig. 3. Chart describing fish productivity in Lake Qaroun Source: Authors after (EEAA/NCS 2007; Ramadan 2018)

As for flora, Lake Qaroun is rich with its flora of unique vegetation growing along some of its shores. This vegetation is a valuable habitat threatened due to pressures on the shores due to human activities (Hussein *et al.* 2008).

As part of the protected area, many actors contribute to environmental conservation in the area of Shakshouk village. This includes the Ministry of State for Environmental Affairs (MSEA) and its executive arm the Egyptian Environmental Affairs Agency (EEAA); especially the Nature Conservation Sector (NCS): the main body responsible for the management of Qaroun Protected Area (EEAA/NCS 2007). Additionally, the General Authority for Fish Resources Development (GAFRD) which is the main body responsible for fish production of the lake. Needless to say, conservationists in the area are not only internal or locally based; but external bodies are also part; such as Bird Life International Agency, RAMSAR, and International Union for Nature Conservation (IUCN).

3.2   The Status of Local Poverty in Shakshouk

This section focuses on the impact of environmental degradation, tough conservation laws and lack of conservation in Shakshouk on the people livelihoods. It highlights how the community suffers from extreme poverty in terms of the multidimensional phenomenon of poverty such as; the lack of education, lack of access to resources, inability to satisfy basic needs, vulnerability to shocks, poor access to sanitation, lack of control over resources, and poor health.

For instance, education and poverty are highly connected in Shakshouk and one leads to the other (Heiba 2016). (CAPMAS 2017) data proves that illiteracy was counted as 48.8%. On one hand, poverty prohibits quite a big number of students from enrolment at schools; and enrolled students (15.5%) leave schools to help parents in gaining money. On the other hand, the lack of education even prohibits Shakshouk's families from enhancing their economic status (Heiba 2016).

In addition, the direct location of the village on the lake without any natural or man-made buffer had a strong impact on people's activities. Almost two thirds of the community used to work in fishery and its supplementary activities (AbdelMaaboud 2018; Ramadan 2018). In this regard, the pollution of the lake jeopardized the main economic-resource base of the locals (NCS/EEAA 2007; Heiba 2012). Despite the fact that boats number increased from 500 in 2009 to 606 in 2018, the price of a boat decreased from 20,000 to 5,000 EGP as a reflection of its return. Nowadays, only few boats are currently working for touristic activities or getting shrimps from the lake (Ramadan 2018) (see Fig. 4). For the past five years, as an environmental conservationist claims, no fish fry was transported to the lake awaiting the diminish of the "Isopoda" parasite (Ramadan 2018). This decision aggravated the situation of fishermen lacking their access to their resource base exacerbating their poverty.

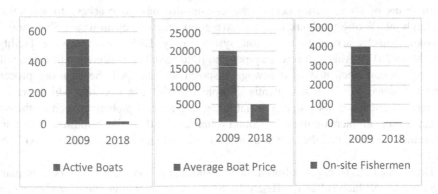

Fig. 4. Fishing between 2009 and 2018. Source: Authors after (El-shabrawy and Dumont 2009; Ramadan 2018)

Furthermore, the community is unable to satisfy its basic needs. This could be attributed to the lack of access to economic-resources coupled with scarcity of irrigation water as well as its pollution. In fact, problems with water quantity and quality indirectly affects third of Shakshouk's population who are working as farmers; since the low quality of their planted crops provides them with minimum earnings (Heiba 2016; AbdelMaaboud 2018). In order to sustain their livelihoods, few numbers of Shakshouk community work in complementary jobs such as fish farming, animals raise, or handmade pottery and handicrafts (lacking quality and marketing) (Heiba 2012; 2016; AbdelMaaboud 2018).

Additionally, the local community lacks control over resources. Despite the fact that the fishermen are directly affected by the lake's situation, they are not decision makers and suffer from lack of control over these resources. Although the NBSAP highlights on the importance of empowering people to have access to their resources, this is not the situation in Shakshouk (Mahdaly 2018). Furthermore, power struggles exist between actors involved in the lake conservation such as: Ministry of Environment, Ministry of Housing, Ministry of Agriculture, the General authority for Fish resources development, Ministry of Water Resources and Irrigation. "These stakeholders do not cooperate for better future to the place", argued the chief of Fishermen in Shakshouk.

Moreover, the community is vulnerable to shocks. The drastic change in economic-base of the community caused shifts in society dynamics. Fishermen migrated to work and left their families in Shakshouk, while women were obliged to work to sustain their livelihoods (Mahdaly 2018). Nowadays, the majority of women help in several economic activities compared to only 1.25% in 2006 (CAPMAS 2006; AbdelMaaboud 2018). They sell fish, feed their poultry, raise animals and peel shrimps in the streets (Youssef 2018). The shrimps are sold to food restaurants and companies, and the shells are sold to companies extracting Chitosan – a chemical extension as an initial component in cosmetics, agriculture, food, textile … etc. (Abdou et al. 2008). Sometimes, women in shrimp peeling sector earn peanut sum of money (25–75 Egyptian piasters/kilo) or shrimp peels to feed their poultry (Heiba 2016; Youssef 2018).

In terms of basic infrastructure, the community has poor access to sanitation. Although 99.8% of Shakshouk families have good access to clean water, Shakshouk's community lacks access to sanitation system (only 1.25% have sewage facility) (CAPMAS 2017). Although sewage pipes and fund have been secured, a problem with land acquisition dedicated as a sewage disposal site stopped the ongoing process (AbdelMaaboud 2018). Consequently, people (96.6%) use trenches which are not regularly cleaned and not properly isolated causing several problems; such as the soil contamination, an increase in underground water level influencing buildings' bases and community's health, and the spread of insects and bad smells (Heiba 2016; CAPMAS 2017).

Due to the high levels of pollution in Shakshouk, the community suffers from many diseases (AbdelMaaboud 2018; Heiba 2018). Lack of sanitation and garbage dissemination lead to hepatitis and kidney diseases (Heiba 2016). In addition, women and kids in direct contact with shrimp peels suffer from respiratory problems, eyes diseases, skin inflammations and bones weakness (AbdelMaaboud, 2018; Heiba 2018). The village includes only one health care unit which lacks doctors and staff (GOPP 2006; Heiba 2016).

3.3   The Status of Economic Development in Shakshouk

This section addresses "economic development" that is generated by economic activities exerted by external actors who are geo-graphically located within the system of Shakshouk; but are implemented by investors not per se locally based. The actors involved in economic development are mainly the Ministry of Agriculture and Land Reclamation, the national Tourism Development Agency (TDA), the Egyptian Salts and Minerals Company (EMISAL), private companies such as Chitosan Egypt, and tourist resorts. In this context, economic development refers to salt extraction industry, shrimp-based industry, and tourism.

Salt extraction industry is one of the largest economic activities on lake Qaroun. The main factories are EMISAL established in 1984 nearby Shakshouk village and future companies in the North shore of the lake (El-shabrawy and Dumont 2009; EMISAL 2018). The salt extraction industry has both positive and negative impacts on the environment and local community. For its positive impacts, it is reported that the salinity of the lake has recently decreased to 35–40 gm/l in 2018 (EMISAL 2018) after reaching to 50 gm/l in 2010 (Hassan 2015). Furthermore, EMISAL claims that it plays an important role in: providing useful kinds of salts for different chemical, food and medical domains and; establishing a leading industrial base in Fayoum. It, additionally, contributes to: enhancing the water quality of the lake; improving the soil quality of surrounding agricultural lands and; raising fund to develop schools, health care unit, or other projects and capacity building initiatives for the local com-munity of Shakshouk (AbdelMaaboud 2018; EMISAL 2018).

Nevertheless, the current salt extraction industry poses negative impacts on the environment and people. This includes the location of the factory in an environmentally sensitive area which threatens fish habitats (AbdelMaaboud 2018), the disposal of some impurities back in the lake after salt production process (Youssef 2018). Furthermore, the unclean dump sites of EMISAL company within the village land which influence the health of nearby residents. Moreover, the power of the company jeopardizes the community to raise their concerns (Youssef 2018).

Shrimp-based industries[2] similarly have positive and negative effects on the poor and the environment. Private companies get shrimp peels from Shakshouk's women to extract Chitosan product (Youssef 2018); to be used in several industries, cosmetics, and organic plantation, etc. This reduces the environment pollution -since the shrimp peels are not thrown in Shakshouk's canals or lake Qaroun; in addition to helping women earn more money for their well-being (AbdelMaaboud 2018). In this regard, a dealer from within the community and his wife are responsible for handling women and providing the private companies (i.e. Chitosan.Egypt, Re-shrimp company) with the shrimp peels. (Youssef 2018). In reality, such activities contributed significantly in the income generation for the households especially with the depletion of fishing and men's escalating migration trend. In this regard, women depend -for affording their

---

[2] Data gathered during a personal interview with Miss. Shahira Youssef, the chief marketing officer from Chitosan Egypt company and a participant in "Social Innovation for Fayoum" workshop: a cooperation between United Nations Development Programme (UNDP) and Misr El Khair foundation.

daily needs- on their income from shrimp peeling (Youssef 2018). However, the fair distribution of the economic benefit is debatable with the activity being controlled by specific dealers. Furthermore, the problem of performing this activity in unclean contexts affected the health status of women and their kids (AbdelMaaboud 2018). Although, Chitosan Egypt tried providing medical insurance for these women. However, Egyptian systems accept providing medical insurance to only employed women with job contracts; and this offer is refused by shrimp dealers since it jeopardizes their authority (Youssef 2018). Hence, the unregulated practices provided unhealthy working conditions, underpaid rates and disconnection from the real poor women; which consequently, contributed to the village multidimensional phenomenon of poverty.

As for tourism - which is an important economic activity in Qaroun Protected area-contributing to the economic growth of poor Shakshouk's communities (Heiba 2016). Many hotels and resorts (i.e. Byoum resort, Panorama Shakshouk Hotel, Auberge hotel… etc.) are concentrated along the southern shore of Lake Qaroun providing their clients with the spiritual and cultural aesthetics of the lake. Nonetheless, the current touristic activities also pose negative impacts on the environment on which they depend, affecting the long term process of development (NCS/EEAA 2007). Firstly, hotels and resorts throw their sewage and wastes in Lake Qaroun through large pipelines (EEAA 2008), which negatively affects the color, quality and smell of the lake; in addition to the indirect impacts on fish production and migratory birds habitats (Heiba 2016; AbdelMaaboud 2018). Secondly, some hotels extended their premises by filling in lake Qaroun which affected the biotic life in the lake. Thirdly, for the sake of horizontal expansion of some resorts, many shores –rich in biodiversity- suffered from erosion and the removal of rich vegetation and birds habitats (EEAA/NCS 2007). Furthermore, hunting violations practices caused loss of biodiversity(NCS/EEAA 2007).

3.4 Shakshouk Between Poverty Reduction Actions and Environmental Conservation Efforts

This section discusses efforts in reducing community poverty and conserving the environment in the context of Shakshouk. Regarding poverty reduction, a number of initiatives were implemented by different entities between 2009 and 2011. This includes the project of Fayoum Agro Organic Development (FAOD) with cooperation with Shakshouk NGO, which focused on minimizing the solid wastes and providing medical care committees to help the community; in addition to educating them handicrafts and potteries during workshops (FAOD 2011). Also, social development projects were implemented by the NCS as a social responsibility towards the poor people of Shakshouk (Heiba 2012). However, the authors argue that these initiatives were short-term projects with neither a clear comprehensive framework for community development nor continuous fund or support.

As for efforts to conserve the environment; several points could be pinpointed. GAFRD decided to stop adding fish fry to the lake till the death of Isopoda parasite under the claim that this decision would eventually increase the fish productivity back to the lake, disregarding the status quo of fishermen (Ramadan 2018). Although NCS introduced regulations against hunting violations, there has been no proper means for implementation or monitoring. Furthermore, water drainage is not filtered before accessing the lake (Mahdaly 2018). Overall, this sheds light on the apparent lack of an effective integrated management of the protected area.

4 Discussion: Mutual Influences in Shakshouk

This part begins with discussing the mutual influences between poverty in the community and economic development in the case of Shakshouk village. Then, the mutual influences between poverty- environment and environment-development are plotted respectively.

4.1 Poverty-Development Mutual Influence

The interrelationships between community and developers could lead to win-win relationship. On the one hand, rural poor communities provide and sustain manpower for such economic development projects. Additionally, the communities could supply raw materials –shrimp peels for example– that is useful for these developers' industries. On the other hand, these developers guarantee the community monthly shares, earnings and job opportunities; or indirectly affect them by offering funds, tool, trainings, etc. to increase economic growth of their settlement. In the case of Shakshouk, salt production factories helped in the schools and houses renovation, in addition to, the agricultural lands' soil and water improvement. Such actions helped the community minimize their poverty to a certain level; in terms of satisfying some of their basic needs.

However, the poor community-developers' relationship is not always smooth. Many stories during field work and secondary data reveal tensions between them. This happens sometimes because of disputes on developers' land pieces left unclean polluting the environment where people live, or affecting the soil which they use. Other times, the factories themselves throw sewage and impurities that negatively affects Lake Qaroun's water quality which in return affects people's natural resource base. As a way to face these disputes, poor people protest, manipulate, libel or spread rumors on these development agencies among the town affecting negatively their businesses. Since these investors have a big authority on the place's economy and the upper hand in many decisions, communities suffer from a lack of freedom of expression as a projection of rural poverty (Youssef 2018) (see Fig. 5).

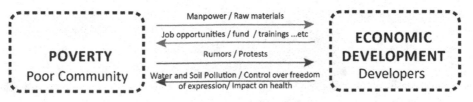

Fig. 5. A diagram summarizing the mutual influence key points between Poverty and Economic-Development. Source: Authors

4.2 Poverty-Environment Mutual Influence

As previously mentioned, the environment guarantees a good base for poor livelihoods, by providing the ecosystem services such as fisheries, water, birds, landscape aesthetics, on which they depend. In this regard, conservationists' efforts in protecting these resources doesn't benefit only the national or global communities; but has – definitely- a positive impact on local people nearby. Nevertheless, conservation actions, or policies could worsen local poverty when excluding people from the resources, and when finding that reducing people poverty is outside of conservationists' core business.

In the case of Shakshouk, before the fish death crisis, pro-environment agencies; such as GAFRD, Shakshouk NGO, had several tensions with the fishermen after catching them over exploiting the fish resources by using nets with tiny holes harvesting fish fry before reproduction. Several campaigns were organized by the NCS with cooperation of Shakshouk NGO refusing this action that threatens the environment. Accordingly, to face this challenge of over-exploitation, some fishermen accepted the regulations in protecting their environment while others refused to listen to this moral and social pressure. Furthermore, it is worth to highlight the recent efforts of NCS who cooperated with the NGO to minimize people's local poverty by providing other opportunities, such as handicrafts, pottery, etc. to take away pressures on the environment. This shows that initiatives from conservation agencies in Shakshouk have some impacts on the community poverty, despite being small scale.

Another tension exists on ground when people do not respect the rules and regulations prohibiting from hunting migratory birds. This situation is aggravated when hunters arrange to come up with manmade lakes or fish farms to attract these migratory birds far from the protectorate boundaries to hunt and sell them to interested external parties. This highlights questions on the management effectiveness of conservationists outside the protectorate's boundaries. Moreover, fish farmers' unwatched behaviors threaten the population of birds and could lead to their mass death.

Moreover, rural communities which have no sanitation systems and throw their wastes and sewage in lake Qaroun severely affect the water quality of the lake by polluting it and changing its quality. Additionally, human behavior during the agriculture process and the usage of pesticides and fertilizers has a negative impact on the soil salinity as well as on the water quality. This provides the perfect environment for parasites reproduction threatening the resource base of fishing, and affects the long term benefits of the environment itself. Once the ecosystem is negatively affected, it jeopardizes the community the other way around making vicious circle of impacts. In this regard, people themselves leave the place and migrate, leaving their families behind searching for non-polluted environments to practice their jobs (see Fig. 6).

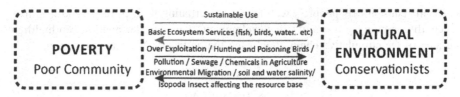

Fig. 6. A diagram summarizing the mutual influence key points between Poverty and Environment. Source: Authors

4.3 Environment-Development Mutual Influence

Being the source of water, fishes, birds, salts, and shrimps, the environment offers the developers the incentive to develop their economies. Moreover, the aesthetical value of the place motivates the tourism industry. Similarly, the economic development itself affects positively the environment; this exists in Shakshouk when salt production industries minimize the salinity level of the lake balancing the salinity load of agricultural drainage. Furthermore, shrimp based industries minimized the village canals' pollution by making use of these wastes. However, the relationship between the environment and economic development is not always a win-win situation. The development projects sometimes break the rules and throw their wastes and sewage in the lake affecting its biodiversity. Moreover, the location of large scale factories and extension of tourist resorts on the lake's shores influence the fish production, vegetation, and birds' habitats of the place. This negative influence on the environment obviously affects the on-going economic development; since polluting the environment affects the quality of tourism, agriculture and shrimp-based industries (see Fig. 7).

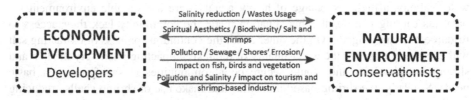

Fig. 7. A diagram summarizing the mutual influence key points between Economic Development and Environment. Source: Authors

5 Results and Conclusion

5.1 Results: The Circular Relationship in Shakshouk

The review of Shakshouk village portraits some relationships between community poverty, environmental conditions, and economic development. This could be observed when both the people and the development affect/are affected by the environment;

which in return affects people's well-being exacerbating their poverty, and negatively affects the on-going process of this development. This circular relationship highlights the idea of the cumulative chain effect each theme has on the others (see Fig. 8).

Fig. 8. A diagram illustrating the circular relationship between the environmental conditions, community poverty, and the economic development. Source: Authors

This section connects the three to establish the dynamic circular relationships among them. For example, poor access to sanitation leave the community with no other option except throwing their sewage in the lake without treatment. This has affected the water quality, increased its salinity, and polluted the environment; which in return threatened tourism and shrimp-based industry affecting the quality of product they deliver. Moreover, the extensive usage of chemicals in the agriculture process by the poor community, in addition to the industrial sewage by developers worsened the environmental conditions of soil and water. A high degree of pollution, an increase in water salinity, a high percentage of heavy metals were the suitable environment for parasites causing fish death. This situation made the community lack their access to resource base and migrate. On the other hand, the continuous process of extracting salt will eventually improve the water quality of the lake; impacting positively the fish and shrimps' productivity and would secure poor communities in satisfying their basic needs. Similarly, the shrimp-based industries that make use of shrimp shells –reducing canals pollution- affects generally the context of the village which would lead to better health conditions if magnified (see Fig. 9). This circular relationship draws a special attention to a continuous loop of strong impacts endlessly affecting each other.

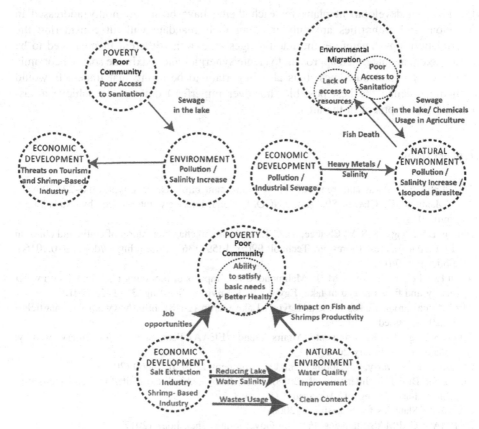

Fig. 9. Examples for the possible interrelationships forming the circular relationship among Poverty, environment and Economic development.

5.2   Conclusion

The purpose of this study is to explore the dynamics of development of poor communities within protected areas, with particular focus on the interrelationships among the community poverty, the natural environment and economic development. These three themes are mutually interlinked affecting and being affected by each other and the circular relationship is generally complex and context specific. Based on the empirical study of the case of Shakshouk village that is part of Qaroun Protectorate, the current conditions of the village could be understood in the light of negative social, environmental and economic forces that have exerted pressure over a prolonged time period as well as the reinforced loop of negative interrelationships among these forces. Within this understanding, conserving the natural environment of Shakshouk is important to the alleviation of long-term poverty; and the on-going process of development.

This research throws light on the gravity of dealing in sectorial manner neglecting the interrelationships between the different themes. This could be explained in light of the fact that development plans for each theme have been commonly addressed in isolation; and authorities are only minding their mandate without considering the interrelationships. Therefore, the interlinkages among the different themes need to be addressed in an integrated approach, to create synergies and maximize social, economic and environmental outcomes. It is also important to be aware that trade-offs would sometimes define the best possible (however imperfect) outcome to achieve a sustainable development in the area.

References

AbdelLatib, W.: Status and trends of selected important bird areas in Egypt, pp.0–22 (2009)

AbdelMaaboud, E.: CEO of Shakshouk NGO, Personal Interview, Interviewed by: Nada Samir, April 2018

Abdou, E.S., Nagy, K.S.A., Elsabee, M.Z.: Extraction and characterization of chitin and chitosan from local sources. Bioresour. Technol. **99**(5), 1359–1367 (2008). https://doi.org/10.1016/j. biortech.2007.01.051

Abou El-Gheit, E.N., Abdo, M.H., Mahmoud, S.A.: Impacts of blooming phenomenon on water quality and fishes in Qarun lake, Egypt. Int. J. Environ. Sci. Eng. **3**, 11–23 (2012)

Afrol: Local group makes mark at Egypt's Lake Qarun (2018). http://www.afrol.com/articles/34229. Accessed 6 Oct 2018

Allam, K., Egyptian Environmental Affairs Agency (EEAA): Personal Interview, Interviewed by: Nada Samir, February 2018

Barbier, E.B.: Poverty, development, and environment **15**(6), 635–660 (2010)

Bird Life: Bird Life International (2018). http://datazone.birdlife.org/site/factsheet/lake-qarun-protected-area-iba-egypt. Accessed 3 Oct 2018

CAPMAS: Statistics for Shakshouk (2006)

CAPMAS: CAPMAS Statistics, Fayoum Governorate, Shakshouk (2017)

Carey, C., Dudley, N., Stolton, S.: Squandering paradise? The importance and vulnerability of the World's protected areas, pp. 1–232. WWF-World Wide Fund for Nature (2000)

DFID et al.: Linking Poverty Reduction and Environmental Management: Policy Challenges and Opportunities (2002)

Dudley, N., et al.: Safety net: protected areas and poverty reduction (2008)

EEAA/NCS: Protected Areas of Egypt : Towards the Future', Development, p. 58 (2006)

EEAA/NCS: Qaroun Protected Area Management Plan (2007)

EEAA: Highlighted Environmental Action Plan Fayoum Governorate (2008)

El-shabrawy, G.M., Dumont, H.J.: The Fayum Depression and Its Lakes, The Nile: Origin, Environments, Limnology and Human Use (2009). https://doi.org/10.1007/978-1-4020-9726-3_6

El-Serafy, S.S., et al.: Qarun Lake fisheries?: fishing gears, species composition and catch per unit effort. Egypt. J. Aquat. Biol. Fish. **18**(2), 39–49 (2014). https://doi.org/10.12816/0011075

EMISAL: The Egyptian Salts and Minerals Company in Fayoum (2018). www.emisalsalts.com

Fisher, R.J., et al.: Poverty and Conservation: Landscapes, People and Power. International Union for Conservation of Nature and Natural Resources (IUCN), Gland, Switzerland and Cambridge (2005)

GAFRD: General Authority for Fish Resources Development - Ministry of Agriculture (2016). http://www.gafrd.org. Accessed 1 Oct 2018

GAFRD: General Authority for Fish Resources Development Fact Sheet (2018). www.gafrd.org. Accessed 3 Oct. 2018

GOPP: Master Plan for Shakshouk Village (2006)

Hassan, R.M.A.: Ecosystem restoration using maintenance dredging in Lake Qarun, Egypt. J. Am. Sci. **11**(12), 55–65 (2015). http://www.jofamericanscience.org

Heiba, A.: Evaluation of Social Development Programmes in Qaroun Protectorate. Ain Shams University (2012)

Heiba, A.: Social and physical problems that hinder tourism in Qaroun reserve. A comparative Study for variety of patterns. Faculty of Tourism and Hotels - Fayoum University (2016)

Heiba, A.: Director of Qaroun Protected Area, Personal Interview, Interviewed by Nada Samir, April 2018

Howarth, R.B.: Sustainability, Well-Being, and Economic Growth, pp. 32–39 (1972)

Hussein, H., et al.: Pollution monitoring for Lake Qarun. Adv. Environ. Biol. **2**(2), 70–80 (2008). https://doi.org/10.1046/j.1439-0426.2003.00456.x

Mahdaly, A.A.: CEO of Shakshouk Local Authority, Personal Interview, Interviewed by Nada Samir, April 2018

Ministry of Environment: Egyptian Biodiversity Strategy and Action Plan, 2015–2030 (2016)

NCS/EEAA: The State of Qaroun Protected Area: An Evaluation of Management Effectiveness, Cairo (2007)

Ramadan, S.: Chief of Fishermen, Personal Interview, Interviewed by Nada Samir, April 2018

RAMSAR: RAMSAR Egyptian Sites (2012). https://www.ramsar.org/countries/egypt?page=4. Accessed 6 Oct 2018

Rosendo, S., Brown, K.: The limits to integration : critical issues in integrated conservation. In: The Commons in an Age of Global Transition: Challenges, Risks and Opportunities, the Tenth Biennial Conference of the International Association for the Study of Common Property, pp. 1–28 (2004). https://dlc.dlib.indiana.edu/dlc/bitstream/handle/10535/482/Rosendo_Limits_040823_Paper207.pdf?sequence=1%5Cn%5Ct

Shahid, S.A., Abdelfattah, M.A., Taha, F.K.: Developments in Soil Salinity Assessment and Reclamation: Innovative Thinking and Use of Marginal Soil and Water Resources in Irrigated Agriculture, pp. 1–808. Springer, Heidelberg (2013). https://doi.org/10.1007/978-94-007-5684-7

State Information Service: Map of Egypt (2004)

UNESCO: Poverty, environment and development: studies of four countries in the Asia Pacific Region. UNESCO Principal Regional Office for Asia and the Pacific. Regional Unit for Social and Human Sciences in Asia and the Pacific (2001)

USAID: Issues in Poverty Reduction and Natural Resource Management, October 2006

Youssef, S.: Chief Marketing Officer, Personal Interview, Interviewed by Nada Samir, September 2018

The Community Participation in the Design Process of Livable Streets

Nourhan Ahmed$^{(\boxtimes)}$, Abeer Elshater⦿, and Samy Afifi

Ain Shams University, Cairo 11517, Egypt
nourhan.ahmed.fathy@gmail.com,
{abeer.elshater,samy.afifi}@eng.asu.edu.eg

Abstract. Urban streets in some countries of global south have been struggling for decades and have several problems. Much money is spent on roads construction and maintenance yearly with no significant interest to create places for public life that is different from a city/place to another. This paper addresses the pressing need to review the principles raised by the Western literature of streets design to help to reach livability in Cairo, Egypt through the community participation rather than building a road for movement and daily commutes. The community participation provides action plans that suit the local context. The current work extends to analysis cases from different cities. The research aims to provide a design toolkit for streets to have public places attached. These places can foster the social interaction, active living and community identity. The present paper offers a descriptive and analytical contribution. Inviting the community in the open-ended questionnaire and semi-structured interview provides a level of details in public realm that highlights the need not only to put the road environment on the level of strategic thinking and policy development as an essential element in towns and cities but also community participation at the design level. The concluded remarks provide room for creating streets in Cairo as more than inter-joined connections that serve car mobility and access. The contribution can make better streets as public spaces to live rather than to commute from point to another.

Keywords: Urban streets design · Community participation · Streets for people initiatives

1 Introduction

Previously, streets have played a critical role in shaping the life of the community. Streets have contributed in defining the cultural, social, economic and political functions of cities. They are the first remarkable and distinctive thing that marks the character of a place, from a chaotic and unplanned settlement to a well-established town or city. In Egyptian cities, especially Cairo, the design of street becomes more abnormal patterns and are followed by the urban sprawl with losing their design principles/criteria which were mostly designed on a livability basis. Before the automobile era, streets often served as the lifeblood of neighborhoods, intermingling together the urban life and places that shape up a community. Today, streets are more

G. Bassioni et al. (Eds.): InterSol 2019, LNICST 296, pp. 144–157, 2019.
https://doi.org/10.1007/978-3-030-34863-2_13

commonly considered barriers between a city's residents. Streets often confine people to their private space or a narrow sidewalk along the fringe. As a result, residential streets can be dangerous and uninviting places due to the threat of speeding traffic. This match to what J. Jacobs mentioned about the streets as being "... most vital organs. Think of a city and what comes to mind? Its streets. If a city's streets look interesting, the city looks interesting; if they look dull, the city looks dull" (Jacobes 1961, p. 37; The World Bank 1994). Recently in Cairo, streets are being planned, designed and implemented without even asking the community about its needs or even involving community in any phase of designing their own streets, which led to streets that does not represent the needs of the community.

The objectives of this paper are to refer to the lack of community participation in designing process as a major problem when it comes to streets, also its importance in many ways and to evaluate case studies which were affected by community participation and local initiatives to help solving their problems and achieve their needs. This paper is organized in three parts; the first discusses the research motivation and reason for selecting the settings. The second part handles the design process of streets as an urban space which had been discussed in literature. The third part discusses the cases that are similar to the cases of the Egyptian context which reach the outcomes that determine the pros and cons of local initiatives.

1.1   On Concepts

There's a difference between roads and streets; roads are being for motor vehicles in the first place, although it's recognized that it should serve a dual purpose (United Nations Human Settlements Program 2013). Furthermore, streets are being for people as a priority. Streets should work as the main element of the community as it represents more than 80% of the public space, so, it must be a place for people to work and socialize (Christ 2009; Elshater and Ibrahim 2014). When streets as a public space do not achieve the main purpose of their existence, problems happen such as chaos, traffic jam, pollution everywhere, citizens and users not having a suitable place to meet and do their daily activities such as communicate with each other, walking, safely crossing, cycling and playing...., etc. (ELshater 2014). In so doing, reports have commented on the community itself may be involved not only in making decisions, but also in participating by every means to make streets a place for them so that they would feel a sense of pride and ownership (UCLA 2011; National Association of City Transportation Officials 2013; Elshater 2013).

Community participation – to include people in street design and appraising – is a new approach which needed to be adopted to reach new attitudes as they have a certain vision for their streets which fulfils their needs. Community means any stakeholder parties in particular street residents, businesses owners and pedestrians...., etc. The current paper groups the taxonomy of people into two categories. Figure 1 shows the producers of street environment and the users of street environments.

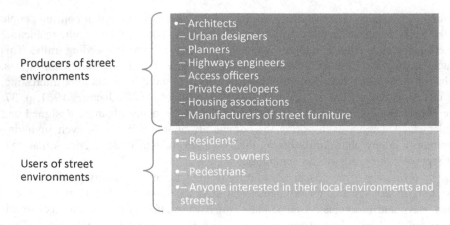

Fig. 1. The taxonomy of people that contact/affect the urban corridors. Source: the authors

1.2   What Is Meant By Community Participation? and Why Is It Important?

The World Bank (1994) defines participation as "a process through which stakeholders' influence and share control over development initiatives, and the decisions and resources which affect them". Community participation can be defined as the involvement of people in community projects to solve their problems and fulfil their needs. People cannot be forced to 'participate' in projects which affect their lives but should be given the opportunity where possible. This opportunity is held to be a fundamental human right and a fundamental principle of democracy. It can have many forms such as expressing their opinions about desirable improvements, formulating objectives, criticizing plans and evaluating the work done, participating in training activities, they can even implement in small initiatives.

Local governments use design manuals which suit their conditions in designing urban streets. All this so that community can use urban streets efficiently and vice versa, effective community engagement can improve the success rates of policies and projects affecting the built environment because it helps the agencies and organizations leading a project understand and respond to local conditions. Agencies that create true community engagement are more successful at adapting to socioeconomic changes that may influence the effort than those that do not conduct effective outreach (Cogan and Faust 2010). When people affected by a project are involved from the beginning of the planning process, the likelihood of unexpected or significant opposition when it comes time to implement the project is reduced (Kimley 2012).

Community members also have unique knowledge of local contexts, including political, cultural, and geographic settings. Effective community engagement also has the power to build social capital—the social systems and communications that encourage support and interchange between residents (Leyden 2003). A community with a high level of social capital is characterized by a culture of neighbors knowing each other, interest and participation in local politics, high rates of volunteerism, and diversity in social connections. These characteristics foster a sense of community, engender trust, enhance innovative problem solving, and increase the likelihood that stakeholders will support financial investments in community projects (Burton and Mitchell 2006).

There are so many benefits that would return on the community through community participation on many sides as mentioned before one of them is community health. Long-term health improvements can be achieved by a group of people, when people become involved in the city and act collectively to make a change (Hanson 1988).

Federal workshops should involve people in the planning method that sets the city on a track via increasing strength of the local community. Active community outreach helps to address unlike passage to better development, including issues such as active living. Through successful community outreach, people of all ages, backgrounds, and social standing can contribute to projects that support the ability to live their life in good environment achieving a healthier environment, well-being, social and economic activities along with many other advantages. They also can help project leaders better understand how social, cultural, and economic barriers that impact historically disadvantaged communities are relevant to include the community in streets planning and design process.

2   Literature Review: Streets Design Process and Public Participation

There is no clear process for street design in urban design field, but there is a design process in general that could be used in designing urban streets as public spaces for people. The design processes used in many countries and cities are similar to these processes discussed in the next figures. General design process in urban design according to (Moughtin 2003), Sir Patrick Geddes' planning method was just a survey, analysis and then a plan, but this process needed to be cyclical having intermediate loops (Figs. 2 and 3).

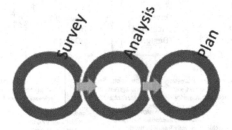

Fig. 2. Design process advocated by planners at first

Design methods advocated by architects are similar in nature to those prepared by planners. The RIBA practice and management handbook (Ostime 2013) divides the design process into four phases:

- Phase 1 Assimilation: The accumulation of general information and information specially related to the problem.
- Phase 2 General study: The investigation of the nature of the problem: the investigation of possible solutions.
- Phase 3 Development: The development of one or more solutions.
- Phase 4 Communication: The communication of chosen solution/s to the client. In this phase designers include clients in the process, but this phase was in the architecture design process not in the planning or urban design process. Street design process needed to have this value, to be able to include the community in the process.

Thomas Markus and Thomas Mayer take the description of design method a little further.

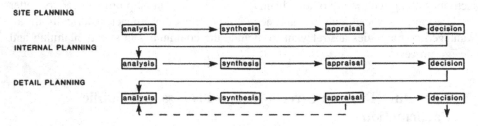

Fig. 3. Architectural method by Thomas Markus and Thomas Mayer

Urban street design process held out in Arabic city of similar conditions to Cairo Abu Dhabi, United Arabs Emirates with no interference from the community in any phase (Fig. 4).

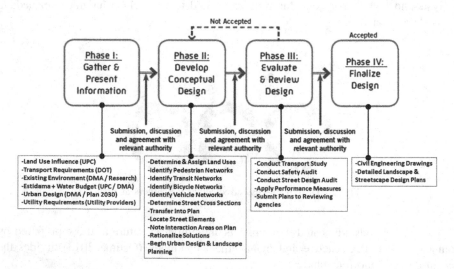

Fig. 4. Urban street design process in Abu Dhabi UAE (Source: Abu Dhabi Urban Street Design Manual, n.d.)

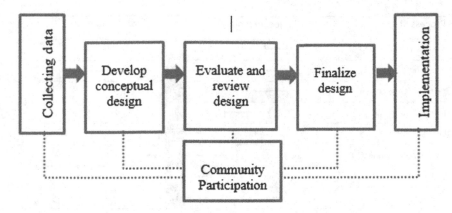

Fig. 5. Integrated design process. Source: the authors

Community participation should be included in each phase in the design process, in developing conceptual design showing their hopes, needs and aspirations. In evaluating the design after it is made by the experts and then to accept it after it finally done and been operated. Community members can even start proposing the projects they see that their community needs to be a better place or sharing initiatives even if it was on a small scale.

Both disciplines of Landscape architecture and Urban Planning and design prepare a development plan for streets in cities and towns. Much of the design and planning of the streets are done by the landscape architect and urban planners without community participation. This practice results in incompatibility of the spaces for the communities; underutilizing or abandoning the streets from pedestrian users, and worse vandalizing the properties of streets. Resulting the streets to be focused on automobiles only neglecting their main purpose.

After discussing all the previous design processes development, the relationship between urban design process and street design process that take place in many cities in the western countries. One of these street design process was discussed in Global Street Design Guide published by Island Press. (National Association of City Transportation Officials 2013) A typical process for shaping streets, while local processes vary in each context using the typical steps in the diagram below Fig. 5 to define and guide for each project before it begins. Street design is an iterative process. Processes should be flexible and relevant, evolving and adapting over time as best practices, specific challenges, and contexts change (Fig. 6).

The Global Street Design Guide is supporting practitioners to redefine the role of streets in cities around the world. Created with the input of experts from 72 cities in 42 countries, the guide offers technical details to inform street design that prioritizes pedestrians, cyclists, and transit riders. While specific processes vary by place, coordination and collaboration during each stage is fundamental, and effective communication and engagement throughout the process is critical. This process includes stakeholders and community members in the whole street design process from project planning phase till post completion phase.

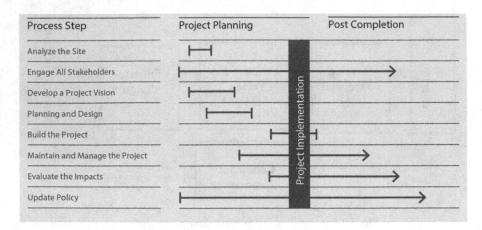

Process Step	Project Planning	Post Completion
Analyze the Site	⊢⊣	
Engage All Stakeholders	⊢————————→	
Develop a Project Vision	⊢———⊣	
Planning and Design	⊢———⊣	
Build the Project	⊢—⊣	
Maintain and Manage the Project	⊢————————→	
Evaluate the Impacts	⊢————————→	
Update Policy	⊢————————————→	

Fig. 6. Urban street design process adapted by global street design guide by NACTO (National Association of City Transportation Officials 2013)

3   Method

This study presents a review of integrating community participation in planning process carried out by non-governmental organizations. The review identified the effectiveness of approaches in dealing with public participation programs done by local governments in three countries: Germany, USA, and the UK. The strategies and approaches reviewed in those counties were compared between system practices in Cairo, Egypt. In the current work, three examples of organizations internationally have been used to illustrate the differences between initiatives of local community internationally and those done locally in Cairo.

The current research extent to collect data from questionnaire which is powered by SurveyMonkey[1]. The investigated issues include questions about the user satisfaction on street design in term of safety and initiatives that took place in the street. The sample target was in Cairo which has almost 9.153 million resident 2017 according to Cairo governate website when calculating the sample with confidence level of 80% as most researches do and margin of error 7% the sample size was 84.

3.1   International Cases

Case Study Parklet, SCHÜTZENPLATZ: Real Experiment, (Future city lab., summer 2016)

In the process, it is examined which ecological, technical and social conditions affect the experiment. In this sense, in doing this experiment for sustainable mobility culture, Stuttgart citizens are confronting challenges in urban mobility and experimenting with strategies of detachment through real experiment. The parklet is an intervention in enhancing public space, like parks and spaces parklets act as publicly

---

[1] https://www.surveymonkey.com/r/NB3HYG5.

accessible and usable spaces. However, they are subjected to the responsibility of residents or professionals. In this initiative, parklet are created using parking spaces in street to provide walk-in friendly city and living space instead of parking space for cars (Fig. 7).

Fig. 7. The first case from Germany. Source: future city lab, university of Stuttgart casas chuetzenplatz group on Facebook (Future Cities Laboratory 2016)

Invitations were sent to the neighbors to decide what to do in the future considering the experiment and it would lead to three options. The first one to break it down or to break it down in winter or the third one to stay as it is. This experiment was made by community member and developed afterwards by local community itself according to their needs and ideas which suit them.

This experiment used many forms of community participation by expressing opinions, formulating objectives, criticize plans, evaluate the work done, training activities and implementing the project themselves and they are considering the future development as well.

Case Study of Play Grounds in the Street in BRISTOL 2011, by (Ferguson 2011)
There is a project held in Bristol by Alice Ferguson one member of the society there. She has created a national organization called playing out supporting a growing UK-wide street play movement. A simple idea of closing part of a street there to through traffic for a couple of hours to give over the space for children. Kids spend time less trapped indoor and adults can make friends with neighbors. It is an easy cheap way to tackle childhood obesity and social isolation as it brought community together. Alice

campaigned to make this possible and changed the rules in Bristol. Streets apply just once, to hold regular sessions. Eight years on more than forty UK authorities use the same system. Inspired, Toronto is the latest city to pilot the scheme. This initiative proves that community participation is an effective tool to make the right changes that the community really needs.

Fig. 8. The public interaction in the second case, Source: http://playingout.net/about/what-is-playing-out/ - playing out group on Facebook

Case Study of Play Streets Program in New York
Streets are temporarily closed to traffic to create new places for play. Play Streets partners: City of New York/Health & Mental Hygiene, Transportation, Parks & Recreation, and Education; Transportation Alternatives; local schools and community-based organizations.

Program summary: Play Streets offer a low-cost way for neighborhoods and schools to create more space for active recreation. The program helps neighborhood organizations and schools identify streets that can be closed to traffic for certain periods of time, in order to create new outdoor play spaces.

Community Play Streets are sponsored by local community organizations and operate throughout the summer months. Nineteen community Play Streets were permitted in NYC during the summer of 2012 with assistance from the Health Department and partners, offering programming such as running groups, dance classes, yoga, and soccer workshops, and simple equipment like jump ropes and hula hoops for unstructured play. During the summer of 2013, the Health Department assisted fourteen community organizations with obtaining Play Street permits.

School Play Streets are designed to create active space for schools with limited or no access to a gymnasium, multi-purpose space, or outdoor recreation facilities. Many schools in the city do not have adequate space to meet the State Education Department's requirements for physical education and physical activity and a Play Street can help to address this issue. Fourteen NYC schools obtained Play Streets permits for the 2012–2013 school year, with assistance from the Health Department and partners. The active design highlights some factors such as streets are converted to temporary recreation spaces for children and families. Programming organized by local organizations builds a sense of community and encourages more vigorous physical activity.

3.2   The case of Cairo, Egypt: Local Initiatives

The previous international cases prove that initiatives made by the community are effective method to achieve their needs and it can be in many different shapes; experiment using neglected spaces or reuse spaces, closing street for children to play out in specific timing,....etc. On the other hand in Cairo, There are many local initiatives in the district of Hadaek el-Quba. The observations raised from the co-habitation indicate the need for social initiative to let citizen participate in the design process. Those initiatives came from the needs of the local residents, one of them were in Masr w El-Sodan Street when a famous landmark with the picture of the previous president Hosny Mubarak was destroyed after the 25th of January 2011 revolution and turned to a dump (Fig. 9 on the right side) as an expression of this event and then the reform campaign that went off through whole of Egypt, they start to repaint the landmark regardless of the type of repair, but they care that they need their landmark back.

Fig. 9. The landmark of Masr w El-Sodan street after the reform of the locals and Fig. 8 after the formal renovation (top). Source: by the author

Elkorba street festival initiative is an annual event that took place each spring in El-Korba, Heliopolis in Baghdad Street by the residents there since 2005. The festival features Egyptian performing artists. It represented all the celebrations events and activities such as Graphite drawings, street paintings, singing bands, meeting friends, walking dogs and pets and overall enjoying the whole day for all the Egyptian as showed in Fig. 10, but it was cancelled since 2010 for reasons of security as it was very difficult to control the whole street. After waiting seven years it has been returned but with new place and settings. This example shows how can the local community be effective and make their own activities which would attract people from all over the country not even the Korba residents.

Fig. 10. The Korba Festival. Source: Mariam Elias

4 Results and Discussion

The responses of the survey were 71. The findings from the survey come from ages that ranges from 28% less than 20's, 1.5% more than 40's and the majority was 70.5% from 20's to 30's. When asking the users who respond to the survey to describe their street in just three words. The two largest percent of keywords were 22% quiet and calm and the other are 20% crowd and noisy. The next two percentages were 13% narrow and 12% wide. There is also 14% of them saying that their street is vital, popular, friendly and livable with multiple activities. From their point of view, as for the rest of the responses were between the street is well serviced or has no services at all, clean or dirty and under construction, accessible or unreadable, safe or unsafe and some of them with low percent was that their streets are planted and green. All those descriptions refer to their perspective of the street they are living in.

As for the last question in this survey, the user's suggestions represented their needs in their local streets to hold green features, gardens, shading trees, seating areas, lighting features, to have landscape designs, pedestrian walkways rather than sidewalks, variety of activities such as kids' playgrounds, bike lanes and shading elements. They also complained about some problems that they face daily that their streets i term of being not paved or the paving is needed to be maintained regularly. In this, they added that they don't have enough parking spaces, so they park their cars on sidewalks blocking the way for pedestrian. If a street is not planned to hold too many cars parking, it would narrow it. For this case, they have complained from cleanness and not having enough garbage bins.

In some areas, people throw their garbage on street. Another problem is that those streets districts are residential streets so when it comes to pass through paths they claimed for the needs of more regulations in term of signs, bumps for reducing cars speed, pedestrian crossing points. They also, face problems with occupancies on sidewalks or on the street itself and with unsuitable activities. In their point of view, some interviewees saw that there are some unsuitable activities of food shops that need to be relocated or organized others saw that they need kiosks and shops as a nearby services. For the surrounding architectural style, some responses indicated an implicit hope not to destruct old buildings and villas and to regulate building heights.

Chart (Fig. 11) shows the daily activities that the user can do such as walking across streets and jog as a majority (48.5%). The rest were distributed between gardens, playing in the street, siting in their front yard or/and biking. There is also large percent of 42.5% had troubles with parking. Chart (Fig. 12) shows the initiatives of the local community when asking the users whether there are initiatives or not. On one side, the majority with the percent was almost 72% who said, 'no there are not any.' On the other side, 18% of them said that there are some but not as much and the rest 10% said there are many initiatives on their streets.

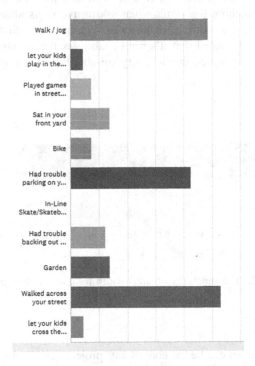

Fig. 11. The normal street activities

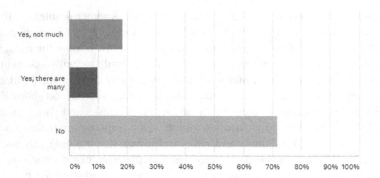

Fig. 12. The local community initiatives

It worth mentioning that the residential streets in the Egyptian context has many local initiatives according to its users' needs. One of these initiatives were when some of the home residents were throwing their waste on the street, the community decide to participate to solve the problem by clearing all the area from the waste and redesigned it to be a zone where they can set and chat or even look for their around merchandize. These notes were matching the result when asking the users about the suitability of their streets in form of the width the majority of 45% answered that it's just right. The next percentage of 38% stated that it's not suitable for the activities that are held in it as for the rest they answered that it's very suitable for them (Fig. 13).

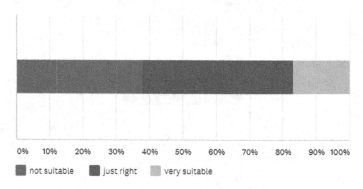

Fig. 13. The suitability of street width for community activities

5 Conclusion

Community participation can be the core of any project that is subjected in each phase of design process till the implementation and the evaluation afterwards. The local community initiatives when they plan and organize the scheme, the design could lead to many benefits. The main benefits are as mentioned before. It can grantee the continuity of any initiative as it has its own engine of local stakeholders that have specific needs, man   power, having   the sense of   ownership   and continuous feedback.

All those factors could lead to the success of any initiative, but sometimes when the local community lack the proper experience or just not organized, it can have some of these factors. Otherwise, not all of them, the citizen would need the help by formal organizations or even the government to achieve those initiatives. In conclusion to reach livable streets, there are some criteria that should be achieved to fulfill the needs of the residents and the users of the street in general and who knows those needs better than the users themselves, when including them in the process it would lead to livable streets.

References

Abu Dhabi Urban Street Design Manual. Abu Dhabi urban planning council UPC, Abu Dhabi (n.d.)

Burton, E., Mitchell, L.: Inclusive Urban Design Streets for Life. Architectural Press, Oxford (2006)

Christ, W.: Access for All: Approaches to the Built Environment. Bsirkhauser Verlag AG, Berlin (2009)

Cogan, E., Faust, S.: Innovative civic engagement tools and practices. In: Land Use Decision-Making (2010)

Elshater, A.: Towards a refined new concept of new urbanism in Egypt. Asian J. Environ.-Behav. Stud. (ajE-Bs) 3(8), 205–220 (2018)

ELshater, A.: Tactical urbanism: a method of community empowerment in Cairo neighborhoods. In: World Sustainable Buildings WSB14. Local Partnerships for Greener Cities and Regions, Barcelona, pp. 28–38 (2014)

Elshater, A., Ibrahim, F.: From typology concept to smart transportation hub. Quality of Life in the Built & Natural Environment, January 2014

Ferguson, A.: Play grounds in the street in Bristol. Playing Out National Organization, Bristol (2011)

Future city lab (summer, 2016 Parklet schutzen platz University of Stuttgart, Stuttgart)

Future Cities Laboratory, Live Project in University of Stuttgart casaschuetzenplatz group on Facebook (2016). https://www.facebook.com/futurecitieslaboratory/. Accessed Dec 2017

Hanson, P.: Citizen involvement in community health promotion: the role application of CDC's PATCH model. Int. Q. Community Health Educ. 9(3), 177–186 (1988)

Jacobes, J.: The Death and Life of Great American Cities. Vitage Books Edition, New York (1961)

Kimley, H.: Broward Complete Streets Guidelines (2012)

Leyden, K.: Social capital and the built environment: the importance of walkable neighborhoods. Am. J. Public Health 93, 1546–1551 (2003)

Moughtin, C.: Urban Design: Street and Square, 3rd edn. Architectural Press, London (2003)

National Association of City Transportation Officials: Urban Street Guide. Island Press (2013)

Ostime, N.: Handbook of Practice Management, 9th edn. RIBA Publishing, London (2013)

The World Bank: The World Bank Annual Report 1994. The World Bank (1994)

UCLA: Luskin School of Public Affairs. Model for Design Manual, Los Angeles (2011)

United Nations Human Settlements Program. Streets as Public Spaces and Drivers of Urban Prosperity. United Nations Human Settlements Program, Nairobi (2013)

A Smart Computing Framework Centered on User and Societal Empowerment to Achieve the Sustainable Development Goals

Athula Ginige[1], Bahman Javadi[1], Rodrigo N. Calheiros[1(✉)], and Sheryl L. Hendriks[2]

[1] School of Computing, Engineering and Mathematics,
Western Sydney University, Sydney, Australia
{a.ginige,b.javadi,r.calheiros}@westernsydney.edu.au
[2] Department of Agricultural Economics, Extension and Rural Development,
University of Pretoria, Pretoria, South Africa
Sheryl.Hendriks@up.ac.za

Abstract. The United Nations has developed 17 Sustainable Development Goals (SDGs) to transform our world. Smart Computing aims to combine advances in Information and Communication Technologies including Internet of Things, cloud computing, mobile computing and social computing to create smart systems to make human life better. Smart Computing is providing a new approach to address many of the complex and challenging problems and is a valuable tool to support progress towards many SDGs. The lack of a suitable framework to handle the complex multi-disciplinary nature of these applications is hindering sustainable development. Based on a series of solutions we have developed for agriculture domain to address the first three SDGs (i.e., No Poverty, Zero Hunger, and Good Health and Wellbeing), we proposed a smart computing framework centered on user and societal empowerment. This framework consists of six dimensions: Economics, Domain Knowledge, Interaction Design, User Interface Design, User Empowerment and Societal Empowerment. As a way of validation, we adopted this framework to design a mobile-based information system to address "Hidden Hunger" in African countries and carried out a preliminary evaluation. Having the framework to guide our thinking and designing of the solution helped us to frame a holistic solution centered on user and societal empowerment. The proposed framework can be adopted to develop effective and innovative solutions to address many SDGs.

Keywords: Smart Computing · User and societal empowerment · Nutrition · Food security · Sustainable Development Goals

1 Introduction

The world is facing several grand challenges and pressing problems. In order to address these challenges and improve the lives of people, countries around the world now have agreed that sustainable development is the best pathway to promote economic

G. Bassioni et al. (Eds.): InterSol 2019, LNICST 296, pp. 158–172, 2019.
https://doi.org/10.1007/978-3-030-34863-2_14

opportunity, better social wellbeing, and protection of environment. This motivated the United Nations to formulate 17 global goals - the Sustainable Development Goals (SDGs), which are aimed to transform the world we live in by 2030.

Smart Computing is an effective method to integrate the capabilities of computer hardware, software, social media and communication networks together with digital sensors, smart devices, Internet of Things (IoT), big data analytics, computational intelligence and intelligent systems to realize various innovative applications [1]. Smart Computing is a multi-disciplinary domain and can be broadly classified into two major areas: how to design and build smart computing systems and how to use computing technology to design smart solutions to make human life better. Smart Computing can be used to provide new solutions to many challenges faced by humanity and address many SDGs.

In order to achieve the SDGs, development programs need to reach billions of people across different continents irrespective of any country's development status. This is a very complex challenge. The lack of a suitable framework to handle the complex multi-disciplinary nature of these applications hinders finding effective and long-term solutions to these issues. What we see today is a very large number of "apps" providing point solutions to various human needs rather than offering an integrated system to solve a complex human problem.

This paper presents an approach to utilize Smart Computing to develop a multi-disciplinary solution to a complex problem using Systems Engineering approach to make human life better. The approach is based on a series of solutions we have developed for the agriculture domain to address the first three SDGs (i.e., No Poverty, Zero Hunger, and Good Health and Wellbeing). It consists of a smart computing framework centered on user and societal empowerment. This framework combines six dimensions, namely Economics, Domain Knowledge, Interaction Design, User Interface Design, User Empowerment, and Societal Empowerment, to formulate a solution.

The proposed framework has been used in the design of a mobile-based information system to address "Hidden Hunger" in African countries. Hidden Hunger is a form of malnutrition arising from diets that, although generally adequate in energy, are inadequate in terms of micronutrients, leading to micronutrient deficiencies [2]. Having the framework to guide our thinking and the design helped us to develop a holistic solution centered on user and societal empowerment. An initial evaluation with domain experts and end-users demonstrated the potential of both the framework and the resulting mobile artefact to address such pressing societal issues.

In summary, the contributions of this paper are twofold. It proposes a framework that enables us to combine six dimensions centered on user and societal empowerment to develop solutions to large-scale and complex humanitarian challenges. It also presents a real case study in the use of the framework to tackle hidden hunger in African countries, from the inception of the system to the end-user evaluation.

This paper is organized as follows: Sect. 2 discusses related work. The proposed framework is presented in Sect. 3. Adoption of the framework for a case study and its evaluation are explained in Sects. 4 and 5, respectively. The conclusions and future research direction are presented in Sect. 6.

2   Related Work

Information and communication technologies (ICTs) have been identified as a valuable tool to tackle problems related to SDGs. In the context of this work, a number of frameworks have been developed that utilize different technologies in agriculture. AgriSuit [3] is a framework for assessment of the suitability of lands for agriculture in Ethiopia. In AgriSuit, data is obtained from satellite data and public data sources and computed in a backend. End-users access the system via a GUI optimized for access via desktops.

Yan-e [4] discusses the design of an agriculture management system based on Internet of Things (IoT). The system is organized around three key functionalities: data collection, data transmission, and data analysis. Input data is generated by a number of sensors spread around a large area. The system not only collects environmental data, but also collects data about the state of crops that are stored after harvesting processing occurs in the cloud. End-users access data via mobile phones, however there is no discussion whether the system has been deployed or tested in the field.

Agri-IoT [5] is an IoT-based semantic framework for e-farming. It focuses in the capability of aggregating streams of data from different sources. Its backend comprises capabilities for real-time data analytics and reasoning. Sources of data comprises not only traditional environmental sensors and public data sources, but also cameras and drones. Output from the system include dashboards and mobile apps. There is no discussion available about deployment of the solution in production environments.

The aforementioned approaches are focused on the technological aspects of the problem with limited consideration for the end-users of such systems. So, it is difficult to evaluate the effectiveness of the approaches and the value brought for these technologies. In fact, most approaches do not consider the end-user's perspective in the design stage. Our approach considers the full spectrum from underlying technology to end-users, and takes into consideration how different agents and actors are affected by the technology and how this information can be fed back to the system to enable change behavior. Without such consideration, there is a risk of failure during the adoption of platforms. Hoppen et al. [6] report on how failure in "buying-in" end-users and key stakeholders may lead to failures in project adoption. The work of Hoppen et al. [6] is particularly relevant because it reports on a framework targeting agriculture in an in-development country, as the approaches discussed so far.

Still in the topic of the importance of community involvement to enable success of ICT-based approaches for agriculture, Janssen et al. [7] presents the requirements for next generation application modeling in agriculture, covering not only technical but also organizational aspects (as in then different stakeholders that need to be involved for successful projects) and the knowledge and wisdom informing the project. Although the work by Jenssen et al. focuses on agricultural applications, our approach is intended to be of general applications within SDGs.

Approaches that actually consider the end-user perspective usually target specific goals. Ag-Analytics [8] is a platform for the acquisition, storage, and analysis of data for end-user researchers in the area of agricultural finance and environmental sciences. Omolayo [9] lists 10 different apps targeting issues related to agriculture in Africa.

Each of these apps targets a specific aspect (such as dairy management, detection of diseases in cattle, marketplace, advise, and others), and were developed by private companies. Because most of these projects are business products, no information is available about the conceptual frameworks (if any) that drove the design and development of the apps. The exception to the above is the EZ-farm app developed by IBM Research [10]. EZ-farm utilizes IoT to help farmers to monitor soil moisture levels and thus manage water resources. The system was deployed in Kenya.

Our framework addresses general aspects related to the management of agricultural data, geolocation, and users to enable a number of different applications, having as objective community and social empowerment with members of the communities affected by the system as the system's end-users. The feasibility of the approach has been demonstrated in a previous project [11] where a Digital Knowledge Ecosystem has been deployed in Sri Lanka to empower farmers to make more economically viable decisions about what, where, and when to plant so duplication of crops is avoided, yielding greater benefits for all the farmers that utilize the system.

Finally, it is worth mentioning that similar frameworks were also proposed for different domains. Vlacheas et al. [12] discuss a framework based on cognitive management and IoT enabling Smart Cities. Bellagente et al. [13] developed a framework for energy management in smart buildings, applied on a University campus. Lu and Cecil [14] applied IoT to enhance productivity in smart manufacturing. These approaches can also benefit from the holistic perspective enabled by our work, although a level of customization would be necessary to tackle domain-specific requirements, objectives, and user needs and expectations.

3 The Proposed Framework

We used the insights gained from developing the mobile-based information system for farmers in Sri Lanka and India [11, 15, 16] to create a generalized framework to effectively use Smart Computing to propose a multi-disciplinary solution to address SDGs targets.

Such insights have shown us the observed problems are only symptoms of a deeper problem; the root cause being coordination failure at multiple levels over a period of time compounding the problem [17]. This coordination failure is due to relevant people or domain stakeholders not having the right information at the right time to make informed decisions. This has created information asymmetry allowing people with information to create profitable operations while disempowering the others.

There have been many attempts to enhance the flow of information using mass media, radio, television, face to face workshops, call centers etc. But a solution that can reach the masses has not been found. The rapid growth of mobile devices among the affected masses now provides a personalized channel to communicate information. Even though many mobile-based applications have been developed for the agriculture domain, none of these applications has been widely adopted. Analysis of such applications revealed that these applications are providing information targeting one or few symptoms in a generic manner, but not a holistic solution addressing the root cause [18].

Using Smart Computing, we can develop artefacts, especially mobile-based information systems, to enhance the flow of information in a domain. Information from sensors, both fixed and embedded in mobile devices such as GPS, can be used to identify some aspects of the context to provide personalized information addressing shortcomings in some of the earlier mobile applications providing generic information. Yet, if these applications fail to empower users and society, then they will not be adopted at large. Finally, solutions that are economical and sustainable will grow while the rest will die over time [19].

To develop a holistic sustainable solution, we need to consider it from multiple dimensions drawing on expertise from multiple discipline areas. The lack of a suitable framework to manage such complexities has hindered the development of sustainable solutions to large-scale challenges and pressing problems we face today. The ability to explore the solution from multiple dimensions and being able to integrate the insights from each dimensions to a holistic solution addresses this drawback. We have identified these dimensions to be Economics, Domain Knowledge, Interaction Design, User Interface Design, User Empowerment, and Societal Empowerment, as depicted in Fig. 1.

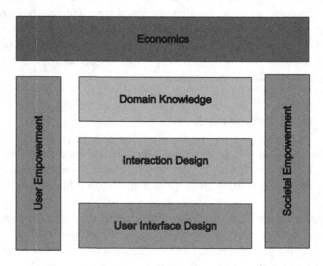

Fig. 1. The proposed framework with six dimensions

Economics: In this dimension, a root cause analysis is done to identify the fundamental problem that gives rise to the visible symptoms. Moreover, a conceptual solution should be devised to address the given problem, which will be based on user and societal empowerment. Solutions to any large complex problem fall beyond an individual and need a community approach. The community will organize themselves into horizontal and vertical value creation networks. In these networks, information, material and finances need to flow. To achieve the optimum flow there need to be coordination at multiple levels. This requires people having access to the right information at the right time to make the right decisions. The decisions should lead to optimal matching of wants and needs with the minimum search cost to achieve the best possible solution.

Issues with the flow of information affect the economic sphere. Initially, these problems can surface as health, production, nutrition, social problems, etc. All these problems have a value associated with not acting or acting on them. This governs whether the investments required to fix the problem will happen or not happen.

Thus, an analysis of the problem from an economic dimension will help in the identification of the root cause as well as conditions that need to be satisfied to address the root cause.

User Empowerment: For a solution to succeed, users need to adopt it at scale. This requires sustained user behavior change. Empowerment Theory [20–22] shows that to bring about a behavior change, we need to empower the person. People can be empowered by being provided choices and other information that can help them to achieve meaningful goals. Thus, in this dimension we need to identify goals that are meaningful to the potential users and identify a set of process that will assist them to achieve these goals. Further, these processes need to be embedded with choices, supported with relevant, accurate and timely knowledge, to enable informed decisions.

Thus, in this dimension, relationship between conditions that needs to be met for the solution to be economical and sustainable and individual user goals are identified. From this, functions and information needs for the users to better achieve their personalized goals can be derived.

Societal Empowerment: As mentioned earlier, the root cause for many of the major problems facing the society is coordination failure at multiple levels. Thus, when formulating a solution, in this dimension we need to examine how the developed solution can lead to enhanced coordination of the activities for all domain stakeholders or the community to achieve an enhanced value from their efforts.

Thus, this dimension studies how best to coordinate the various related activities to achieve a better outcome due to new ways available for individuals to make decisions and due to mobile system's availability to support this behavior.

Domain Knowledge: Having understood where critical coordination failure has happened and the economic dimensions of the problem, it is then necessary to identify how the various tasks are carried out in the application domain and what information is required to make optimal decisions to achieve better coordination. Domain experts are needed to advise on various aspects of the solution and provide relevant discipline-specific information. In general, we found the needed information could be divided into two categories: (i) quasi static – information that can be derived from published literature and only changing periodically; and (ii) dynamic or real time – information changing rapidly such as current production levels that needs to be generated in real time.

Thus, in this dimension, how the activities in application domain is happening and what new scenarios are possible is studied.

Interaction Design: This is the dimension that has been revolutionized by Smart Computing. In this dimension, we need to identify ways in which users can interact with information. This is best explained using the evolution of GPS as an example. Before GPS, people used printed maps to go to places. The maps were useful, but not very easy to use while driving a vehicle and not many people new how to effectively use a map. The early GPS contained the same information that was in a printed map but now in a vector form. Once the destination was keyed in, it was able to work out a suitable route and at various junctions it was able to inform the user to turn left or right or go straight. We can visualize the GPS as a multi-layer device; at the bottom layer is the printed map converted to a set of spatial vectors. The next layer is the smart sensor layer that senses the user's location is real time and generates actionable information by reading the vector information that match with location data in the form of next action to be performed. This change in interaction enabled more people to navigate using GPS compared to a printed map.

When more people start using GPS for navigation, the capabilities of the GPS got further enhanced. Using sensors, it was possible to find out the time it took to a user to travel a specific road segment. Thus, a third layer was added to the GPS, which is real time traffic map. Now, the actionable information that is generated at each junction not only looks at the shortest distance to the location; but also determines the route to get to the location in the shortest possible time.

Thus in this dimension making use of Smart Computing capabilities, the optimal way for a user to interact with information is worked out. The approach is to explore the optimal way to present the quasi static information needs and get users to interact with this information in a way to generate the dynamic or real time information needed to achieve optimal coordination.

User Interface Design: This is another dimension that requires a different set of expertise. The flow of information from the system to user and vice versa happens through the user interface. These interfaces could be textual, visual or graphical and auditory. The design of the interface needs to take in to account the language, culture, and literacy and education level of the users, among other things.

Thus, analyzing and finding solutions to the problem in these six dimensions will result in a holistic solution. It may appear that the activities in each of the dimensions tend to follow a sequential order, but this is not the case. They can happen in parallel or in any order depending on the problem and the skills of the team members applying the framework.

4   Case Study: Mitigation of Hidden Hunger

In this section, we describe our experience applying the framework in the domain of hidden hunger in African countries, which in turn demonstrates the generality and broader applicability of the proposed framework.

Hidden Hunger is a challenging health and wellbeing issue in Africa where the population do not get enough nutrients in their daily diet. Sub-Saharan Africa has one of the highest levels of child malnutrition globally and it has been estimated that 39% of children in East Africa, 32% in West Africa and 28% in Central Africa are stunted (short for their age) [23]. These statistics reflect a state of undernourishment in early life and leads to irrecoverable physical and mental development problems. Overcoming micronutrient deficiencies requires the diversification of diets and an increase in the consumption of micronutrient-rich foods.

4.1 Framework Adoption

We investigated a solution to overcome this problem within a multidisciplinary team to understand the root cause and possible solutions. We present our investigation in the context of the proposed framework as follows:

Economics: The root cause of the hidden hunger is not getting enough nutrients, while generally having enough daily intake of calories. This comes from the lack of food diversity. In many areas, there are highly nutritious indigenous foods that can be grown, but information on these crops and their nutritional value is not readily accessible. The conceptual solution is based on increasing awareness about hidden hunger and providing information and knowledge for sustainable access to diverse food sources including growing local crops and trade foods within the local communities.

User Empowerment: While improving the health and wellbeing was the immediate goal of decreasing hidden hunger, access to food and affordability are primary user concerns. The health-promoting benefits of eating these foods could be a second interest to the users. The proposed solution was based on a research, showed that household production of fruit and vegetables could reduce the incidence of hidden hunger in South Africa [24]. The project developed an application for the selection of diverse crops that could address hidden hunger. This approach is referred to as nutrition-driven agriculture.

Societal Empowerment: Nutrition-driven agriculture could be more effective if the community were empowered to take advantage of sharing and trading more nourishing products and creating more awareness around hidden hunger. We extended the current solution to a social network where individuals can get information about available nutritious foods and products in their local area and be able to have more sustainable and affordable food access. This brings more sustainability in terms of motivation and scalability to the proposed solution and can be adopted in other countries.

Domain Knowledge: The proposed solution needed expertise in the area of food, nutrition and agriculture to provide relevant information to address the issue. This information includes available local crops suitable for a specific agriculture/ geographical zone as well as nutrition information about the foods. Having this information, the solution can recommend what crops can be grown to address nutrient deficiencies.

Interaction Design: In this dimension, we need to devise a workflow to interact with users. Based on the domain knowledge results, we developed a dietary diversity survey for users so they enter their intake for last 24-hours [25]. The data were classified into 16-food categories. Where the diet was deficient in some of the food groups, the application identified crops that could grow in that area that could fill this gap. We used mobile information to identify the user location. Given the societal empowerment requirements, we plan to develop an optimizer to maximize the food diversity within the community by recommending various crops.

User Interface Design: Given the low level of literacy and education in many rural communities in Africa, we designed a visual food survey as well as graphical navigation tools to develop the solution. The developed application is a mobile app with a graphical user interface where users can see the pictures and select their intake. They are able to see the list of local crops and recommended crops with the relevant pictures.

4.2   System Prototype

In this section, we present the detail of the system prototype, which was developed based on the proposed solution in six dimensions. Figure 2 shows the workflow of the system prototype. We designed the workflow at household level where users will provide information about their household diet as the main input. We collect the dietary survey information from users and identify the missing food groups. Then we create a mapping table to identify the list of crops that grow in the user location that can address the dietary deficiency. The list of crops along with relevant information is provided to users. This provides enough options for users to select appropriate crops to grow based on their requirements and available resources.

The system prototype has been developed as a mobile app (called Ustawi [26]) for Android devices with relevant information about three African countries (Kenya, Nigeria and South Africa). Users are able to register to the application, providing their location and personal information, including the number of people in the household. The survey is conducted at the household level and users can select the foods that have been consumed by the household members in the last 24 h using a visual interface as shown in Fig. 3. After completion of the survey, the results tables show food categories that are missing in their diet. Users are able to see the result of last survey including date and the missing food groups. This is part of user empowerment to increase their knowledge about their food habit.

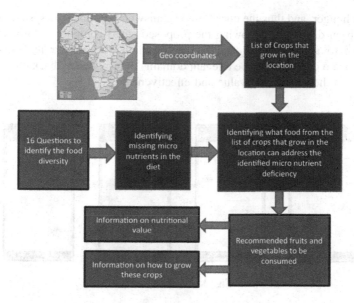

Fig. 2. The workflow of the system prototype

Users can continue their navigation through the app and access the recommended crops based on the missing food groups as shown in Fig. 4. Information about each crop, including season and production guidelines are provided to users. The system prototype also has a data analytics backend where researchers are able to look at the various data with various filters including date, food groups, and geographical region. In addition, there is an option for management of registered users by an administrator.

5   Evaluation and Discussions

We asked the question whether the proposed Smart Computing framework could address problems beyond the domain [11, 15, 16] that motivated its development. In order to answer this, we applied the conceptual framework to address hidden hunger at the household level in Africa. In this section, we aim to answer if it achieves its objectives of enabling end-user empowerment and achieving SDGs.

To carry out this evaluation, we look at two important aspects: its effectiveness in solving the target problem and its effectiveness in promoting change behavior in end-users. It takes a long time in this type of project to measure the actual economic and social impacts. But what is essential to take place, and measurable in shorter timespans, is the change in user behavior.

5.1   Addressing the Hidden Hunger Issue

The first aspect that requires investigation is the effectiveness of the solution in solving the problem that triggers the application of the framework. In this example, the problem was hidden hunger, and thus the question to be answered is: does the system prototype, which has been developed following the proposed smart computing framework, have the potential to address the hidden hunger problem? To answer the question, we employed a team of experts in the relevant domains to provide feedback on the features of the app and their perceived value and effectiveness.

Fig. 3. Food survey

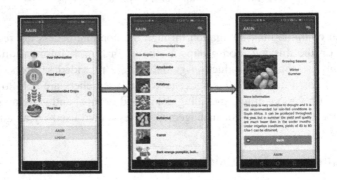

Fig. 4. Crops information

Experts included several food and nutrition scientists as well as two crop scientists. Feedback received from crop scientists was the suggestion to expand the amount of practical crops covered in the survey and to remove exotic foods and vegetables as well as narrow down recommended crops to take into consideration the microclimate of the users. This way, not only geolocation but also maximum temperature, rainfall, seasonality, and frost issues are taken into consideration when crops are suggested. Other feedback from crop scientists were more of a general nature – provide nutritional information delivered by each food group and more information about the household member filling the survey (e.g., age, gender).

The food and nutrition scientists provided feedback concerning expanding the app capabilities to provide direct access to the recommended crops (for example, by directly linking the app to online markets); include insects in the food survey; enable the capture of seasonal behavior (harvest time and between-harvest time); include more details in recommended crops (including cost and time to grow). The market capabilities in the app and seasonality in user behavior are interesting aspects to be explored in future works. To ease addition of information of crops, backend functionality has been added to assert that databases and user interfaces are completely separated from the underlying data that can be made available.

Finally, another feedback from the food scientists was enabling a social network to expand the reach of the application. In fact, we had this feature as part of the framework, but this feature needed to be delayed because it is a complex functionality that depended strongly in user adoption to succeed. Thus, it was a logical decision to focus initially in singular users (users and households) and, if the app succeeded at this point, expand it to community level. The positive reaction of end-users to the app (described in the next section) provided the motivation for prioritizing this feature in next development cycles, and the feedback from the food scientists gives us confidence that the time and cost for developing this feature is well-justified.

In summary, expert feedback provided us insights that we were in the right direction in the early prototype, although adjustments were needed to better reflect the particular food habits of the target groups and to maximize the amount of valuable information provided by the app. However, the most decisive factor in the success of the app lies in end-users adopting and benefitting from the app, which is discussed in the next section.

5.2 Promoting Behavior Changing in End-Users

Effectiveness of the framework in promoting change behavior in end-users is affected by a number of reasons. First, as reported by Hoppen et al. [6], there is the problem of convincing end-users of the relevance of the problem and the solution, as this will result in the end-user buy-in necessary for initial adoption of the solution. Second, the initial buy-in is not enough to guarantee that the objectives are met. As discussed in Sect. 3, even if end-users are willing to adopt the solution, but the solution fails in empowering them, the solution is also likely to fail. We therefore evaluated the point where the proposed framework interfaces with end-users: the prototype mobile app.

Usability study of the mobile app has been carried out at the Department of Informatics at University of Pretoria, South Africa [27]. Six end-users (workers from the experimental farm of the University of Pretoria) participated in the study. There was equal representation of men and women in the observed group. Their ages ranged from 25 to 50 years. Participants were asked to carry out certain activities in the app and the effectiveness was observed in terms of which tasks they were able to complete. The tasks participants completed were:

- Start the app and complete registration
- Change location in their user profile
- Complete the 24 h recall food survey
- Analyze the summary provided after survey completion
- Analyze the "recommended crops" portion of the app
- Explain the information presented in the household diet

This initial evaluation provided some insights in minor language localization issues and other minor usability issues. For example, utilization of pre-filled forms confused some users while others had difficulty with the fact that the virtual keyboard of the phone covered part of the app screen.

Another aspect that required improvements was the mapping of the original paper-based questionnaire to the app: the original questionnaire only asks if at least one food of a given group was consumed or not; there was no need to record how many food items (and which ones) were consumed from the group. The first version of the app reproduces this concept by progressing to the next food group once one food of the group was selected. However, during the evaluation, users were confused about this feature, and thus the design was changed so users can record all the consumed foods of a given group. Likewise, a majority of usability-related issues and feedback were addressed in the second development cycle of the app.

Overall, the app has been positively received by the users, which provided information about extra features they would like to see in future versions of the app. This is a great example of valuable feedback from end-users: they see value in the app as is, and they signaled other types of information that they currently miss and that they see as relevant to help them improve their diet. Some of the extra information they see as valuable include information on how to prepare meals with the recommended crops, which crops are easier to grow, information on fertilizers and pesticides, and even a section with tips for healthy living (for example, exercising).

A particular evidence of relevance of the app for end-users came from one of the users that, while carrying out the usability test, reached the crop information about potatoes and realized that the method he was utilizing was incorrect, thus impairing his efforts. The usability test allowed him to benefit from the knowledge enabled by the app, and led to the user to change the way he grows his crops, an information that, although seems trivial, was not easily available to these farmers.

These results confirm previous findings [11, 15, 16] that the main issue faced by rural communities, and that hinders a better lifestyle for them, is lack of basic information. Our Smart Computing framework is a step towards better and timely availability of information for end-users, what can be a powerful tool for their empowerment and solution of SDGs.

6   Conclusions and Future Work

In this paper, a Smart Computing framework based on user and societal empowerment is proposed. This framework has six dimensions and was created based on series of previous experiences to address SDGs. In order to show the applicability of the proposed framework, a case study to address the hidden hunger issue in Africa was presented. Having the framework to guide the thinking and designing of the solution helped us to frame a holistic solution centered on user and societal empowerment. The system prototype and its evaluation also presented and revealed that this framework can be adopted to develop effective and innovative solutions to address other SDGs.

As future work, we intend to develop the hidden hunger application further and add social computing components to complete the societal empowerment. Evaluation by testing the application in different communities across African countries is also part of our future plan. We also would like to adopt this framework for other SDGs and refine the framework further.

Acknowledgements. The authors would like to specifically acknowledge the participation and contribution of Prof. Helene Gelderblom, from the University of Pretoria's Department of Informatics, who passed away on the 7 April 2018. This research has been partially supported by funding from the Australia-Africa Universities Network (AAUN) and the South African National Research Foundation.

References

1. Bartels, A.H.: Smart computing drives the new era of IT growth. Forrester Inc. (2009)
2. Kennedy, G., Nantel, G., Shetty, P.: The scourge of "hidden hunger": global dimensions of micronutrient deficiencies. Food Nutr. Agric. **32**, 8–16 (2003)
3. Yalew, S.G., van Griensven, A., van der Zaag, P.: AgriSuit: a web-based GIS-MCDA framework for agricultural land suitability assessment. Comput. Electron. Agric. **128**, 1–8 (2016)
4. Yan-e, D.: Design of intelligent agriculture management information system based on IoT. In: 2011 Fourth International Conference on Intelligent Computation Technology and Automation, pp. 1045–1049 (2011)
5. Kamilaris, A., Gao, F., Prenafeta-Boldu, F.X., Ali, M.I.: Agri-IoT: a semantic framework for Internet of Things-enabled smart farming applications. In: 2016 IEEE 3rd World Forum on Internet of Things (WF-IoT), pp. 442–447 (2016)
6. Hoppen, N., Klein, A.d.C.Z., Rigoni, E.H.: Sociomaterial practices: challenges in developing a virtual business community platform in agriculture. BAR – Braz. Adm. Rev. **14**, 1–22 (2017)
7. Janssen, S.J.C., et al.: Towards a new generation of agricultural system data, models and knowledge products: information and communication technology. Agric. Syst. **155**, 200–212 (2017)
8. Woodard, J.: Big data and Ag-Analytics: an open source, open data platform for agricultural & environmental finance, insurance, and risk. Agric. Finance Rev. **76**, 15–26 (2016)
9. http://venturesafrica.com/these-10-apps-will-boost-agriculture-in-africa/
10. Kshetri, N.: The economics of the Internet of Things in the Global South. Third World Q. **38**, 311–339 (2017)
11. Ginige, A., et al.: Digital knowledge ecosystem for achieving sustainable agriculture production: a case study from Sri Lanka. In: The 3rd IEEE International Conference on Data Science and Advanced Analytics Montreal, Canada (2016)
12. Vlacheas, P., et al.: Enabling smart cities through a cognitive management framework for the internet of things. IEEE Commun. Mag. **51**, 102–111 (2013)
13. Bellagente, P., Ferrari, P., Flammini, A., Rinaldi, S.: Adopting IoT framework for Energy Management of Smart Building: a real test-case. In: 2015 IEEE 1st International Forum on Research and Technologies for Society and Industry Leveraging a Better Tomorrow (RTSI), pp. 138–143 (2015)
14. Lu, Y., Cecil, J.: An Internet of Things (IoT)-based collaborative framework for advanced manufacturing. Int. J. Adv. Manuf. Technol. **84**, 1141–1152 (2016)

15. De Silva, L., et al.: Interplay of requirements engineering and human computer interaction approaches in the evolution of a mobile agriculture information system. In: Ebert, A., Humayoun, S.R., Seyff, N., Perini, A., Barbosa, Simone D.J. (eds.) UsARE 2012/2014. LNCS, vol. 9312, pp. 135–159. Springer, Cham (2016). https://doi.org/10.1007/978-3-319-45916-5_9

16. Ginige, T., De Silva, L., Walisadeera, A., Ginige, A.: Extending DSR with sub cycles to develop a digital knowledge ecosystem for coordinating agriculture domain in developing countries. In: Chatterjee, S., Dutta, K., Sundarraj, R. (eds.) Designing for a Digital and Globalized World, vol. 10844, pp. 268–282. Springer, Cham (2018). https://doi.org/10.1007/978-3-319-91800-6_18

17. Ginige, A.: Systems engineering approach to smart computing: from farmer empowerment to achieving sustainable development goals. In: International Conference on Smart Computing and Systems Engineering 2018, Colombo, Sri Lanka (2018)

18. De Silva, L., Goonetillake, J., Wikramanayake, G., Ginige, A.: Towards an agriculture information ecosystem. In: 25th Australasian Conference on Information Systems. ACIS (2014)

19. Ginige, A.: Digital knowledge ecosystems: empowering users through context specific actionable information. In: 9th International Conference on ICT, Society and Human Beings (ICT 2016), Madeira, Portugal (2016)

20. Bandura, A.: Self efficacy mechanism in human agency. Am. Psychol. **37**, 122–147 (1982)

21. Zimmerman, M.A.: Psycological empowerment: issues and illustrations. Am. J. Community Psychol. **23**, 581–600 (1995)

22. Deci, E.L., Schwartz, A., Sheinman, L., Ryan, R.M.: An instrument to assess adults' orientations toward control versus autonomy with children: reflections on intrinsic motivation and perceived competence. J. Educ. Psychol. **73**, 642–650 (1981)

23. Akombi, B.J., Agho, K.E., Merom, D., Renzaho, A.M., Hall, J.J.: Child malnutrition in sub-Saharan Africa: a meta-analysis of demographic and health surveys (2006–2016). PLoS One **12**, e0177338 (2017)

24. Hendriks, S., et al.: The current rain-fed and irrigated production of food crops and its potential to meet the year-round nutritional requirement of rural poor people in North West, Limpopo, KwaZulu-Natal and the Eastern Cape. Water Research Commission Project number K5/2172/4 (2016)

25. Swindale, A., Bilinsky, P.: Household dietary diversity score (HDDS) for measurement of household food access: indicator guide. Food and Nutrition Technical Assistance Project, Academy for Educational Development, Washington, DC (2006)

26. http://ustawi.scem.westernsydney.edu.au

27. Gelderblom, H.: Report on the Usability Evaluation. Informatics Design Labs, University of Pretoria, South Africa (2018)

Towards an Efficient Prediction Model of Malaria Cases in Senegal

Ousseynou Mbaye[1], Mouhamadou Lamine Ba[1(✉)], Gaoussou Camara[1,2],
Alassane Sy[1], Balla Mbacké Mboup[3], and Aldiouma Diallo[4]

[1] LIMA,Université Alioune Diop, BP 30 Bambey, Senegal
{ousseynou.mbaye,mouhamadoulamine.ba,gaoussou.camara,
alassane.sy}@uadb.edu.sn
[2] Sorbonne Université, IRD, UMMISCO, 93143 Bondy, France
[3] Région Médicale de Diourbel, Diourbel, Senegal
bmmboup@yahoo.fr
[4] Vitrome, IRD. campus universitaire Hann maristes, BP 1386 Dakar, Senegal
aldiouma.diallo@ird.fr

Abstract. One amongst the most deadly diseases in the world, Malaria
remains a real flail in Sub-saharan Africa. In underdeveloped countries,
e.g. Senegal, such a situation is acute due to the lack of high quality
healthcare services and well-formed persons able to perform accurate
diagnosis of diseases that patients suffer from. This requires to set up
automated tools which will help medical actors in their decision making process. In this paper, we present first steps towards an efficient
way to automatically diagnosis an occurence or not of Malaria based on
patient signs and symptoms, and the outcome from the quick diagnosis
test. Our prediction approach is built on the logistic regression function.
First experiments on a real world patient dataset collected in Senegal,
as well as a semi-synthetic dataset, show promising performance results
regarding the effectiveness of the proposed approach.

Keywords: Malaria · Diagnosis · Data imputation · Prediction model

1 Introduction

Malaria is one amongst the most deadly diseases in the world, especially in
underdeveloped countries located in the sub-saharan Africa area such as Senegal. Malaria is caused by parasitic single-celled microorganisms belonging to the
Plasmodium group; it is an infectious disease which is transmitted to human
being through bites from infected female Anopheles mosquitoes. When a person
suffers from Malaria, she may present symptoms typically include fever, tiredness, vomiting, and headaches. In its severe form, the disease can cause yellow
skin, seizures, coma or death.

© ICST Institute for Computer Sciences, Social Informatics and Telecommunications Engineering 2019
Published by Springer Nature Switzerland AG 2019. All Rights Reserved
G. Bassioni et al. (Eds.): InterSol 2019, LNICST 296, pp. 173–188, 2019.
https://doi.org/10.1007/978-3-030-34863-2_15

Research Problem and Motivations. As stated in the last report [26] about the propagation of Malaria disease around the world, released in November 2017 by the World Health Organization (WHO for short), 216 millions of cases have been reported in 2016. Consequently, the number of cases has significantly increased regarding the 211 millions of reported Malaria patients in 2015. On the other side, the number of death due to Malaria does not decrease between 2015 and 2016 (446.000 vs. 445.000) despite the huge effort made by governments and non-governmental organizations to enhance healthcare services and the awareness strategies, especially in critical areas. Analyzing the statistics above in details, one can easily remark that the burden of the Africa region of the World Health Organization is colossal. Indeed, 90% of Malaria cases and 90% of deaths due to the disease were located in this area in 2016. More specifically, 80% of the burden in terms of morbidity is distributed in fifteen countries, all located in Sub-saharan Africa except India. This demonstrates that Malaria is a real flail in Sub-saharan Africa states and Senegal is not spared at all. We investigate in this study an efficient approach to predict, using machine learning, the occurence or not of Malaria when a patient has to be diagnosed. Given the patient signs and symptoms, as well as the result from the quick diagnosis test, our solution should be able to automatically tell if he suffers from Malaria or not with a high accuracy.

Malaria is an acute problem in Senegal due mainly to the lack of high quality healthcare services and well-formed staffs able to perform accurate diagnosis of diseases that patients suffer from. Over the past years, the government with the help of international organizations have tried to eradicate Malaria by implementing various proactive and reactive solutions to fill the gap in terms of services and human resources [2]. However, the mortality rate is still very high, e.g. in underserved areas, areas without required healthcare needs, uneducated people, population with low income, etc. Most of these deaths cases are reported to be caused by inaccurate diagnosis, sometimes incomplete leading to a bad prediction of the exact type of Malaria. On the other hand, Malaria occurence or complication can often occur during popular events (for instance religious events such as the Grand Magal of Touba [20]) which gather thousands of persons from everywhere in the country during a short time period. During those popular events, non-permanent medical points are set in order to assist and treat ill persons; the staff in a given health point might be composed sometimes by only volunteers without advanced medical skills. Each of these medical points might receive and treat hundreds of patients every day with some of them potentially suffering from Malaria. This requires to find and set up automated tools to help medical actors in their decision making process, and thereby to improve provided healthcare services.

Proposed Model. In this paper we present first steps towards an efficient manner to automatically diagnosis Malaria occurence or not based on patient signs and symptoms, and the outcome from the quick diagnosis test. We define our diagnosis task as a classical binary classification problem by considering two classes: *"malaria"* and *"not-malaria"*. Given a patient data, our main goal is to properly find to which class the patient belongs. To solve this classification problem we rely on machine learning and use the logistic regression function as the basis of our prediction approach. Machine learning has been largely used in several domains (e.g. Health Informatics [10]) for various purposes whereas logistic regression has demonstrated its efficiency when dealing with a binary classification problem. As an application scenario, we focus on predicting Malaria cases in Senegal. At this end, we use a large volume of patient dataset collected during the most popular religious event in Senegal (i.e. the Grand Magal of Touba) from the different installed health points, namely more than hundred points which receive every days several patients. The contributions of this work are as follow.

- A full-fletched data preparation pipeline in order to (i) explore patient data for profiling purpose; (ii) indentify records related to Malaria cases; (iii) clean and transform attributes, as well data values, into the raw dataset; (iv) extract the relevant Malaria features from the raw data; and (v) impute missing values using a prediction algorithm. Such a data preparation pipeline has been set up based on OpenRefine (formely Google Refine) for data profiling, cleaning, and transformation and missForest, a robust algorithm for imputing missing data of various types.
- The proposal of a prediction model for Malaria cases built on the logistic regression function.
- A practical validation of the efficiency of our model through a series of experiments on a real world patient dataset, augmenting with a semi-synthetic dataset.

Paper Organization. The rest of the paper is organized as follows. We review the literature of the existing research works on Malaria prediction in Sect. 2. In Sect. 3, we introduce our full-fletched data preparation pipeline. We then present our prediction model for Malaria cases in Sect. 4. Experiments and the performance of our model on several datasets are detailed in Sect. 5 before we conclude in Sect. 6.

2   Related Work

In this section, we summarize the state-of-the-art research on Malaria in general, and in particular the use of machine learning techniques to tackle the various aspects related to one of the major healthcare problems worldwide which is Malaria.

As it is well-known, Malaria is caused by the bite of the female Anopheles, the most dangerous of which is Plasmodium falciparum. Many early works have been consequently focused on the study of the evolution and the distribution of the responsible mosquito, mainly with the goal to detect or diagnosis the severity of the disease given an infected patient [6,11]. Recent research on Malaria have largely adopted machine learning and showed its ability to solve various aspects of the disease. Most of these machine learning based techniques are centered on the analysis of blood data obtained from high-definition microscopic screenshots as in [13]. The authors in [13] propose an unsupervised learning algorithm that detects and determines the types of infected blood cells. Used prediction approach consists of quantifying the amount of plasmodium parasites in a blood smear. Using the same intuition of harnessing blood, the Jordan-Elman neural network classifier is introduced in [8] to quickly determine the occurrence of Malaria and its severity level as well: the neural network analyzes the features of the blood data of the patients. Still using ML, DIAZ et al. have proposed in [9] a semi-supervised algorithm able to quantify and classify the erythrocytes infected by Malaria parasites through microscopic images. The originality of this work comes from its usability even in the presence of thin blood dandruff infected by falciparum Plasmodium for the quantification and the classification tasks. Besides blood data, sign and symptom records were also used to study Malaria with ML methods. Indeed, decision trees based approach has been proposed in Nigeria [24] to predict the occurrence of Malaria given diagnostic data. However a decision tree suffers from various limitations as a classifier. Indeed it can easily overfit or can be extremely sensitive to small pertubations in data for instance. Even though we both rely on signs and symptoms, the prediction model in [24] differs from ours on numerous facets: our model is built upon logistic regression and is trained using also inputs from the quick diagnosis test. In addition, we apply our method in the context of patients living in Senegal. An example of previous work that has used logistic regression is that of Farida et al. in [4]. The logistic regression is exploited there for the selection of features in order to construct stable decision trees. The decision trees are then used to predict the severity criteria of Malaria in the context of Afghanistan.

In the same line of works applying machine learning, in [17], Pranav et al. propose Malaria likelihood prediction model built on a deep reinforcement learning (RL) agent. Such a RL predicts the probability of a patient testing positive for Malaria using answers from questions about their household. In the presented approach the authors have also dealt with the problem of determining the right question to ask next as well as the length of the survey, dynamically. Moreover, statistically enhanced rule-based classification model to diagnose Malaria has been proposed in [7]. A corresponding prototype which incorporates the rules and statistical models have been implemented; the main goal of the study was to develop a statistical prototype to perform clinical diagnosis of Malaria given its adverse effects on the overall healthcare, yet its treatment remains very expensive for the majority of the patients to afford.

To the best of our knowledge this is the first work in Senegal that attempts to provide a prediction model for identifying the occurrence of Malaria given patient data.

3   Data Preparation

In this section, we detail the data preparation pipeline followed to obtain a proper Malaria dataset for the prediction phase. We start by presenting the used data cleaning and normalization techniques.

3.1   Data Cleaning and Normalization

In order to set up an efficient prediction model for Malaria cases in Senegal, we have relied on a real-world patient dataset for validation purposes. The dataset was extracted in 2016 during the Grand Magal of Touba [20]. An estimated 4–5 million individuals gather each year in the holy city of Touba, Senegal during the Grand Magal religious pilgrimage.Several health points are set during the Grand Magal to receive and treat hundreds of ill people, some of them suffering from Malaria. The patient data we are using here have been manually recordered from these points in registers as no electronic health management system does exist.

In detail, the raw dataset consists of thousands of patient records having each 16 attributes. Some of these attributes (also known as features) comprise personal data about the patient, but also patient signs and symptoms reported by the doctor who took in charge the patient. The other attributes describe clinical data such as information about the final diagnosis of the doctor (the disease that the patient suffers from), the income of the quick diagnosis test, and the status (i.e. admission, dead or put under observation) of the patient. For privacy concerns and some restrictions in data use, we have disregarded personal data about the patient during this work. Due to the fact that patient records have been collected manually in registers, we have noticed many inconsistencies such as misspellings, same attribute values with different writings (e.g., "DIARRHEE INFECTIEUSE" and "INFECTIEUSE DIARRHE" and multi-valued attributes (e.g. sign and symptom reported values). As a result, we have used OpenRefine [1,14] to first clean and then normalize values in the patient dataset.

OpenRefine is a powerful open source tool that allows researchers or scientists to accomplish the data wrangling activity, i.e. working with messy data: cleaning it; transforming it from one format into another; and extending it with Web services and external data. We used the following methods in OpenRefine to pre-treat our raw dataset.

- **Text filter function:** text filter enables to explore attribute values, clean them, and to identify those that may have many variants.
- **Transform functions:** OpenRefine provides two different Transform functions: preset transformations for resolving trivial formatting issues like trimming whitespaces and advanced transformations based on the OpenRefine Expression Language (GREL) to normalize data in batch or split them. This second class of transformations is very useful, especially when the number of piece of data values to normalize is very important (doing the same task manually would be time-consuming and prone to errors).
- **Cluster and edit function:** Clustering option in OpenRefine also provides users with methods to merge and normalize variations across the dataset. The power of clustering is that it is able to automatically detect small data variations which follow a certain pattern.

For the particular case of multi-valued attributes such as symptom and sign columns in our raw dataset, we splitted them into multiple values in distinct columns. Indeed, in the raw dataset information like the symptoms a given patient suffers from were stored in a single column, separated with the special character '+', e.g. "DOULEUR ARTICULAIRE" + "DOULEUR PELVI-ENNE"+ "VOMISSEMENTS".

After this step of data cleaning and normalization, we have proceeded to the extraction of Malaria features.

3.2 Extraction of Malaria Features

To properly study Malaria, one needs to have a patient dataset with the main features of the disease. Unfortunately, some of these Malaria features were not explicitly specified in our raw dataset. As a result, we have inferred twelve new attributes that better describe the signs and symptoms of Malaria according to experts in the health domain. Those new attributes are: *lack of appetite, tiredness, fever, cephalalgia, nausea, arthralgia, digestive disorders, dizziness, chill, myalgia, diarrhea,* and *abdominal pain.* We have then added the new attributes in our dataset and transformed this latter accordingly by filling the value of each new attribute based on the list of reported signs and symptoms for every patient.

A medical diagnostic is the results of an interpretation of the reported signs and symptoms; in general such a diagnostic is further confirmed by a medical test. Since our raw dataset does not contain only information about Malaria, this yields to records with various diagnostics. For the purposes of our study, we replaced any diagnostic that is not Malaria by the class *"not-malaria"*. At this step of our data preparation pipeline, we came up with a patient dataset that contains required Malaria features. However, our preparation process was not yet complete and ready because of values missingness. As a last step, we have completed our dataset by using a robust data imputation approach.

3.3 Missing Data Imputation

As shown in Table 1, we observed many missing values in our dataset, affecting the majority of the data attributes. Such missing values should not be ignored as data completeness and quality are very important when dealing with a prediction problem; this could negatively impact the accuracy of our prediction and should be treated appropriatey. One has to note that machine learning relies on complete dataset. The sources and types of missing values can be various [23]. In our context, missingness is *not completely random* and can be due to an incomplete knowledge of the patient data, the fact that the medical staff do not specify an attribute value when it is not observed, or a difficulty for the patients to properly describe some piece of information (e.g. related to the signs or symptoms of their diseases) at the diagnostic time. Since it might have a certain relationship between attribute values for the same patient, or even a correlation between patient records, we decide to solve our problem of missing values by using imputation algorithms instead of choosing arbitrary values or removing records with missing values.

Table 1. The number of missing values per attribute

Attribute name	#missing_values
Lack of appetite	21068
digestive disorders	21062
Loss of weight	21017
Arthragia	20940
Chill	20925
Nausea	20874
Myalgia	20870
Tiredness	20713
Diarrhea	20481
Vomit	20051
Abdominal pain	19770
Dizziness	19628
Fever	18245
Temperature	17636
Arterial pressure	16924
Cephalalgia	15370
Diagnostic	2875
Quick diagnostic test	76

Data imputation is often used in the machine learning field when dealing with missing information. Many algorithms have been proposed in the literature [19,23], depending on the nature of the missingness or the type of data. MissForest [22] has been proved to be efficient at the presence of various types (e.g. numerical data, string, categorical data, etc.) of data simultaneously as in our case. The algorithm missForest relies on Random Forest, a non-parametric prediction method that is able to deal with mixed-type data and allows for interactive and non-linear regression effects. Such an imputation algorithm aims at handling any type of input dataset by minimizing (when possible) assumption about the structural aspects of the data. Given an input dataset, missForest solves the missing data problem using an iterative imputation scheme by training a Random Forest on observed values in a first step, followed by predicting the missing values and then proceeding iteratively until convergence.

We have applied missForest on our Malaria patient dataset by using its opensource Python implementation [3]. We have then measured the accuracy of the prediction made by the algorithm with the help of the normalized root mean squared error metric; the obtained performance was rather satisfactory.

4   Prediction Model

To learn from labelled patient dataset and be able to properly predict the occurence or not of Malaria given a new patient, we harness the logistic regression function as our classifier. We next briefly recall the basic of the logistic regression function and how it can be used as a binary classifier. We start by introducing the binary classification problem we are solving in the study.

4.1   Binary Classification Problem

Let us assume two given classes of Malaria diagnostic: *malaria* and *not-malaria*. We also consider P and C as respectively the set of patients and a prediction model. A patient p in P is defined by a set of pairs $(a_1, v_1), (a_2, v_2), \ldots, (a_n, v_n)$ where a_i and v_i, for each $1 \leq i \leq n$, respectively corresponds to a given Malaria feature and its associated value defined as follows.

$$v_i = \begin{cases} 1 \text{ if } a_i \text{ is observed} \\ 0 \text{ otherwise} \end{cases} \tag{1}$$

Definition 1. *(Our prediction problem) We define our binary classification problem for the prediction of the occurrence or not of Malaria on a given patient dataset as a mapping* C *of every patient p in* P *to one and only one class in* {malaria, not-malaria}. *Formally, we present such a mapping as* C: P $\mapsto$ {malaria, not-malaria}.

We define and use C with the help of the logistic regression for the specific purpose of our study.

4.2   Logistic Regression

The logistic regression (also known as the logit function) is a statistical model used in the machine learning domain for binary classification [18]. It is based, in its basic form, on a logistic function to describe a binary dependent variable [12, 21]. The logistic regression takes as input qualitative or/and ordinal predictive variables (e.g. the presence or not of fever given a patient) in order to measure the probability of the outcome (e.g. the occurrence or not of the Malaria) by using the *Sigmoid function*.

The logistic regression is one of the most used multi-valued models in epidemiology [5,16]: the variable to explain is often the occurrence or not of an event like a disease and the explanatory variables are those that highly impact the occurrence of this event. The main interest of using logistic regression is its ability to quantify the strength of the relationship between each explicative variable and the variable to explain, given the other variables integrated to the model [5].

Formalization. Let us consider Y as the variable we are trying to explain in this study, i.e. the variable which models the occurrence or not of Malaria and whose two possible values *malaria* and *not-malaria* are respectively denoted by M+ and M-. If only one explicative variable a is used (which case corresponds to a simple regression), formally the model is written as follows.

$$\text{PR}(\text{M+} \mid a) = \frac{e^{\alpha+\beta \times a}}{1 + e^{\alpha+\beta \times a}} \tag{2}$$

where the coefficients α and β are the parameters of the model. $\text{PR}(\text{M+} \mid a)$ measures the probability of the occurrence of Malaria if the variable a is observed. gain, the main interest of this function lies in the simplicity of reaching an estimation of an odds ratio (OR) which measures the strength of the association between the disease and an exposure variable in a regression analysis. Indeed if the value exposure variable is either 0 (the variable is not observed) or 1 (the variable is observed) as in our setting, the model enables to obtain after some simplifications $\text{OR} = e^{\beta}$. The coefficient β of the exposure variable in the logistic model is then the logarithmic of the odds ratio which measures the relationship between the explanatory variable (sign or symptom) and the disease (Malaria); this eases the analysis of the results of the logistic regression.

An extension of the simple regression to a model with multiple variables (called multiple regression) is straightforward as we show with the formula below.

$$\text{PR}(\text{M+} \mid a_1, a_2, \ldots, a_n) = \frac{e^{\alpha+\sum_{i=1}^{n} \beta_i \times a_i}}{1 + e^{\alpha+\sum_{i=1}^{n} \beta_i \times a_i}} \tag{3}$$

where to every variable a_i is associated a coefficient β_i. The corresponding odds ratio OR_i, quantifying the relationship between a_i and M+ is equal to e^{β_i}.

Optimal Model. The question that generally raises when using a multiple regression approach is how to select the minimum set of variables amongst the a_i's that better explain the variable Y. Several optimization strategies are possible to obtain the best final prediction model which takes into account the maximum of information while restricting as much as possible the number of explanatory variables in order to ease the analysis of the results: *stepwise descendant* and *stepwise ascendant* are the most used approaches. Both approaches apply an iterative regression and we use stepwise descendant in our experimentations which considers the entire set of variables at the beginning and gradually excludes from the model variables which do not significantly improve the determination coefficient.

We next present the results of our prediction of Malaria cases by using our logistic regression model above on real-world patient datasets.

5   Experimentation and Results

In this section, we prove the efficiency of our prediction model for Malaria occurrecne through an analysis of the results of the tests we have conducted on real-world datasets and a semi-synthetic dataset. We start by presenting our experimentation setting.

5.1   Experimentation Setting

We ran tests on three different datasets using the Python Implementation of the logistic regression function.

Our Datasets. We collected and used a real-world patient dataset from the different health points which were set during the Grand Magal of Touba in 2016. We also generated and used two variants of this real-world dataset. The description of the characteristics of our raw real-world dataset, as well as the data preparation pipeline that we have proposed in order to clean, normalize and impute information, are given in Sect. 3; we refer to this cleaned and complete real-world patient dataset by DT1.

We generated the first variant, denoted by DT2, of the raw real-world patient dataset by removing records with missing attributes, instead of using an imputation algorithm that will predict values for missing information. Such a variant will help to study the impact of removing records with missing values in the prediction accuracy.

The second variant, called DT3, is a semi-synthetic dataset which has been set up by using a sampling strategy over our raw real-world dataset. Indeed when we have performed some explanatory analysis on the real-world dataset they have revealed that the dataset was not balanced, i.e. it shows strong class imbalance; the amount of records about patients suffering from Malaria was largely less than the number of patients that do not suffer from Malaria as shown in Fig. 1. Harnessing sampling approaches may enable to obtain a balanced semi-synthetic dataset regarding the two classes to predict. To solve our problem of imbalanced dataset, we used the algorithm SMOTE [25], which is a synthetic minority oversampling technique, through its Python implementation in the package *imbalanced-learn* [15]. SMOTE consists of predicting a sample of synthetic dataset based on the value of the minority class of the targeted class (here the attribute Diagnostic). It randomly chooses the k-nearest neighbours of a given record in order to randomly create new observations. We have applied an over-sampling of the minority class into our patient dataset for generating a semi-synthetic dataset DT3 containing the same number of records for both classes.

Prediction Model Setting. In order to set up our logistic regression-based classification model, we rely on the Python implementation of the logistic regression in the *sklearn* library[1]. This python package defines the logistic regression

---

[1] https://scikit-learn.org/stable/modules/generated/sklearn.linear_model.LogisticRe gression.html.

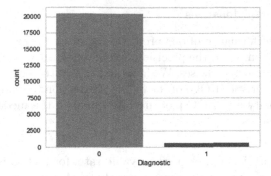

Fig. 1. The number of records by class

with the required input parameters, as well as optimization strategies, to properly perform binary classification using an optimal model. For the purposes of our tests, we have used the following input parameters of the logistic regression:

- **random_state**: it models the seed of the pseudo random number generator to use when shuffling the data. Its value is set to 0 as we do not need to shuffle data in our experimentations.
- **class_weight**: weights associated with classes. We set it to *None*, i.e. all classes are supposed to have weight one.
- **dual**: dual or primal formulation. Dual formulation is only implemented for l2 penalty with liblinear solver. This parameter is set to *False* as the number of samples is greater than the number of features.
- **fit_intercept**: useful if a constant (a.k.a. bias or intercept) should be added to the decision function. Consequently, we fixed the fit_intercept to *True*.
- **intercept_scaling**: this parameter, set to 1, is useful only when the solver "liblinear" is used and fit_intercept is set to True.
- **max_iter**: maximum number of iterations taken for the solvers to converge.
- **multi_class**: if the option chosen is "ovr" hen a binary problem is fit.
- **n_jobs**: number of cpu cores used when parallelizing over classes if multi_class="ovr". This parameter is ignored when the solver is set to "liblinear" regardless whether "multiclass" is specified or not.
- **penalty**: this parameter is used to specify the norm in the penalization. We fixed the penality to its default value l2.
- **solver**: it enables to specify the strategy used to solve the optimization underlying our model. For the solver we fix it to *liblinear*.
- **tol**: tolerance for stopping criteria which is set to 0.0001.
- **verbose**: for the liblinear solver set verbose to any positive number for verbosity.
- **warm_start**: when set to *True*, reuse the solution of the previous call to fit as initialization, otherwise, just erase the previous solution. Useless for liblinear solver.

As the logistic regression performs a supervised learning we have used 60% for the training set and 30% for the test set.

5.2   Performance Measures

To evaluate the performance of our prediction approach over the different used datasets, we have computed the precision, recall (or sensitivity), F-measure, and specificity of the predicted classes. We have also drawn the graph of the Receiver Operating Characteristic (ROC) of the logistic regression to study its shape. The sensitivity, specificity and ROC plot are often used in the medecine domain as performance measures.

Precision. The precision p, or positive value rate, for a class is the number of true positives (i.e. the number of cases correctly labeled as belonging to the class M+) divided by the total number of cases labeled as belonging to the class M+ (i.e. the sum of true positives and false positives, which are incorrectly labeled as belonging to the class).

$$p = \frac{\sum_{i=1}^{|R|} Entity(i)}{R}. \tag{4}$$

$Entity(i)$ is a binary function that returns true if the predicted class for the i-th case is correct (w.r.t test set) and false otherwise. R is the sum of the number of predicted true positive and false positive cases.

Recall. The recall r (also known as sensitivity) is defined as the number of true positives divided by the total number of cases that actually belong to the class M+ (i.e. the sum of true positives and false negatives, which are cases which were not labeled as belonging to the class M+ but should have been).

$$r = \frac{\sum_{i=1}^{|R|} Entity(i)}{G} \tag{5}$$

G is the sum of the number of predicted true positive and false negative cases.

F-measure. The F-measure, denoted by F_1, is a metric that measures the accuracy of a test in statistical analysis of a binary classification. It is computed using both the precision p and the recall r of the test as the ratio of the number of correct positive results and the number of all positive results returned by the classifier.

$$F_1 = 2 \times \frac{p \times r}{p + r} \tag{6}$$

Specificity. The specificity, or true negative rate, measures the proportion of actual negatives that are correctly identified as such (e.g., the percentage of people not suffering from Malaria who are correctly identified as not having the condition).

Receiver Operating Characteristic. A receiver operating characteristic, or ROC in short, is a graph that shows the diagnostic ability of a binary classifier system as its discrimination threshold is varied. The ROC curve is created by plotting the *true positive rate* (i.e. recall) against the false positive rate (1 - specifity) at various threshold.

5.3 Experiments and Analysis of the Results

For each given dataset, we have performed two kinds of tests with our prediction model by considering or not the outcome of the quick diagnostic test (or QDT for short) as an input feature. We first describe below the obtained results for each dataset and then present a comparative analysis.

Experiments with DT1. Table 2 and Fig. 2 respectively show the performance measures and the ROC curve of the results of our classification approach tested on dataset DT1. The results on Table 2(a) and Fig. 2(a) are obtained without considering the quick diagnostic test output in contrast of measures in Table 2(b) and Fig. 2(b). One can easily see that the accuracy of our prediction model is sensibly the same when considering or not the QDT; this accuracy is quite good as proven by the precision which is greater than 90%.

Table 2. Performance measures of the prediction on DT1

(a) Prediction without the QDT			(b) Prediction with the QDT		
Precision	**Recall**	**F-measure**	**Precision**	**Recall**	**F-measure**
0.97	1.0	0.99	0.98	1.0	0.99

Experiments with DT2. Table 3 and Fig. 3 respectively show the performance measures and the ROC curve of the results (with or without taking into account the QDT) of our classification approach tested on dataset DT2. The accuracy measures on Table 3(a) et Fig. 3(a) respectively compare to those in Table 3(b) and Fig. 3(b) show that our classifier does well when considering the QDT as a feature; without the QDT the precision of the prediction decreases a lot which result can be explained by the fact we do not have enough examples to properly train the model.

Experiments with DT3. Similarly to results on DT2, performance measures on DT3 show a better prediction accuracy (See Table 4 and Fig. 4) when the QDT is considered as a feature.

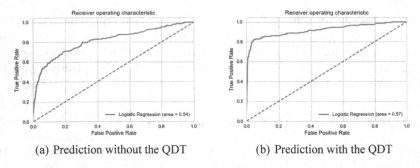

(a) Prediction without the QDT　　　　(b) Prediction with the QDT

Fig. 2. The curve of the Receiver Operating Characteristic for prediction on DT1

Table 3. Performance measures of the prediction on DT2

(a) Prediction without the QDT			(b) Prediction with the QDT		
Precision	**Recall**	**F-measure**	**Precision**	**Recall**	**F-measure**
0.75	1.0	0.86	1.0	1.0	1.0

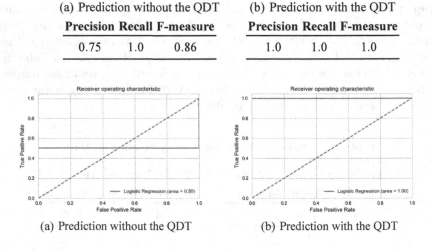

(a) Prediction without the QDT　　　　(b) Prediction with the QDT

Fig. 3. The curve of the Receiver Operating Characteristic for prediction on DT2

Table 4. Performance measures of the prediction on DT3

(a) Prediction without the QDT			(b) Prediction with the QDT		
Precision	**Recall**	**F-measure**	**Precision**	**Recall**	**F-measure**
0.77	0.82	0.79	0.87	0.90	0.89

Comparative Analysis of the Results. In sum, the first experimentations detailed above prove that our logistic regression based prediction model does well in general and in particular when the outcome of the quick diagnostic test is considered as a feature for the learning process. More specifically, the precision of our prediction is greater than 90% for datasets DT1 and DT2, reaching 100% for DT1. For the specific case of the real-world patient dataset with missing data filled using an imputation algorithm this accuracy does not decrease even though the QDT is not considered during the prediction process, and only the

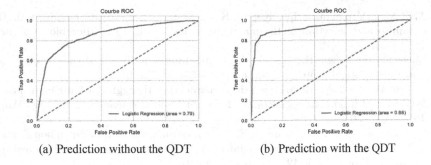

(a) Prediction without the QDT   (b) Prediction with the QDT

Fig. 4. The curve of the Receiver Operating Characteristic for prediction on DT3

Malaria features, i.e. signs and symptoms are taken into account. As a result, we can conclude that there is a hope to construct an efficient prediction model for Malaria without the need to perform the quick diagnostic test in order to declare a given patient he is affected by the disease.

6 Conclusion

In this paper we have studied the problem of predicting the occurrence or not of Malaria given ill-patient dataset in the context of Senegal and by using machine learning techniques. To tackle this problem we have first presented a data preparation pipeline that enables to clean, normalize and impute missing values given a real-world dataset using efficient tools and algorithms. We also introduced a manner to extract the features that characterize the Malaria disease. We have then proposed a prediction model based on the logistic regression to determine the occurrence of Malaria. The performance of such a model has been demonstrated through extensive experimentations on real-world and semi-synthetic datasets. As a research perspective we plan to first include a prevalence factor into our prediction function in order to improve its accuracy. Second, we will use other binary classification models such as Support Vector Machine (or SVM in short) and compare their results to those obtained with the logistic regression based model.

References

1. Openrefine. http://openrefine.org/. Accessed 30 Oct 2018
2. Programme national de lutte contre le paludisme. http://www.pnlp.sn/. Accessed 15 Jan 2019
3. Python implementation of missforest. https://pypi.org/project/predictive_imputer/. Accessed 31 Oct 2018
4. Adimi, F., Soebiyanto, R.P., Safi, N., Kiang, R.: Towards malaria risk prediction in Afghanistan using remote sensing. Malaria J. **9**(1), 125 (2010)
5. Aminot, I., Damon, M.: The use of logistic regression in the analysis of data concerning good medical practice. Rev. Med. Assur. Mal. **33**(2), 143–157 (2002)

6. Aly, A.S., Vaughan, A.M., Kappe, S.H.: Malaria parasite development in the mosquito and infection of the mammalian host. Ann. Rev. Microbiol. **63**, 195–221 (2009)
7. Bbosa, F., Wesonga, R., Jehopio, P.: Clinical malaria diagnosis: rule-based classification statistical prototype. SpringerPlus **5**(1), 939 (2016)
8. Chiroma, H., et al.: Malaria severity classification through Jordan-Elman neural network based on features extracted from thick blood smear. Neural Netw. World **25**(5), 565 (2015)
9. Daz, G., Gonzlez, F.A., Romero, E.: A semi-automatic method for quantification and classification of erythrocytes infected with malaria parasites in microscopic images. J. Biomed. Inf. **42**(2), 296–307 (2009)
10. Dua, S., Acharya, U.R., Dua, P.: Machine Learning in Healthcare Informatics. Springer Publishing Company, Incorporated (2013)
11. Ferguson, H.M., Mackinnon, M.J., Chan, B.H., Read, A.F.: Mosquito mortality and the evolution of malaria virulence. Evolution **57**(12), 2792–2804 (2003)
12. Hosmer, D.W., Lemeshow, S.: Applied Logistic Regression. Wiley (2000)
13. Kunwar, S.: Malaria detection using image processing and machine learning. ArXiv e-prints. January 2018
14. Kusumasari, T.F., Fitria: data profiling for data quality improvement with open-refine. In: 2016 International Conference on Information Technology Systems and Innovation (ICITSI), pp. 1–6, October 2016
15. Lemaître, G., Nogueira, F., Aridas, C.K.: Imbalanced-learn: a Python toolbox to tackle the curse of imbalanced datasets in machine learning. J. Mach. Learn. Res. **18**(17), 1–5 (2017)
16. Preux, P., Odermatt, P., Perna, A., Marin, B., Vergnengre, A.: Qu'est-ce qu'une regression logistique ? Revue des Mal. Respir. **22**(1, Part 1), 159–162 (2005)
17. Rajpurkar, P., Polamreddi, V., Balakrishnan, A.: Malaria likelihood prediction by effectively surveying households using deep reinforcement learning. CoRR abs/1711.09223 (2017)
18. Robert, C.: Machine learning, a probabilistic perspective. CHANCE **27**(2), 62–63 (2014)
19. Silva, L.O., Zárate, L.E.: A brief review of the main approaches for treatment of missing data. Intell. Data Anal. **18**(6), 1177–1198 (2014)
20. Sokhna, C., et al.: Communicable and non-communicable disease risks at the Grand Magal of Touba: the largest mass gathering in Senegal. Travel Med. Infect. Dis. **19**, 56–60 (2017)
21. Sperandei, S.: Understanding logistic regression analysis. Biochem. Med. **24**, 12–18 (2014)
22. Stekhoven, D.J., Bhlmann, P.: MissForest: non-parametric missing value imputation for mixed-type data. Bioinformatics **28**(1), 112–118 (2012)
23. Swalin, A.: How to handle missing data. https://towardsdatascience.com/how-to-handle-missing-data-8646b18db0d4. Accessed 31 October 2018
24. Ugwu, C., Onyejegbu, N.L., Obagbuwa, I.C.: The application of machine learning technique for malaria diagnosis. Int. J. Green Comput. **1**(1), 68–77 (2010)
25. Wang, J., Xu, M., Wang, H., Zhang, J.: Classification of imbalanced data by using the smote algorithm and locally linear embedding. In: 2006 8th International Conference on Signal Processing, vol. 3, November 2006
26. WHO: World malaria report in 2017 (2017)

Author Index

Printed in the United States
By Bookmasters